P9-BTY-111

GOVERNMENT IN BRITAIN

GOVERNMENT IN BRITAIN

BY

G. T. POPHAM, B.SC(ECON), PH.D, DPA

Lecturer in Politics, University of Aston in Birmingham

PERGAMON PRESS

OXFORD · LONDON · EDINBURGH · NEW YORK
TORONTO · SYDNEY · PARIS · BRAUNSCHWEIG

PERGAMON PRESS LTD.,
Headington Hill Hall, Oxford
4 & 5 Fitzroy Square, London W.1
PERGAMON PRESS (SCOTLAND) LTD.,
2 & 3 Teviot Place, Edinburgh 1
PERGAMON PRESS INC.,
Maxwell House, Fairview Park, Elmsford, New York 10523
PERGAMON OF CANADA LTD.,
207 Queen's Quay West, Toronto 1
PERGAMON PRESS (AUST.) PTY. LTD.,
19a Boundary Street, Rushcutters Bay, N.S.W. 2011, Australia
PERGAMON PRESS S.A.R.L.,
24 rue des Écoles, Paris 5e
VIEWEG & SOHN GMBH,
Burgplatz 1, Braunschweig

First edition 1969
Library of Congress Catalog Card No. 69-19843

Printed in Great Britain by A. Wheaton & Co., Exeter

08 013417 3 (flexicover)
08 013418 1 (hard cover)

CONTENTS

PREFACE

THIS book is intended to meet the needs of students preparing for certain papers in the finals stage of the diplomas in Municipal and Government Administration of the Local Government Examinations Board. I hope it may also be of interest to undergraduates who are studying British Government.

In dealing with so vast a subject one must be selective. I have concentrated on certain areas of central government and have touched on local government only with respect to the provision of social services.

A hazard of writing this kind of book is that information is apt to become quickly out of date. The discerning reader will concentrate on the basic issues involved.

I wish to thank the many officials who kindly supplied information. I must also thank Maurice Hookham, of the University of Leicester, who commented on parts of the manuscript, and my former colleague Bruce Grocott, who read the whole work. I am responsible for any remaining errors of fact and defects of style.

Those who attempt to keep pace with developments in government confirm Thoreau's remark that most men lead lives of quiet desperation. In the interval between completing the text and publication it has proved necessary to add a postscript and an appendix.

University of Aston
Birmingham

G. T. P.

CHAPTER 1

THE CABINET

Parties and Prime Ministers

The Cabinet is the natural starting point in any account of British Government; it has been aptly described as "the main-spring of all the mechanism of government". Yet the Haldane Report on the Machinery of Government, from which these words are taken, makes no direct reference to the fact that the Cabinet is a creature of party politics.[1]

Cabinets owe their very existence to parties since they are composed of members of the party, or coalition of parties, which is supported by a majority of Members of Parliament who sit in the House of Commons. Occasionally men have entered the Cabinet without having strong party connections or before they have obtained a seat in Parliament. Sir John Anderson, later Lord Waverley, who first became a minister in Neville Chamberlain's pre-war Cabinet, is a case in point. But if a man is to remain a minister for any considerable period, in time of peace, he must become identified with a party. And in becoming identified with a British party he associates himself with certain broad policies, programmes, and attitudes, which are of some significance for the harmonious working of Cabinet government.

Most politicians enter the Cabinet via membership of the House of Commons. The few who do not, assuming they are not amongst the usual three or four peers, chosen from the non-elected House of Lords, must, by convention, ultimately obtain a seat in

[1] *Report of the Machinery of Government Committee*, Cmd. 9230, 1918, pp. 4–6. For comment see W. J. M. Mackenzie, in *British Government Since 1918*, Allen & Unwin, 1950, p. 59.

the Commons. It is true that General Smuts became a member of the War Cabinet in 1917 without a seat in the British Parliament, but occasional exceptions, made for a short time and in unusual circumstances, do not invalidate conventions. Mr. Patrick Gordon Walker's failure to win a seat in the Commons for some time after his defeat in the general election of 1964 forced him to resign from his Cabinet post as Foreign Secretary, a position for which he had long been groomed when his party was in Opposition. Thus the composition of the Cabinet is to some extent influenced by the availability of safe seats and the will of the electorate.

This dual membership of a parliamentary party and the Government, applicable to Cabinet and non-Cabinet ministers alike, is responsible for the close union of executive and legislative power to which Bagehot drew attention in his classic study.[2] Constitutionally, the Crown in Parliament, i.e. the Commons, Lords, and Monarchy together, makes statute law. But for political reasons the will of the majority in the Commons, the elected chamber, prevails over the other parts of Parliament. And the Cabinet, which dominates the executive, controls the legislative process through its party majority in the Commons. No British Government with a working majority in the Commons can envisage that its policies will be totally frustrated by a recalcitrant legislature. To this extent the party system makes for effective Cabinet government. It also makes for responsible government in the sense that the leaders of the party in power are clearly the persons to blame for the results of legislation.

Of course, no Government can legislate as it pleases merely because it is founded on a party majority in the Commons. The possible reactions of the electorate will be borne in mind; majorities may become minorities. Powerful interest groups will be consulted and placated. Concessions will probably be made to meet the criticisms of the Government's own backbench supporters. Neither of the two major parties in Parliament is in any sense a monolithic unity. On close inspection both parties tend to dissolve into groups or factions having widely differing positions

[2] W. Bagehot, *The English Constitution*, Fontana Paperback edn., 1963, p. 65.

on many issues. British parties are remarkable for the way in which they manage to reconcile unity and diversity. And the divisive and unifying aspects of parties leave their mark on the Cabinet.

One may say that Conservative Members of Parliament are united by a belief in the rightness of the capitalist system; but positions may range from attachment to extreme *laissez-faire* to the acceptance of a considerable degree of planning and control by the State. Conservative MPs are also united by social background. So far, they have been overwhelmingly drawn from the upper and middle classes. But this does not prevent differences within the party on economic affairs, foreign policy, or social matters. The Parliamentary Labour Party reveals the same diversity and unity. If its members are committed to some form of socialism its nature is extremely vague. A party which embraces individuals as diametrically opposed in their philosophies as Mr. Woodrow Wyatt and Mr. Eric Heffer can scarcely be preoccupied with ideological conformity. The PLP is more socially divided than the Conservative Party in Parliament. It has a virtual monopoly of working-class representation in the Commons, but over the years the number of Labour Members with middle- or upper-class backgrounds has tended to increase. Inside both parties there are divisions along age group and occupational lines.

The various groupings in the two major parliamentary parties tend to coalesce round particular MPs who become the recognized leaders. Such Members enjoy a sort of baronial power and prestige. Their standing may be enhanced by connections outside Parliament, in the local constituency organizations, or the trade unions. In the Labour Party, men like Ernest Bevin or George Brown cannot be easily ignored because of the support they enjoy, not only amongst MPs but also in the trade union movement. Neither can Richard Crossman, nor Barbara Castle, so long as they have the confidence and support of the left of the party and the activists in the constituencies. In the Conservative Party, Mr. Quintin Hogg is popular in the constituency associations. Reginald Maudling appeals to the younger intellectuals in the

Parliamentary Party. Sir Alec Douglas-Home has the support of aristocratic coteries, which are still influential.[3]

It follows that although constitutional convention gives a Prime Minister authority to decide who will be in his Cabinet, his choice is circumscribed by party political realities. Certain prominent party men "choose" themselves. To exclude them would be to risk exposing party differences on the floor of the Commons. In some cases it could lead to difficulties outside Parliament. It was convenient for Mr. Wilson to keep Frank Cousins in the Cabinet for as long as he could, knowing that the latter was the natural leader of trade union opposition to the Government's incomes policy. Lord Attlee, when he was Prime Minister, went out of his way to secure a Cabinet which would be representative of the various groups and opinions in the PLP.[4] Party influences make for strange bedfellows in the Cabinet. To make it into a working team, exhibiting an outward show of complete unity, in the face of fairly well-known individual differences, is a task that calls for some skill on the part of the Prime Minister.

It is sometimes suggested that the power of the Prime Minister is so great that Cabinet government is no longer an appropriate term to apply to the British system. Instead, it is contended, Prime Ministerial government would be a more accurate description.[5] But this claim must be seen in the context of power within political parties and in the light of actual experience.

A Prime Minister is obviously in a different position from any other member of the Cabinet. Within the limits outlined above he chooses the members and determines the size of the Cabinet. He allocates the various departmental and other responsibilities. He may reconstitute the Cabinet or demand resignations. The Prime Minister controls the agenda of meetings. He may interest himself in any aspect of government. He may decide to be his own Foreign Secretary or Defence Minister. Promotion in the Cabinet

[3] On groupings within parties see R. Rose, Parties, factions and tendencies in Britain, *Political Studies*, Feb. 1964.

[4] F. Williams, *A Prime Minister Remembers*, Heinemann, 1961, p. 81.

[5] For example, see R. H. S. Crossman's Introduction to Bagehot, *op. cit.*, pp. 48–56.

hierarchy depends very much upon his favourable opinion of a colleague. He is the leader of the Parliamentary Party as well as the party outside Parliament. Elections increasingly revolve round the choice of the Prime Minister. His personality and performance are bound up with the image of the party. He has access to television and other media to an extent denied other ministers. He makes the final decision on the right moment to seek a dissolution of Parliament, a decision which can crucially affect the prospects of a party in the subsequent election.

It seems true enough, therefore, that a Prime Minister who plays his cards well, and who is popular with his Parliamentary Party, occupies an impregnable position. But these conditions do not always hold; they may be present for a time and then circumstances change.

Prime Ministers in the twentieth century have been at their weakest in peacetime coalition Cabinets. Lloyd George had autocratic tendencies, but after 1918 a Cabinet founded on an uneasy liaison between a Liberal faction and Conservative Party leaders was a very shaky power base. It took all his considerable political skill to keep it in being as long as he did. For a time his reputation as a wartime leader enabled him to carry on. He was active in many spheres of government, especially foreign policy, which caused some resentment in the Cabinet. In the long run, however, his fate depended on the balance of power in the Conservative Party and in 1922 his career as a minister came to an end. Ramsay MacDonald, after his expulsion from the Labour Party, was entirely dependent on the co-operation of parties of which he was not the recognized leader. His services were dispensed with at the earliest opportunity by his Conservative colleagues and he went into ignominious decline.[6]

Peacetime coalitions are unusual in Britain. In a wartime coalition, when party political differences are to some extent put

[6] On Lloyd George see Beaverbrook, *The Decline and Fall of Lloyd George*, Collins, 1963; and T. Wilson, *The Downfall of the Liberal Party*, Collins, 1966, chs. 9 and 10. For comment on both Lloyd George and Ramsay MacDonald see J. P. Mackintosh, *The British Cabinet*, Stevens, 1962, pp. 355–80 and 412–13.

into cold storage, the authority of a Prime Minister may be great, assuming the war is being successfully prosecuted. If it is not, it is the Prime Minister's reputation above all others which suffers. The fall of both Asquith and Neville Chamberlain demonstrate the point that in wartime the position of Prime Minister is vulnerable. More than in other professions, the man at the head of the system must show results if he is to continue in power.

The behaviour of Prime Ministers is influenced, like that of other politicians, by custom and convention. The office of Prime Minister is institutionalized; that is to say, there is an expected way of doing things and conducting Cabinet business, irrespective of the person who holds the position. True, each Prime Minister has his own individual style, but he works within a tradition. Some Prime Ministers appear to be especially conscious of the propriety of collective decision taking. Balfour, Baldwin, and Asquith resembled committee chairmen rather than self-willed autocrats. Churchill, in wartime, was careful to observe constitutional practice. In his post-war Cabinets he is reported to have offended some ministers by relying on an "inner" Cabinet. He is also said to have lost touch with the party rank and file in the Commons. Attlee, though always in firm control, usually worked more in the tradition of Asquith.[7]

Attlee's decision to approve the production of a British atomic bomb, taken before the full Cabinet was informed, has been cited as evidence of the demise of Cabinet government. Mr. G. R. Strauss, the Minister who then headed the Ministry of Supply, the department mainly responsible for implementing the decision, has denied that the Cabinet was kept in ignorance. Formally, the matter was eventually reported to the Cabinet; in that sense the decision received its approval, or at least its negative consent.[8] In

[7] See Sir Charles Petrie, *The Powers Behind the Prime Ministers*, Macgibbon & Kee, 1958, p. 163; Sir Ivor Jennings, *Cabinet Government*, Cambridge, 1951, pp. 180–1; H. Wilson, *Pressure Group*, Secker & Warburg, 1961, pp. 97–100; B. E. Carter, *The Office of the Prime Minister*, Faber, 1956; Mackintosh, *op. cit.*, pp. 426–37.

[8] See R. H. S. Crossman, Introduction to Bagehot, *op. cit.*, pp. 54–55; and letter from Mr. Strauss in *New Statesman*, 10 May 1963.

this instance the balance of argument rests with those who stress the increasing power of the Prime Minister. But the customary practice of Cabinet government by no means dictates that the full Cabinet be consulted prior to every major decision. In the field of foreign affairs particularly, where events move quickly, it is often necessary to act without seeking the opinion of the full Cabinet. Precisely who should be initially consulted, and when to inform the whole Cabinet, are matters of political judgement.

Sir Anthony Eden, now Lord Avon, is said to have committed the Cabinet to the Suez operation of 1956 without full discussion. Lord Avon, in his memoirs, suggests that this was not so. At least one commentator takes the view that the Cabinet was informed in time about policy and could have influenced events "unless Eden's report is flatly wrong". According to Lord Butler, then a Cabinet minister, the Cabinet came very little into the Suez crisis until towards the end. In his opinion, the Cabinet "could have blown up if it had wanted to". It did not do so because there was no widespread opposition to the policy in the Conservative Party in the Commons. Opinion within the Parliamentary Party sets limits to any dictatorial ambitions of Prime Ministers.[9] Naturally, to be effective, such opinions need to be organized and led; other Cabinet ministers might well exploit the situation, out of a conviction that the Prime Minister is wrong, or to pay off old scores, or out of personal ambition.

The six years of Mr. Macmillan's premiership are full of interest. This relatively long period in office gave him unusual authority. He had pulled the Conservative Party out of a difficult situation after Suez. He led it to victory in the election of 1959. He had served a long political apprenticeship and had an inside

[9] Lord Avon, *Full Circle*, Cassell, 1960, Book 3; L. D. Epstein, *British Politics in the Suez Crisis*, Pall Mall, 1964, pp. 69–72; Lord Butler, in conversation with Norman Hunt on Cabinet Government, *The Listener*, 16 Sept. 1965, pp. 409–10. The whole Cabinet probably did not realize the full implications of the Suez operation when it was endorsed. Only an inner circle was initially aware of collusion with France. Even when the Cabinet did discuss the use of force there were said to be "layers" of knowledge. See H. Thomas, *The Suez Affair*, Weidenfeld & Nicolson, 1966, pp. 96–97.

knowledge of the major departments of State. There was no serious challenger for the leadership of the Conservative Party. If ever a Prime Minister was in a position to dominate the Cabinet it was Mr. Macmillan. But his handling of affairs did not go unchallenged. He reshuffled his Cabinets in 1959, 1960, and 1961, thereby unsettling the Conservative Party in Parliament. His choice of a relatively unknown peer as Foreign Secretary, in 1960, was viewed with suspicion. It was suggested that he was deliberately excluding more suitable persons because they were potential rivals or successors. He upset some backbenchers, who thought that a modern Foreign Secretary should be directly accountable to the Commons. Finally, in 1962, he replaced seven Cabinet ministers; some of them, like Mr. Selwyn Lloyd, had considerable support in the Parliamentary Party.

The motives which inspired Mr. Macmillan at various times have yet to be fully explained. Perhaps they never will be. But it remains the case that his strength lay in correctly assessing feeling within the Conservative Party in Parliament. If, in 1962, he had not found able politicians willing to step into the shoes of the dismissed ministers, he could not have acted as he did. Some bitterness and disunity in the party resulted from his apparently off-hand treatment of loyal followers. At least one observer close to the scene, in general an ardent admirer of Macmillan, has suggested that the reconstruction of the Cabinet in 1962 was a crucial stage in the decline of his authority in the Parliamentary Party.[10] Subsequent events contributed to his loss of prestige. The winter of 1962–3 brought a high level of unemployment; de Gaulle vetoed Britain's application to join EEC; opinion polls revealed a fall in the Prime Minister's standing. In June 1963 the resignation of Mr. Profumo adversely affected not only the image of the Conservative Party but also that of the Prime Minister. When the Profumo affair was debated in the Commons, twenty-seven Conservatives abstained, expressing their lack of confidence in the Government. Illness completed the series of events which led

[10] R. Bevins, *The Greasy Pole*, Hodder & Stoughton, 1965, pp. 133–8. See also H. Daalder, *Cabinet Reform in Britain*, Oxford, 1964, pp. 124–6.

to Macmillan's decision to resign, announced at the Conservative Party conference in October.

Sir Alec Douglas-Home followed Mr. Macmillan as Prime Minister and leader of the Conservative Party, but only after a succession struggle, for once conducted partly in the open.

Sir Alec had the misfortune to face a confident and skilful Leader of the Opposition whose party, at that time, was more united than his own. The new Prime Minister had only recently renounced his peerage, and his experience of Parliament had hitherto been mainly confined to the different atmosphere of the House of Lords. Sir Alec's career as Prime Minister is seldom referred to by those who contend that modern Cabinets are almost wholly dominated by whoever holds that office.

It is too early to attempt an assessment of Mr. Wilson's relationship with other members of his Cabinets; little reliable or impartial information is available. When he reshuffled his Cabinet in January 1967 he was criticized in some quarters for not being a "good butcher", but it should be remembered that wholesale sackings from the Cabinet make better copy for political commentators. One subsequent episode deserves mention. It appears that in December 1967 a majority of the Cabinet Defence and Oversea Policy Committee, not representative of all shades of opinion in the full Cabinet, favoured lifting the embargo on the supply of arms to South Africa. The Prime Minister, supported by other Cabinet ministers, opposed this. Mr. Wilson is said to have encouraged the build-up of backbench opinion against lifting the embargo to which he had committed the Government in November 1964. But although Mr. Wilson had his way, he did not succeed without a fight. The precise division of opinion in the Cabinet is not known.[11]

Concern over the power of the Prime Minister may derive from a too literal acceptance of the dictum that he is, or should be, merely *primus inter pares*. In practice, the authority of Prime Ministers must be greater than that of their Cabinet colleagues.

[11] See *The Economist*, 14 Jan. 1967, and report on arms embargo in *The Times*, 16 Dec. 1967.

A cabal of party politicians, often with different points of view, and dealing with complex issues, needs a firm controlling hand to maintain at least an outward show of unity. Whether the power exercised by a particular Prime Minister, at a particular moment of time, is excessive or not can only be discussed in the political context which then exists.

What one can be certain of is that the situation in the relevant party or parties will strongly influence the power structure in the Cabinet. Each Cabinet minister has his independent link with Parliament via his membership of a party. This connection of ministers with Parliament, and especially the Commons, is the essence of the Cabinet system in Britain. If the power of the Prime Minister is to be checked or limited, the means may be found in his relations with his party as a whole rather than in his relations with other members of the Cabinet. What the latter can or cannot do will turn very much on the party situation. Daalder's remark that Prime Ministers govern "at the mercy of party" needs to be stressed.[12]

If a Prime Minister, or any member of the Cabinet, loses touch with the Parliamentary Party he is apt to run into trouble at some stage. Mr. Enoch Powell, when Minister of Health in Mr. Macmillan's Cabinet, took great pains to maintain good relations with the Health Committee of the Conservative Party in Parliament. He put his ideas about future policy before members of the committee and tried to ensure that policy was seen as growing out of their views. Mr. Emanuel Shinwell reports that he lost his Cabinet post of Minister of Fuel and Power, in Attlee's Cabinet, because sections of the Parliamentary Labour Party disliked his handling of the fuel crisis of 1947.[13]

[12] Daalder, *op. cit.*, p. 248. Also see D. N. Chester, Who governs Britain?, *Parliamentary Affairs*, 1962, pp. 519–26; H. J. Laski, *Reflections on the Constitution*, Manchester University Press, p. 136; and J. P. Mackintosh, The Prime Minister and the Cabinet, *Parliamentary Affairs*, Winter 1967–8.

[13] Enoch Powell, conversation with Norman Hunt, in *Whitehall and Beyond*, BBC Publications, 1964, pp. 49–50; E. Shinwell, *Conflict Without Malice*, Odhams, 1955, p. 186.

It is evident that membership of the Cabinet, relations within it, and the way in which it performs its functions are influenced by party. It is not suggested that party considerations are the only ones that matter or that they are invariably more important than other influences. But they are certainly important. The size of the Cabinet, for example, is not unrelated to party. And the size of the Cabinet is generally held to affect the whole of its operations.

The Size of the Cabinet

Obviously, the unity of the Cabinet and relations within it are affected by size. But what is the "ideal" or "right" size? L. S. Amery, an experienced politician, thought six. The Haldane Committee suggested ten, and certainly not more than twelve. In practice, since 1945, Cabinets have ranged from sixteen to twenty-three. In part, this reflects the increased functions of the State and the creation of new government departments; but the ministers who head new departments are not automatically members of the Cabinet. Sir Winston Churchill had a Cabinet of sixteen in 1951. Sir Alec Douglas-Home and Mr. Wilson have had Cabinets of twenty-three. Before he became Prime Minister, Mr. Wilson declared his intention of reducing the size of the Cabinet, but in 1967 he still had a Cabinet of twenty-one.

In Amery's scheme about six Cabinet ministers, relieved of departmental chores, would concentrate on long-term policy and planning. His ideas derive from his experience in the secretariat attached to Lloyd George's Cabinet in the First World War. That Cabinet had only five members, including the Prime Minister. It is extremely doubtful, to say the least, that such a small Cabinet would be acceptable in peacetime. It would certainly mean the exclusion of ambitious party politicians who could cause a lot of trouble in the Commons. The overriding objective of winning the war tended to produce a unity which would be more difficult to achieve in normal times. According to Laski it was not relief from departmental responsibilities, nor its small size which unified the

Lloyd George war Cabinet. Rather it was the fear of offering Asquith any opportunity of overthrowing the coalition.[14]

A Cabinet composed entirely of non-departmental ministers, though nominally responsible for policy, would have to rely heavily on information provided by departmental ministers. Moreover, policy cannot be realistically formulated without direct experience of its day-to-day implementation. It is the departmental ministers who have to see that policy is put into effect and, since they are individually responsible for their departments, it is their reputations which are at stake if policies fail to produce satisfactory results.

These problems of information and responsibility recur when one turns to other ideas for reducing the size of the Cabinet. In 1947 Lord Samuel proposed a Cabinet of ten. Six were to be without departments, acting as chairmen of sub-committees on such matters as defence, external affairs, economic policy, and social services. The Foreign Secretary, the Chancellor of the Exchequer, the Home Secretary, and the Lord Chancellor, all with departmental responsibilities, were to be included. But the Foreign Secretary and the Chancellor of the Exchequer were to be subordinate to the chairman of the appropriate committees. How such powerful departments as the Treasury and the Foreign Office would react to the downgrading of their political heads is unknown, since no Prime Minister has followed Lord Samuel's scheme. There would be some confusion in the minds of civil servants since they would be subject to two ministers whose precise responsibilities would be blurred.[15]

Although he was too experienced to tangle with the Treasury or Foreign Office, Sir Winston Churchill did experiment with supervising ministers, popularly called "overlords". In 1951, Lord Woolton, whose duties as Lord President of the Council were far from onerous, was given the task of supervising the work of the Ministry of Food and the Ministry of Agriculture, whose

[14] L. S. Amery, *Thoughts on the Constitution*, Oxford, 2nd edn., 1953, pp. 90–91; Laski, *op. cit.*, pp. 142–4.

[15] Daalder, *op. cit.*, pp. 284–5.

ministers were not in the Cabinet. Lord Leathers was given similar responsibility over the Ministries of Transport and Fuel and Power. Lord Cherwell had general responsibility for scientific research and development throughout the Government as a whole.

It was unfortunate that these supervising ministers were all members of the House of Lords. Not only did this wound the *amour-propre* of the Commons, but it also lent force to Opposition criticisms that elected representatives were being deprived of the opportunity to question the ministers ultimately responsible for policy, traditionally regarded as an important means of securing the accountability of the executive. The precise division of responsibility between the "overlords" and the ministers they supervised was far from clear since their respective duties were not defined in any statute.

Lord Morrison, at that time a leading member of the Opposition in the Commons, contends that had the "overlords" been merely co-ordinating ministers, with no powers to decide matters, there would have been little objection. Their powers should have been clearly restricted to persuasion, suggestion and guidance. But, he argues, the term "supervising", used in connection with the system, indicates a person with power to issue directions to a subordinate. In his opinion such a relationship is incompatible with the constitutional principle of individual ministerial responsibility.[16] This principle, and the closely associated concept of collective responsibility, will be discussed later. For the moment we shall merely observe that individual ministerial responsibility involves the notion that a departmental minister is primarily responsible for the policy and general efficiency of his department. Obviously such a principle is difficult to reconcile with the existence of "overlords", whose influence must affect the running of departments. The principle therefore inhibits the use of "overlords" as a means of reducing the size of the Cabinet.

[16] Lord Morrison, *Government and Parliament*, Oxford Paperback, 3rd edn., 1964, pp. 58–68. Note opinion of Lord Woolton, quoted on p. 62, to the effect that co-ordinators were responsible to the Cabinet, not Parliament.

According to Daalder, it was Churchill's intention that the "overlords" would have powers of direction in their respective spheres and that they would be answerable to him. The system would thus increase the power of the Prime Minister. But the departments resisted the authority of the "overlords", insisting on their customary right to appeal to the whole Cabinet when a difference of opinion could not be settled in any other way. Daalder also suggests that some younger departmental ministers never really accepted the authority of the "overlords". The Prime Minister rarely discussed matters with them or with Cabinet ministers who were not members of his intimate inner circle.[17] These tensions within the Government, together with the criticisms of the Opposition, brought about the end of the "overlord" experiment in 1953.

Nevertheless, a co-ordinating minister existed between 1946 and 1964 in the shape of the Minister of Defence. Supported by a small department he attempted to supervise the work of three separate Service departments whose political heads were not in the Cabinet. He differed from the "overlords" in that his functions were defined by statute. The organization of defence is discussed in greater detail in a subsequent chapter. Here we need only note that the size of the Cabinet was reduced by the exclusion of Service ministers; but it is likely that they would not have been included anyway in a peacetime Cabinet. In 1964 a new Ministry of Defence was created and the separate Service departments were abolished.

Before leaving the subject of "supervising" and "co-ordinating" ministers, it might be as well to note that the distinction drawn between them, by Lord Morrison and others, though fairly clear on paper, may not be so in actual practice. A "suggestion" emanating from a co-ordinating minister, who has the backing of the Prime Minister or some influential clique in the Cabinet, might prove difficult to distinguish from a directive in the mind of the recipient. On the other hand, a supervising minister, without adequate staff, is in a weak position. And it is uneconomical to

[17] Daalder, *op. cit.*, pp. 119–20.

duplicate the staff available to a departmental minister. A departmental minister can concentrate on a relatively narrow range of issues. A supervising or co-ordinating minister may be saddled with special or unexpected problems when they do not clearly fall within the province of any particular department.[18]

But there are ways of reducing the size of the Cabinet which do not involve the use of supervising ministers. The number of ministers in the Cabinet is related to the number of departments which exist. The increase in the number of departments, over the years, reflects the increase in the functions of the state, and their complexity. The Haldane Report, with its recommendation for a Cabinet of ten, was produced at a time when there were far fewer departments than there are now. However, the number of departments may be reduced by merging two or more of them; or a department might be broken up and its functions distributed amongst other departments.

The absorption of the three Service departments by the Ministry of Defence did not reduce the size of the Cabinet because the Service ministers were not members. But it might be possible to combine, say, the Ministry of Power and the Ministry of Technology. Alternatively, responsibility for science, which at present lies with the Department for Education and Science, might be reallocated to Technology and the Secretary of State for Education dropped from the Cabinet. In short, there would be a tendency towards bigger and more complex departments represented in the Cabinet. Those who favour a small policy Cabinet will obviously object that ministers would be so bowed down with departmental

[18] See D. N. Chester, *Lessons of the British War Economy*, Cambridge, 1951, p. 28. Since Mr. R. H. S. Crossman took charge of social service matters in the Cabinet, he has often been described as an overlord. His immediate task was to arrange the merger of the Ministry of Health and the Ministry of Social Security. When this is complete he is expected to become minister of the new department and to assume unambiguous ministerial responsibility. In the transitional period responsibility is somewhat blurred. Other ministers without departmental responsibilities have previously acted as social service co-ordinators in Mr. Wilson's Cabinets. For a time Mr. Wilson himself acted as economics overlord but the Opposition failed to exploit the constitutional issue. See Appendix (1).

duties that they would have little time for the consideration of long-term overall policy.

The appropriate size of a department is difficult to determine. The ideal, according to one view, is that size which enables the minister and his most senior civil servant, the Permanent Secretary, to effectively control all the business involved; work should flow smoothly across their desks.[19] But this does not seem to be a very helpful criterion. Ministers vary in their capacity to handle work, and permanent secretaries manage their departments with different degrees of competence. Furthermore, work may be flowing smoothly across desks because too little notice is taken of the effects of decisions on other people or departments.

Cabinet ministers are certainly hard pressed even when they are in charge of relatively small departments. A small department, in terms of numbers, may be dealing with complicated and difficult problems. This is the case with the Treasury and the Department of Economic Affairs. Ministers must not only run their departments and attend meetings of the Cabinet and some of its committees, they must appear in Parliament to answer questions and participate in debates and divisions. They must attend party meetings. If they are in the Commons they cannot afford to neglect their constituencies. They will nurture contacts with pressure groups. Increasingly, they may spend much of their time abroad at international conferences.

Obviously, unless he is to sink into an early grave, a Cabinet minister needs assistance in the form of junior ministers. If he makes full use of their talents, a large or complicated department can be managed effectively. Much depends on the availability of junior ministers with the necessary qualities. If a Cabinet minister with departmental responsibilities struggles along without much assistance from political juniors, more power is likely to accumulate in the hands of officials. They must be permitted, and expected, to take more decisions on their own initiative, including those of a manifestly political nature. Since the Minister is constitutionally

[19] D. N. Chester and F. M. G. Willson, *The Organization of British Central Government*, Allen & Unwin, 1957, p. 343.

answerable for these decisions, he must have confidence in his officials. The corollary of larger departments, which may reduce the size of the Cabinet, is an increase in the power of civil servants.

This does not mean that officials will necessarily welcome departmental mergers. Organizational change may adversely affect the career prospects of some civil servants. At the very least the outcome is uncertain and feelings of insecurity result. Promotion prospects in each department vary and officials are very conscious of this.[20] A permanent secretary who receives personnel from a defunct department is confronted with a delicate managerial problem when fitting them into his organization. It is thus possible that many officials will oppose change; and they are certain to receive support from those politicians who believe they too are losing in power and status.

The number of departments is affected as much by political as by administrative considerations. A Ministry may be kept in being, and its political head in the Cabinet, because of the influence of a particular pressure group, or because some part of the country is important from the electoral point of view. No Prime Minister is anxious to offend the farmers by abolishing the Ministry of Agriculture and Food or dropping its Minister from the Cabinet. Pressure from ex-servicemen, amongst other things, kept the Ministry of Pensions and the Ministry of National Insurance separate for some time, though they were eventually integrated. The Secretary of State for Scotland seems assured of a department and a seat in the Cabinet, partly because Scotland has 71 of the 630 seats in the Commons.

In sum, there are frequently more pressures working for the preservation and creation of departments than for their integration or abolition. Politicians often advocate smaller Cabinets and fewer departments, but in the event they tend to create larger Cabinets

[20] On this see A. Dunsire, The passing of the Ministry of Transport and Civil Aviation, *Public Law*, Summer, 1961, p. 154. Also, H. V. Rhodes, *Setting Up a New Government Department*, British Institute of Management, 1949, p. 14. Even reorganization within a department can cause quite a stir, e.g. see *5th Report from Estimates Committee, 1963–4*, HMSO, paras. 991–1001.

and set up new departments. And some new departments, created with a flourish of trumpets, are almost certain to be represented in the Cabinet. In 1964 it would have been virtually impossible for Mr. Wilson to have excluded the newly created Secretary of State for Economic Affairs from the Cabinet. It would have been almost as difficult to leave out the new Minister of Technology.[21]

The possibility of reducing the size of the Cabinet by rationalizing departmental structures therefore appears limited. In addition the co-ordinating function of the Cabinet tends to maintain its size. Co-ordination is used here in the sense of ensuring that departmental policies and actions do not conflict. Nearly all governmental activity involves several departments. Even if one limits the Cabinet's main responsibilities to economic policy, overseas affairs, and defence, many departments are involved. In economic matters, the Treasury, Department of Economic Affairs, Board of Trade, Department of Employment and Productivity, Ministry of Transport, Ministry of Power, Ministry of Technology, and Ministry of Agriculture have different but related functions. The Secretary of State for Education and Science might be included in the economic category, partly because scientific research is vital for economic progress and partly because the organization of higher education affects the supply of trained manpower.

Some of the economic departments are also concerned, directly or indirectly, with defence and foreign policy. The Foreign Office and the Ministry of Defence must obviously be represented in the Cabinet. The Home Secretary is usually a Cabinet Minister. The Scottish Office, which is responsible for the economic and social policies relating to Scotland, is certain to be represented at Cabinet level. Wales, too, is likely to have a separate Cabinet Minister—the Secretary of State for Wales—who heads a smallish office. The reason for his inclusion is pretty obviously political. No party likes to lose votes by offending Welsh national pride.

[21] Also see Daalder, *op. cit.*, pp. 270–4.

If we add the Prime Minister to the heads of the departments mentioned, this gives a total figure of fifteen. Furthermore, one must expect the inclusion of other departmental ministers. There is always the possibility that a social service department will be represented. The Ministry of Health, for example, may be the centre of political controversy, or the Minister may happen to be a politician of some standing and ability. Aneurin Bevan, a Minister of Health under Attlee, would have been difficult to exclude from any Labour Cabinet. His resignation, ostensibly over health charges, produced bitter factionalism in the parliamentary party. Mr. R. H. S. Crossman, Minister of Housing and Local Government in Mr. Wilson's Cabinet of 1964, later Lord President of the Council, is an almost automatic choice for Cabinet office, whatever position he holds, partly because of his ability and partly because he is potential leader of a left-wing opposition within the PLP.

The Lord Chancellor is customarily a member of peacetime Cabinets. And there are likely to be one or two members with only nominal duties, such as the Lord Privy Seal, who can chair committees or take on special problems as they arise. A Cabinet of at least nineteen is a distinct probability. It might be possible to get it down to around seventeen; there is certainly some fat in the sphere of economic affairs. To attempt to reduce it still further might create more political and administrative problems than it solved.

In point of fact it remains to be proved that a Cabinet of fifteen is to be preferred to one of twenty. A small Cabinet is supposed to permit fuller discussion of major policy. Perhaps it does; but there are also fewer points of view brought to bear on complex matters and the Cabinet is less representative of shades of opinion in the party. A large Cabinet also has political advantages because there are more members to face the bowling in the Commons; responsibility is diffused rather than concentrated. Furthermore, a Cabinet of twenty, if properly serviced and organized, can get through a great deal of business in a relatively short time.

The Cabinet Secretariat and Cabinet Committees

Until April 1968 the normal practice was for the full Cabinet to meet about twice a week for a few hours, though special meetings might also be called. Then Mr. Wilson announced he intended to reduce the frequency of full Cabinet meetings by making greater use of Cabinet committees. These relieve pressure on the full Cabinet, as does the Cabinet Secretariat, through its preparatory work.

The Secretariat is the most important part of the Cabinet Office. The Cabinet Office, composed of career civil servants and certain special advisers drawn from outside the public service, assists the Cabinet in its work. It serves the Cabinet as a whole. The Prime Minister has a separate small group to assist him, though there is an overlap of personnel.

The Secretariat has its origins in the assistance provided for the Committee of Imperial Defence, set up early in the twentieth century. In 1916 Lloyd George took over this assistance, using it for more general purposes. The functions of the Secretariat have been defined as the preparation of agenda for meetings, the keeping of minutes, the recording and circulation of decisions, and the following up of decisions with departments.[22] The Head of the Secretariat, the Secretary of the Cabinet, at present Sir Burke Trend, is clearly in a position of great influence. His predecessor, the late Lord Normanbrook, often accompanied Prime Ministers when they made official journeys overseas. From this it has been inferred that he acted as an intimate adviser to a greater extent than did his predecessors.[23] It is difficult to believe that a Prime Minister would fail to take the Secretary of the Cabinet into his confidence or that he would disregard his advice or judgement.

The more senior members of the Secretariat, and certain special advisers on such subjects as economic or scientific policy, are in close contact with the Prime Minister and his most intimate

[22] Sir Ivor Jennings, *op. cit.*, pp. 227 and 256.
[23] *The Times*, 16 June 1967.

colleagues. The Secretariat services Cabinet committees as well as the Cabinet itself. It is therefore associated with deliberations on all sorts of problems. An active Prime Minister might well be intent on building up the Secretariat, and his own Office, to the detriment of departmental independence.

Shortly before he became Prime Minister, Mr. Wilson indicated that he intended to make greater use of the Secretariat and of special advisers if the Labour Party came to power. And, indeed, the Civil Estimates for 1967–8 show the size of the Secretariat as eighty-five, just about double what it was in 1963. He has also made use of special advisers from outside the civil service; for example, he appointed an Oxford economist with Labour Party sympathies, Dr. Balogh, to be Adviser on Economic Affairs.[24]

It was the opinion of Mr. Wilson that the Cabinet should not have to rely on a departmental brief presented as a consolidated view by the Minister concerned. Policy should be judged at every level, not solely within a department. In answer to questions, however, Mr. Wilson admitted that the Secretariat would itself have to rely on the departments for most of the information it needed. And, since it is in the interest of departments to keep their internal differences to themselves, the Secretariat would scarcely increase its popularity if it took up the cudgels on behalf of factions overruled in their departments, encouraging them to renew the battle at Cabinet level. It is doubtful if the Secretariat would care to interpret its role in quite this light.

The Secretariat is itself staffed by men seconded from departments for relatively short periods of time except at the highest levels. They have been described as "migratory birds", who will soon return to their departments; they are not a separate and distinct administrative elite with different attitudes from those of other civil servants. It is unlikely that they would go out of their way to interfere unduly in the internal struggles of departments. On the other hand, where the interests or policies of two or more

[24] Harold Wilson, conversation with Norman Hunt, in *Whitehall and Beyond*, BBC Publications, 1964, pp. 18–24. Also see further conversation in *The Listener*, 6 April 1967. Dr. Balogh has since been given a life peerage.

departments conflict, the Secretariat's reputation as an impartial body may well be of value in helping the Cabinet to resolve the problem.[25]

It has been suggested that the Cabinet Secretariat might usefully take over some functions of the Treasury. The general control of the civil service has been mentioned in this connection. This would leave the Treasury free to concentrate on economic policy.[26] Whether the Secretariat is equipped for such a task, or would welcome it, is another matter.

Apart from the Secretariat, the Cabinet Office includes the Central Statistical Office and an Historical Section. The latter is of little significance for current administration. The Statistical Office is the rump of the Economic and Statistical Section, set up during the Second World War. The economists were transferred to the Treasury shortly after the war. The Statistical Office produces figures when requested, usually when they are not already available from a government department. Like the Secretariat, it serves Cabinet committees, which have tended to grow in number and importance.

Membership of Cabinet committees is not confined to Cabinet ministers; departmental ministers not in the Cabinet may be included. Committees may be "standing" or *ad hoc*; the former are more or less permanent, though they may undergo modification; the latter are set up to deal with some particular problem and dissolved when they have served their purpose. The Defence and Oversea Policy Committee is an example of a standing committee. *Ad hoc* committees may deal with such matters as events in Rhodesia or Britain's application to join the Common Market.

The use of standing committees has increased since the 1930's. Lord Morrison recalls only one standing committee, apart from the Committee on Imperial Defence, during the Labour Govern-

[25] M. Beloff, *New Dimensions in Foreign Policy*, Allen & Unwin, 1961, pp. 165–6.

[26] W. A. Robson, The reform of government, *Political Quarterly*, April–June 1964, p. 202. Also see postscript on Civil Service Department, p. 225.

ment's period of office between 1929 and 1931. Pressure on the small War Cabinet, in the Second World War, and its concentration on matters directly relating to the conduct of the war, encouraged the use of a committee system. The Labour governments of 1945–51 carried the development still further. For example, in addition to a Defence Committee, chaired by the Prime Minister, there was a Social Services Committee presided over by the Lord Privy Seal. There were also committees on Economic Policy, Production, and other subjects.[27]

Through committees, departmental ministers may become aware of aspects of policy which they might otherwise have overlooked. Preliminary work by committees and the circulation of their reports and papers may save Cabinet time, and junior ministers may acquire valuable experience.

But committees can also waste time or make excessive demands on the time of some ministers. The Chancellor of the Exchequer, for example, is inevitably a member of numerous committees. A committee may be unable to reach agreement and decisions may be delayed or take the form of some weak compromise. Committees tend to proliferate, partly because new functions arise, partly because awkward problems are referred to new committees or sub-committees, and partly through the tactical manœuvres of those who feel things are not going their way. There may be considerable overlap and duplication of work and hence problems of coordination. According to one estimate there were over a hundred committees served by the Cabinet Office in the early fifties. The Cabinet Secretariat is charged with the task of winding up committees, subject to the approval of the Prime Minister and other ministers concerned.[28]

Some committees have been instituted not to relieve pressure on the Cabinet but to supervise inexperienced or mistrusted departmental ministers. An Emergency Fuel and Power Committee, chaired by the Prime Minister, was set up to help the highly regarded Mr. Gaitskell when he first became Minister of Fuel and

[27] Morrison, *op. cit.*, ch. 2.
[28] Daalder, *op. cit.*, pp. 245–6.

Power. When Mr. Neville Chamberlain was Prime Minister he had no confidence in Anthony Eden, who was his Foreign Secretary for a time. Accordingly, he appointed a Foreign Affairs Committee. Ironically, Eden himself made use of a special committee during the Suez affair. Initially the full Cabinet did not know of its existence. The workings of such committees are obscure. Minutes and records are likely to be incomplete and membership depends on the personal inclinations of the Prime Minister rather than on departmental responsibilities. The main purpose of the Suez committee was to achieve a unified clique which could steamroller the full Cabinet.[29]

Some committees, then, owe their existence to personal and factional differences in the Cabinet. They confirm the remark of Sir Henry Taylor that "Not one in ten of the measures taken by the cabinet can win the sincere assent of every member of the cabinet".

In April 1968 Mr. Wilson set up a new Parliamentary Committee of the Cabinet to act as the main policy-making body of the Government. It has a nucleus of about ten senior ministers. The Prime Minister's motives were variously interpreted. Some commentators saw the committee as a device for rearranging the party political balance in the Cabinet; others as a means of overcoming the disadvantages of working with a Cabinet of more than twenty.

The committee should put to rest the fiction that the Cabinet is a body of political equals. But it would be premature to write off Cabinet government as a thing of the past. If the Parliamentary Committee is divided, the minority will wish to appeal to the full Cabinet. It has been reported that dissenting members of committees will need the consent of the Prime Minister before they are allowed to reopen issues in the full Cabinet. But the Prime Minister himself may sometimes wish to do this, and it is easy to

[29] See Mackintosh, *op. cit.*, pp. 390 and 397; Daalder, *op. cit.*, p. 75; Lord Butler, *The Listener*, 16 Sept. 1965, p. 409; D. C. Watt, Divided control of British foreign policy, *Political Quarterly*, Oct.–Dec. 1962, pp. 376–7; and Thomas, *op. cit.*, *passim.*

foresee serious Cabinet splits if he is too niggardly in granting permission. One may doubt whether certain influential Cabinet ministers will tamely accept collective responsibility for policies emanating from a committee of which they are not members.[30]

Collective Responsibility and Ministerial Responsibility

The concept of collective responsibility is of vital importance in the British system of government. It is the basis of a Government's strength and it tends to unify the various parts of the administrative machine. If it is something of a myth, it is nevertheless too important to be lightly discarded. The essence of collective responsibility is that all politicians who are members of the Government are expected to support its policies in public. What they feel privately or say within government circles is another matter. Any member of the Government who wishcs to disassociate himself from policy, in public, is expected to resign office. If he publicly opposes policy before he has resigned he faces the probability of dismissal. In May 1967, for example, seven parliamentary private secretaries were dismissed by their ministers, at the Prime Minister's prompting, for abstaining in a Commons division on Britain's application to join the Common Market.

Collective responsibility is conducive to compromise. Some enterprising ministers may find their most original ideas emasculated by more cautious colleagues. It may be that a good deal of enterprise and vigour is lost to government as a result. But the doctrine has its virtues. First, it tends to counteract departmentalism and separatism, characteristics of all large-scale organizations. Each minister has an interest in every aspect of policy because his own reputation and future are involved. They may be

[30] See *The Economist*, 13 April 1968, and editorial in *The Times*, 10 April 1968. With greater use of committees it is reasonable to desire more information about their number, membership, and functions. With a few exceptions such information has hitherto been hard to come by, ostensibly because it is supposed to undermine the doctrines, or myths, of collective and individual ministerial responsibility.

adversely affected by the blunders of a colleague. Thus every minister is inclined to keep an eye on activities which are not strictly concern of his department.[31]

Secondly, because of collective responsibility, a departmental minister is less likely to be unduly influenced by the civil servants in his department. Cabinet and other colleagues will bring their points of view to bear on policy. And if a minister decides to stick to an unmodified departmental policy, he will nevertheless have to argue his case before a politically interested body. But not all aspects of policy are discussed at Cabinet level.

The Cabinet spends some of its time resolving differences between departments. Departments are expected to keep such differences to a minimum, but at least the Cabinet is made aware of the issues involved. The Cabinet as a whole may be relatively uninformed about aspects of policy which have been settled by ministers and civil servants at a lower level. There may be some sort of assent by the Cabinet but it is of a negative type. Yet the ministers who have actually decided the matter are wrapped in the protective blanket of collective responsibility. It has been suggested that there is an incentive to remove decision taking from the Cabinet sphere, and that, paradoxically, collective responsibility weakens the power of the Prime Minister and the Cabinet.[32]

There is some substance in this line of thought. In practice, however, if the Cabinet attempted more than it already does it would be overwhelmed. Against the certain advantages of a reasonable division of labour and delegation of authority one has the dubious prospect of an increase in the power of the Cabinet, or, more probably, the Prime Minister. And it seems highly unlikely that Cabinet ministers would fail to hear informally of departmental plots or conspiracies which were of political importance. In the long run policy must reveal itself; and a Cabinet minister who had not dealt openly with his colleagues might well find himself isolated and ultimately sacrificed.

[31] See Enoch Powell, *Whitehall and Beyond*, pp. 56–60.

[32] R. E. Neustadt, 10 Downing Street: Is it out of date?, *The Sunday Times*, 8 Nov. 1964.

This does not mean that all ministers have an equal part in the process of decision making. Major decisions may be taken before they appear formally on any Cabinet agenda. Much depends on the issue involved. In foreign affairs, for example, events move with such speed that the Cabinet may be presented with a *fait accompli* by some specially responsible group. Even so, the probable reactions of the Cabinet will be borne in mind by such a group. And if a member of the Cabinet feels strongly about the matter he can certainly make his views known; in the last resort he may resign, causing the Government embarrassment.

Obviously a minister cannot be equally enthusiastic about every aspect of policy. In spite of the understanding that no member of the Government shall publicly attack its policies, individual differences of opinion are fairly well known. A minister who feels increasingly out of sympathy with some major aspect of policy is in something of a dilemma. The temptation to remain in the Government and do what one can to advance one's views is naturally great. Eventually, however, a minister who is consistently in a minority on a matter about which he feels strongly may decide that he has had enough of the doctrine of collective responsibility. It neutralizes influence which he might otherwise have outside government circles, a fact that will not have escaped the notice of the Prime Minister and other interested parties.

Resignations, as it were, regenerate and renew the unity of the Government and make a reality of collective responsibility. But a dissident ex-minister may enhance the effectiveness of a faction opposed to government policy by providing it with an acknowledged leader.

The Opposition is also affected by the doctrine of collective responsibility. It must match the Government's cohesion. If it is to offer a serious challenge as an alternative government, it must have a reasonably united front bench and a coherent set of policies to present to the electorate.

Between elections the Government is mainly responsible, formally, to the Commons. There are two shades of meaning, at least, associated with the word "responsibility"; there is responsibility *for* policy and there is responsibility *to* the Commons and, ultimately, to the electorate.[33] If the Government is defeated in the Commons, on a matter of policy, it must resign *en bloc* or submit to a general election. But the party system in Britain renders a government defeat in the Commons highly unlikely. The majority of the Commons are supporters of the Government or members of the Government. However much certain policies are disliked by backbenchers of the party in office they will not make common cause with the Opposition to bring the Government down, except possibly in a time of national crisis such as war.

There may be as many as ninety ministers in the Commons, a considerable proportion of the majority party.[34] Furthermore, the backbenchers of the government party know that if they were to condemn the Government by voting with the Opposition they would be hazarding their own political future. A divided party seldom, if ever, does well at the polls. Even the most disgruntled local constituency organization is going to look askance at an MP who prefers to see the Opposition in power rather than his own party leaders. The relationship of collective responsibility and party discipline in the Commons is very close.

The effect of the doctrine of collective responsibility on the cohesion of the Government can scarcely be overlooked. The significance of individual ministerial responsibility is less certain.

Although ministers are collectively responsible for policy, they are said to be individually responsible for the administration of their departments and the implementation of certain aspects of policy. In theory they, and they alone, are answerable if their departments prove to be incompetent or unsatisfactory in some other way.

In practice it is not always easy to distinguish clearly between policy and administration but, in addition to this, more than one

[33] On various meanings of "responsibility" see A. H. Birch, *Representative and Responsible Government*, Allen & Unwin, 1964, pp. 17–21.

[34] See H. V. Wiseman, *Parliament and the Executive*, Routledge, 1966, pp. 39–40.

department is likely to be involved in most administrative matters. Defence, for example, is a field where the work of the Foreign Office and Treasury is often as important as that of the Ministry of Defence.

The interrelationships of modern government undermine the concept of individual ministerial responsibility. It is often difficult to determine where collective responsibility ends and individual responsibility begins. On the whole, it is to the advantage of ministers to protect themselves by making an issue one of collective responsibility. Where doubt exists it is the Cabinet itself which decides.[35] In reaching a decision expediency is apt to prevail over logic. But since criticisms of individual ministers tend to rub off on the Government as a whole, even incompetent ministers may anticipate a stay of execution. And sentence is passed by governmental colleagues rather than by the Commons. The outcome may be no more than transfer to some other department after the shouting has died down.

If the reality of individual ministerial responsibility turns on the ability of the Commons to force ministers to resign, then it is not much in evidence. In 1963 the Secretary of State for War, Mr. Profumo, resigned after admitting that he had lied to the House over his relationship with a lady who was simultaneously engaged in an affair with a Russian diplomat. Yet, in spite of a patent failure of security, no other minister resigned. But in this case there were doubts as to which minister was responsible. It was commonly believed that the Prime Minister was responsible for security, but the Home Secretary was also involved.[36]

Mr. Shinwell did not resign from the Ministry of Fuel and Power in 1947 although he was severely criticized in the Commons during the fuel crisis of that year. In 1959 the Colonial Secretary

[35] Daalder, *op. cit.*, pp. 301–2; also Mackintosh, *op. cit.*, p. 446.

[36] See Lord Denning's Report, Cmd. 2152, HMSO, 1963, paras. 182, 239, and 286. It is exceptionally difficult to enforce ministerial responsibility against a Prime Minister. Mr. Macmillan's resignation would have been too much for the Labour Opposition to have hoped for and would have created a major government and party upheaval. But the competence of a Prime Minister may come to be doubted as a result of criticism in the House.

was under pressure to resign following the deaths of eleven prisoners at Hola Camp in Kenya, but he did not do so. These are typical rather than exceptional cases.[37]

It should also be remarked that there is a fairly rapid turnover of departmental ministers in Britain. By the time some example of incompetence or maladministration has come to light a minister may well have been moved to a different department; he may have left the Government altogether. His successor in his original department may admit responsibility to the extent of answering questions, defending decisions, or rectifying mistakes. But he will not feel obliged to resign in the face of criticism.

But it would be wrong to conclude that the concept of individual ministerial responsibility is of slight importance only. It is of some significance that MPs can seek information from departmental ministers and can mount attacks on them when their performance seems unsatisfactory. Although such attacks may have no immediate result, they tend to discredit a minister in the long run if they are kept up. He may be discreetly dropped when the government leaders feel no loss of face will result. And, for the sake of good public relations, ministers will not be indifferent to the views and opinions of the elected representatives.

The effect of individual ministerial responsibility on the Cabinet is clearly less marked than that of collective responsibility. However, we have previously remarked that it does tend to inhibit the use of co-ordinating ministers and "overlords"; this follows from the belief that there should be one minister answerable for a department or some aspect of administration. In passing, one may note that the Cabinet may find the idea of individual ministerial responsibility useful when it becomes necessary or expedient to offer a sacrificial victim to appease public criticism.

Obviously the concept of individual ministerial responsibility

[37] See S. E. Finer, The individual responsibilities of ministers, *Public Administration*, Winter 1956; also G. Marshall and G. Moodie, *Some Problems of the Constitution*, Hutchinson, 1961, pp. 78–84; and Birch, *op. cit.*, pp. 139–49, especially on the now untypical Crichel Down case.

gives each departmental minister an incentive to keep himself informed about the general running of his department. Modern departments are so large and complex that it is inconceivable that a minister will be familiar with more than a part of departmental activity. Nevertheless, he takes responsibility for the whole of it, and cannot complain provided that the behaviour and decisions of civil servants comply with his known policy. But a minister may publicly condemn what he considers the wrongful behaviour of subordinates, especially in the face of Parliamentary criticism. He may disclaim personal culpability or moral responsibility for particular decisions. Even so, he remains constitutionally responsible in the sense of *either* defending *or* repudiating departmental actions and clearly he must have general confidence in his civil servants.[38]

In Britain civil servants are career officials, expected to serve impartially any minister, irrespective of party. The general character of the civil service, and the basis of the confidence which usually pertains between ministers and civil servants, must now be discussed.

[38] See Morrison, *op. cit.*, pp. 333–4; and Marshall and Moodie, *op. cit.*, pp. 84–87.

CHAPTER 2

THE CIVIL SERVICE *

The Structure of the Service

According to official figures, the strength of the non-industrial civil service on 1 April 1967, excluding post office workers, was 457,563, an increase of more than 24,000 on the previous year's total.[1] An organization of this size, performing many different functions, is certain to exhibit a great deal of diversity in its structure. It is true that the civil service is formally unified, the Treasury exercising general control over management and organization, but it is by no means homogeneous. The numerous classes and categories of the service are composed of officials with widely differing backgrounds and qualifications. Contrary to popular belief, the "typical" civil servant does not exist. Within each class or category of the service there is a sense of unity, but there are different types of personnel even within each class.

The "General" or "Treasury" classes of the service consist of the administrative class, the executive class, and the clerical class. Numbers vary from year to year, but in 1967, in the Home Civil Service, there were just under 2500 members of the administrative class, and just over 46,000 in the general executive class. The general clerical class is by far the largest, numbering slightly less than 77,000; if the clerical assistant grade is included with the clerical class this adds another 55,000 in round figures.[2] But, since the clerical class is occupied with the more routine tasks, subse-

* See also Chapter 8, Postscript: The Fulton Report.

[1] *Memorandum by Financial Secretary on Estimates, 1967–8*, Cmd. 3227, HMSO, Mar. 1967, p. 50. The Post Office is scheduled to be run as a nationalized service. Its personnel will not then be civil servants.

[2] *Ibid.*, pp. 52 and 56.

quent discussion will concentrate on the administrative and executive classes.

The most senior officials of the administrative class are those with the rank of permanent secretary. Next in order of seniority are deputy secretaries, under-secretaries, and assistant secretaries. Together they make up about half of the administrative class. In general these are the officials who are most influential in the determination of policy. But some assistant secretaries may be employed on routine duties and have little influence on policy.

The remainder of the administrative class consists of officials with the rank of principal or assistant principal. The latter are relatively new entrants to the service who are still undergoing training. The power, status, and influence of principals will vary according to the precise job on which they are engaged. It is conceivable that a principal who is acting as secretary to a minister is more influential than some assistant secretaries.

The members of the executive class are mainly concerned with the day-to-day conduct of government business within the framework of established policy. It is unlikely that they will be in close contact with a minister or influence policy directly. As with the administrative class, there are several ranks within this category. The most senior, principal executive officers and above, may well be doing work that calls for as much experience and ability as is required of, say, principals in the administrative class. The executive class is important for several reasons.

First, it provides about 40 per cent of the administrative class via promotion. Secondly, administrative class officials who advise on policy are to some extent dependent on information supplied by the more senior ranks of the executive class. Thirdly, the implementation of policy, its success or failure, depends very much on the competence of the executive class. Fourthly, the executive class is in close contact with the general public. The "image" of the civil service is thus affected by the behaviour of the executive class officials. Fifthly, officers of this class manage regional offices or large sections within departments; they can profoundly affect the prospects and morale of numerous subordinates.

The "general" classes of the civil service are so called partly because they need have no professional or vocational qualifications. But in the main "general" means they may be called upon to work in any department. They are supposed to be moved fairly frequently to broaden their experience, but this is not always practicable. In contrast to the "general" classes there are "departmental" classes. These consist of officials whose careers are tied mainly to one department; they are naturally more specialized than the generalists. The departmental classes are divided into categories and ranks which resemble those of the general classes. The more senior enjoy a status equivalent to that of a chief executive officer.

Some government departments have posts classified as special departmental classes—for example, H.M. Inspectors of Taxes in the Department of Inland Revenue. Amongst the departmental executive classes are found the assistant auditors in the Exchequer and Audit Department, who examine public accounts and report on the way departments spend their money, and the immigration officers of the Home Office who are posted at ports and airports to control the movements of aliens entering or leaving the country.

The competence of the departmental classes greatly affects the efficiency of particular departments. Their specialist knowledge and experience may confer on them more power and influence than their formal place in the hierarchy of a department would indicate. But such influence is exercised within one department. In spite of their professional or technical qualifications few, if any, are likely to reach the higher ranks of the administrative class, which dominates the service as a whole. But probably few aspire to do so, though they may resent the predominance of non-specialists.

In a somewhat similar position to the specialists of the departmental classes are the members of the Scientific Civil Service. This branch of the civil service comprises some 17,000 officials. As usual, these are assigned to a particular class within the service. The scientific officer class is the smallest and is the scientific equivalent of the administrative class. The experimental officer class and the scientific assistant class resemble the executive and clerical classes in status and pay. As specialists, and possibly members of research teams, officials of the Scientific Civil Service are less mobile between departments than the generalists. It will be apparent that the term "scientist" conceals a great deal of variety of personnel, embracing physicists, chemists, biologists, meteorologists, and so on.

In addition the civil service employs numerous messengers, engineers, librarians, photographers, and other people who do not fit neatly into any of the classes so far mentioned. There is a small statistician class, some 225 strong, and an even smaller economist class. There are lawyers, museum experts, doctors, and psychologists.

Some departments, such as the Treasury, are staffed mainly by the general classes. Others, such as the Ministry of Defence, are much more complex. The Ministry of Defence employs administrative class officials and other generalists, but it is also manned by scientists and by members of the armed forces. Each group within a department tends to have its own distinctive interests and outlook. The more numerous and diverse the categories, the greater the possibility of internal conflicts and tensions.

The Diplomatic Service is distinct from the Home Civil Service, but its basic structure is similar. It was created in 1965 by the amalgamation of the former Foreign Service, Commonwealth Service, and Trade Commissioner Service. There are five branches but only the administrative and executive and clerical branches will be mentioned here.

The administrative branch of the Diplomatic Service, like the administrative class of the Home Civil Service, fills the senior posts which are directly concerned with policy. Its separation from the executive branch is obscured by a system of grading posts numerically. Thus grades 1 to 5A are in the administrative branch, whereas grades 5E and 7E, for example, are part of the executive branch. The majority of administrative branch recruits enter at grade 8.

The grades of the Diplomatic Service have evidently affected

Treasury thinking on the structure of the Home Civil Service. It has put forward proposals for a similar blurring of the sharp line which at present divides the executive class from the administrative class. The distinction between the principals of the administrative class and the senior ranks of the executive class is sometimes difficult to discern. The smallness of the administrative class, and the increasing scale and complexity of government functions, have meant that some members of the executive class must exercise considerable initiative and discretion.

The Treasury's proposals were submitted in May 1966 to a committee on the civil service chaired by Lord Fulton, Vice-Chancellor of the University of Sussex. The committee, which has not yet reported at the time of writing, is charged with the task of examining the structure, recruitment, training, and management of the Home Civil Service (see p. 254). Under the proposals, the administrative and executive classes would be merged in a single "management" structure. Grade 1 of the new structure would be composed of permanent secretaries. The other end of the scale, grade 8, would consist of officials with the existing rank of executive officer. The present dividing line between the administrative and executive classes would become blurred at grade 4, which would comprise assistant secretaries and principal executive officers. Some principal executive officers, however, would remain in grade 5 along with chief executive officers.

It is difficult to believe that the implementation of these proposals would have more than a superficial effect on relationships within the service. Calling everybody a "manager" does not disguise the fact that entry to the elite of grades 1–3 is going to be more or less confined to the sorts of people who already attain the rank of under-secretary or above. Thus, the Treasury suggests that graduates entering the service should include a number of "starred" recruits; admission to this group would depend on academic record and performance at the selection stage. Both graduates and non-graduates would enter at grade 8, but the career expectations of non-graduates would be grade 6.

The Society of Civil Servants, the recognized staff association of the general executive class, although attracted by the idea of a management structure, opposed "starred" graduate entrants; the majority of executive class recruits do not have degrees.

The Treasury paper suggested that increased opportunities for management training would facilitate movement of specialists into the proposed management grades, but the Institution of Professional Civil Servants, which represents senior specialists, thought there would be little change. In its view, nothing short of the abolition of class divisions in the Higher Civil Service would suffice.[3]

Most scientists, technologists, and professionally qualified men are naturally attracted to the Scientific Civil Service or the more specialized departmental classes. The few who consider an administrative career in the general classes realize that different methods of recruitment greatly reduce their chances of successful application. The division between generalists and specialists begins at the recruitment stage and continues after entry, with separate career prospects and different methods of training.

Recruitment to the Civil Service

The various methods of recruitment employed for different grades and classes reflect the structure of the civil service. Recruitment is largely in the hands of the Civil Service Commission, which works closely with the Treasury. Most papers in what is called method 1, described later, are set and marked by university academics.

The members of the Civil Service Commission have sole responsibility for declaring who is successful in competitions. They arrange examinations and tests in consultation with the Treasury. In the case of the Diplomatic Service they work closely with the Foreign Office. Thus patronage and nepotism are removed from the hands of politicians and the officials who head departments.

[3] Treasury paper to Fulton Committee is reprinted in *Public Administration*, Winter 1966. Reactions of Society of Civil Servants and Institution of Professional Civil Servants are set out in evidence to Fulton Committee.

The Commissioners are civil servants, but they are appointed by Order in Council and are not answerable to any minister. Constitutionally, therefore, their position is a curious one. The basis on which the Commissioners themselves are nominated and selected is something known only to those involved in the process.[4]

The task of recruiting for the civil service is related to the alternative opportunities open to potential candidates. Private enterprise concerns, overseas organizations, local authorities, and the universities fish in the same waters as the Civil Service Commissioners; often their bait is found more attractive. In comparison with some other occupations the work of the civil service is difficult to glamorize. In an era of full employment and private pension schemes, many of the traditional attractions of a civil service career have disappeared.

The methods of recruitment for the Scientific Civil Service, and for technical and professional posts, are fairly flexible. The scientific officer class, the most senior class, is recruited from persons with first- or second-class honours degrees in appropriate subjects. The experimental officer class draws on those who have national certificates, or A-level passes in the General Certificate of Education. The scientific assistant class is recruited from persons with O-level passes. A professional qualification is required for those who apply for posts as accountants, town planners, and so on.

The majority of scientific, professional, and technical entrants come in on an unestablished footing—that is to say, they are initially appointed on a temporary basis. Many seek establishment later when they have decided they wish to stay in the civil service permanently. They must do so, normally, by the time they are 31 years of age. The applicant for establishment applies through the Civil Service Commission; he may find himself competing for a post with outside applicants. Selection is by

[4] See Sir George Mallaby, The Civil Service Commission: its place in the machinery of government, *Public Administration*, Spring 1964. Also see *6th Report*, *Estimates Committee*, *1964–5*, HMSO, pp. 1–8 and 19–31. See Appendix (2).

interview. In the scientific officer class, however, there are generally fewer suitable applicants than there are places available. In such cases there is no element of competition and the Commission merely satisfies itself that the applicant is up to the standard required for the class.

In the generalist classes similar educational distinctions apply. Those who wish to enter the clerical class are exempt from competitive examination if they have five ordinary passes in the GCE. The upper age limit for direct entrants is around 20 years. Direct entrants to the executive class may not normally be older than 28 and they will be required to have five passes in the GCE examination, two of them at A-level. Generally, only those who have continued in full-time education up to the age of 18 are likely to have two A-level passes; some of these will go on to university. Some university graduates who fail to get into the administrative class are prepared to enter the executive class. They presumably hope to enter the administrative class later by way of promotion.

The prospects of those who enter the administrative class via promotion are not so good as those of the direct entrants, who constitute about 60 per cent of the total. The latter tend to be younger and naturally do not regard the rank of principal as the height of their ambition, as might older men who have fought their way up through the ranks of the executive class.

The open competition for direct entry into the administrative class may be taken by persons between the ages of 20 and 28. There are two methods. In both methods 1 and 2 there is a qualifying examination. This consists of three papers, namely, an essay, English, and a general paper. Candidates who have first-class honours degrees or higher degrees, and who are competing by method 2 only, are exempt from the qualifying examination. All other candidates must obtain a minimum number of marks in the qualifying examination before being allowed to proceed to the next stage.

In method 1 those who survive the qualifying examination sit a written examination in subjects normally included in honours degree courses at universities. There is a wide choice. In addition, candidates appear before an interview board, which awards marks; it assesses the past record, intelligence, and personal qualities of candidates. Persons with first-class honours or higher degrees are exempted from the written examination in chosen subjects. Those who are not of at least second-class honours standard have little chance of success.

In method 2 the qualifying examination is followed by a number of tests and interviews, arranged by the Civil Service Selection Board. Those who pass this stage are interviewed by the Final Selection Board. Candidates under method 2 must have, or obtain during the year of the competition, a first- or second-class honours degree.

There is a strong tendency for candidates to favour method 2. In January 1966, in the qualifying examination stage, 31 candidates sat for method 1 only, against 366 for method 2; 143 sat for both methods.[5] These methods are also used for recruitment to grade 8 of the Diplomatic Service.

As remarked earlier, the executive class provides about 40 per cent of the administrative class by way of promotion. Such promotion normally depends on success in a competitive examination limited to executive class candidates. The prospects of crossing the class barrier are remote for the vast majority of the executive class. Only some 3 per cent of young direct entrants to the executive class are really in the running. Persons over 30, and those who have been promoted from the clerical classes, stand very little chance.[6]

Better prospects of entering the administrative class might attract more recruits to the executive class. Careful selection and training in the early stages of an executive class official's career, together with a reconsideration of the functions of the class as a whole, might produce more people of potential administrative class calibre. The general impression of executive class work

[5] *Civil Service Commission, Annual Report*, HMSO, 1966, p. 9.

[6] *6th Report Estimates Committee, 1964–5*, pp. 118–19; and evidence of Professor W. J. M. Mackenzie, pp. 132–4.

in universities is that it is largely routine and carries little status.

But evidence shows that even the "image" of the administrative class is found unattractive by students in provincial universities. That executive class work and conditions are found unsatisfying by a number of entrants is evidenced by the high wastage rate. In 1963 some 22 per cent of male executive class officers under the age of 30 left the civil service, and fewer than half of those under 25 are stated to be satisfied with their jobs.[7] It might be argued, however, that this implies that the other half actually like their jobs. If this is so, it could indicate a high degree of satisfaction as compared with, say, private enterprise, local government, or the nationalized industries. Comparative information is not available.

One cannot but feel that the executive class it is still closely identified with the more routine and mechanical, though complicated, side of public administration. The distinction in the civil service between those concerned with "intellectual" work, the administrative class, and those concerned with allegedly mechanical routine, dating back to the Northcote–Trevelyan Report of 1854, is still very much in evidence.[8] And although the principle of promotion by merit is broadly accepted, this usually means promotion within the class to which one is originally recruited.

Since we are here mainly concerned with promotion from one class to another, usually, though not invariably, determined by success in a limited competition, it is not proposed to enter into the question of what constitutes merit. One may remark, however, that qualities which are considered meritorious in one class may be thought inappropriate for a different class. And, in order to permit executive class officers to demonstrate merits which are believed to be needed in the administrative class, opportunities

[7] *6th Report Estimates Committee, 1964–5*, pp. 113 and 207; and evidence of Society of Civil Servants to Fulton Committee.

[8] On Northcote–Trevelyan Report and other aspects of the civil service, see H. R. G. Greaves, *The Civil Service in the Changing State*, Harrap, 1947.

have to be provided. The work and prospects of the executive and related departmental classes need more investigation than they have hitherto received.[9]

It nevertheless remains true that a large number of administrative class principals are promotees. Most of them will differ in certain respects from the young direct entrants coming in as assistant principals. The latter conform more closely to the popular or customary image of the class as a whole.

In contrast to other groups in the civil service, the educational and social backgrounds of the direct entrants to the administrative class have received a fair amount of attention. A comparison of the periods 1948–56 and 1957–63 revealed that the proportion of successful candidates from boarding schools, i.e. private schools, rose from 31 to 37 per cent. The proportion from State, or State-aided, schools fell from 42 to 30 per cent. The proportion of successful candidates whose fathers were middle or upper class, in terms of occupation, rose from 38 to 46 per cent. Those with fathers in manual occupations fell from 22 to 15 per cent.[10]

In Britain the child of middle-class parents has about six and a half times the chance of a working-class child of obtaining a university place, regardless of intelligence.[11] The above findings are therefore scarcely surprising, given that recruitment is largely confined to those with a university education. The effect of interviews on the fate of applicants is difficult to assess in the absence of information about unsuccessful candidates; some of these may do well in the written examinations. Writing about the situation in the early fifties, one researcher found that the open competition was characterized by a class bias, concealed and subtle, particularly with regard to the conduct of interviews.[12]

[9] Virtually the only study dealing at any length with the executive class is F. Dunnill, *The Civil Service: Some Human Aspects*, Allen & Unwin, 1956. This gives the position for the early fifties. Also see N. Walker, *Morale in the Civil Service*, Edinburgh University Press, 1961.

[10] *6th Report Estimates Committee, 1964–5*, pp. vi–vii.

[11] A. H. Halsey, Education and equality, *New Society*, 17 June 1965.

[12] R. K. Kelsall, *The Higher Civil Servants in Britain*, Routledge, 1955, p. 73. See also Professor Kelsall's evidence to Estimates Committee, *6th Report*, pp. 85–94, especially paras. 396–8.

In the period 1952–62, 70 per cent of successful applicants for the senior ranks of what is now the Diplomatic Service came from independent private schools, attendance at which is mainly the privilege of the wealthier sections of the community. There was a slight trend in favour of applicants from State schools in the first three years of the sixties, but candidates from private schools were still obtaining about 60 per cent of the successes. Between 1948 and 1956, slightly more than 90 per cent of successful condidates came from families with fathers in the top two classes of the Registrar-General's classified list of occupations.[13]

There is no immediate prospect of a more open or socially representative administrative elite. The direct entrants to the administrative class and the Diplomatic Service grade 8 of the late fifties and early sixties are certain to occupy most of the senior positions in due course. We shall return to the subject of social class, but it might be argued that what matters most is not social class but the subjects in which successful candidates graduated. If these are relevant to public administration social class may not matter.

It is sometimes suggested that since the State is concerned with economic and social matters some preference should be shown candidates who have studied the social sciences. Others believe that in an industrial and technological age there should be more emphasis on scientific and technological subjects. The members of the administrative class are often described as "amateurs", because the majority have neither scientific nor vocational qualifications in the usual sense of these terms.

In this connection it must be remembered that the Civil Service Commission and the Treasury regard the present open competitions as designed to test general intellectual ability and not specialist knowledge. In principle no distinction is made between the graduate in economics and the graduate in Ancient Greek. In their comparison of the periods 1948–56 and 1957–63 the

[13] D. C. Watt, *Personalities and Policies*, Longmans, 1965, p. 188 and p. 189 footnote. Also *Report of the Committee on Representational Services Overseas, 1962–3*, Cmd. 2276, HMSO 1964, p. 86, para. 357, and appendix K.

members of the House of Commons Estimates Committee found that the proportion of successful candidates who took degrees in classics rose from 21 per cent to 24 per cent. Those with social science degrees fell from 24 to 17 per cent. The proportion with degrees or qualifications in mathematics, science subjects, or technology dropped from 4 to 3 per cent.[14]

Other investigations confirm these findings. A study of the intake into the administrative class during the five-year period 1960–4 shows that history and the humanities were read at university by 60 per cent of those successful. Social scientists constituted slightly more than 14 per cent of the recruits. Very few scientists and technologists applied and only eighteen were successful.[15] The annual reports of the Civil Service Commission since 1964 indicate that there has been no marked change in the situation.

The Diplomatic Service also attracts the arts graduate. Out of the 102 successful candidates entering the senior branch of the then Foreign Service between 1955 and 1961, 64 per cent had graduated in classical languages, philosophy, or history. There is an element of specialization required in the Diplomatic Service, namely evidence of ability to speak a foreign language. Some 14 per cent had degrees in foreign languages. The remainder had read such subjects as English, mathematics, geography, law and economics.[16]

In the period 1960–4 some 60 per cent of all candidates for the administrative class came from Oxford and Cambridge. Graduates of these universities formed over 83 per cent of those successful. In 1966, however, the proportion of successful candidates from universities other than Oxford and Cambridge rose to 35 per cent as compared with 24 per cent in 1965. Even in 1966, however, Oxford and Cambridge are left with 65 per cent of successes. Again, 1966 was the first year in which the number

[14] *6th Report*, p. vii.

[15] C. H. Dodd, Recruitment to the administrative class 1960–4, *Public Administration*, Spring 1967, p. 68. See also J. F. Pickering, Recruitment to the administrative class: Part 2, *Public Administration*, Summer 1967.

[16] D. C. Watt, *op. cit.*, p. 191.

of applicants from other universities exceeded the combined total of applicants from Oxford and Cambridge.[17]

The dominance of Oxford and Cambridge in the higher ranks of the Diplomatic Service is even more marked. Between 1952 and 1962 they provided just under 95 per cent of successful candidates.[18]

Just why Oxford and Cambridge graduates apply in greater numbers, and are more successful, is not entirely clear. They undoubtedly attract a high proportion of the brightest students in the country, especially on the arts side, where they are likely to be the first choice of an aspiring undergraduate. In other universities greater emphasis may be placed on scientific or technological studies, and, as we have seen, graduates in these subjects are not attracted to the administrative class or the Diplomatic Service. Furthermore, many of the staff and students in universities other than Oxford and Cambridge are either not aware of opportunities within the civil service, or have a distorted image of what its members do. They are sometimes inclined to believe that the scales are weighted in favour of Oxford and Cambridge graduates and that therefore application is not worth while.[19]

Whatever the reason, the predominance of Oxford and Cambridge lends weight to the belief that the higher ranks of the civil service form part of an "establishment" largely, but not exclusively, composed of Oxford and Cambridge graduates, which also occupies many key positions in industry, commerce, politics, and the armed forces.

The idea of an "establishment", however, is even vaguer than concepts like "class" and "elite", either or both of which may be used to explain the existence of an establishment. Whilst admitting their ambiguity, we shall nevertheless make use of the terms "class" and "elite" when discussing firstly, the functions of the

[17] C. H. Dodd, *op. cit.*, p. 68; *Civil Service Commission, Report, 1966*, p. 8.

[18] *Report of the Committee on Representational Services Overseas, 1962–3*, p. 86, para. 358, and appendix L.

[19] See *6th Report Estimates Committee, 1964–5*, evidence of Acton Society Trust, pp. 194–219.

State and secondly, the relationships of ministers and administrative class officials.[20]

The Administrative Class and the Functions of the State

Societies need some degree of internal stability if they are to survive and prosper and it is one of the oldest functions of the State to maintain order internally. Societies also need protection against foreign aggression. The State, as the most inclusive association, serves this collective purpose. Because it is charged with the functions of preserving order and defending a certain geographical area against foreign attack, the State ultimately depends on force or the threat of force.[21]

In practice, States are divided into governors and governed. Those who actually govern are inclined to use the State, consciously or unconsciously, in the interests of a particular group or class with which they identify. There is no reason to suppose that the politicians and civil servants who form the central government in Britain are free of group or class bias. They would not be human if they were.[22] But they are also subject, in varying degrees, to the influence of other groups and classes.

Even in the mythical heyday of *laissez-faire* the State was concerned with more than defence and law and order. Social problems, associated with developing industrialization, had to be dealt with on a collective basis. Housing, sanitation, and health were matters in which the State took an early interest. This interest received added impetus with the concentration of working populations in towns. Efforts were also made to humanize

[20] For a discussion of "class" and "elite" see T. B. Bottomore, *Elites and Society*, Watts, 1964. Also see J. Blondel, *Voters, Parties and Leaders*, Penguin, 1963, ch. 9; and G. Sartori, *Democratic Theory*, Praeger, 1965, ch. 6.

[21] See M. Weber, Politics as a vocation, in *From Max Weber*, edited by H. H. Gerth and C. W. Mills, Routledge, 1948, pp. 77–78. But States are not based solely on coercion; see H. R. G. Greaves, *The Foundations of Political Theory*, Bell, 2nd edn., 1966, ch. 1.

[22] See H. J. Laski, *The State in Theory and Practice*, Allen & Unwin, 1935, p. 111.

the effects of industrialization by factory inspection and the regulation of the employment of women and children.

In other words, practical social problems modified *laissez-faire* and laid additional functions on the State. Nevertheless, the dominant industrial middle class saw the functions of the State as strictly limited. An active civil service was not particularly desired. By the last quarter of the nineteenth century important changes had been made in methods of recruitment to the civil service; but it was a civil service which largely appealed to an industrial middle class with a belief in limited utilitarianism. An efficient service was thought of as one which would be economical to run. To break the corruption and patronage associated with the rule of the older aristocracy entry by open competition was introduced. But for the higher ranks competitions were not to be too open, for some degree of social compatibility was thought necessary for the co-operation of the political and administrative elites.[23]

Political developments ensured that the functions of the State would further increase in number and complexity. The effects of the extensions of the franchise to the working classes, in 1867 and 1884, began to manifest themselves. Party political leaders gave heed to working-class needs because they depended on the votes of that class to achieve, and retain, control over the legislature. In 1900 the Labour Representation Committee, which developed into the Labour Party, met for the first time. Financed by the trade unions, and under the influence of Fabianism, the Labour Party, by 1918, was identified with State ownership of economic property. It also stood for the extension of State-provided social services and security.

But the older parties pioneered the social service state. Arthur Balfour, Conservative Prime Minister in 1902, saw social legislation as the most effective antidote to socialism. The Liberal Government of 1906 introduced a programme of social reform comparable to that of Labour governments between 1945 and 1951. Thus, in the period 1895–1905 both of the then major parties

[23] Greaves, *The Civil Service . . .*, chs. 1 and 2.

turned with varying degrees of enthusiasm towards State intervention in social affairs.[24]

The move away from *laissez-faire* towards collectivism was traced by A. V. Dicey in a work first published in 1905. Behind the trend, he thought, lay Tory philanthropy, the changed attitudes of the working class, household suffrage, and the characteristics of modern commerce. By the characteristics of modern commerce he meant the development of joint stock corporate enterprises, their regulation by the State, and the belief that monopolies should be brought under the control of the State.[25]

It was apparent before the end of the nineteenth century that economic progress, and success in competing with other countries for world markets, depended on a supply of skilled and semi-skilled labour. The increasing scale of operations called for more persons with professional and technical qualifications and administrative skills. These demands could not be met without the provision of State elementary, secondary, and technical education.

Trade depressions and unemployment, for political and social reasons, could not be ignored by governments. The State regulated tariffs as a means of protecting home markets and maintaining full employment. Hence it was necessarily involved in international commerce, which could not be isolated from domestic production. In the economic sphere the State was active even when classical capitalism was at its height.

At home the growth of large-scale enterprises, and monopolistic and oligopolistic trends, meant that the consumer could no longer rely on competition to protect him against exploitation by producers. Thus the consumer looked to the State for the protection no longer afforded by the operation of a free-market economy of small producers and suppliers.

Two world wars have had a marked impact on the civil service. During the Second World War in particular there was an influx

[24] J. D. Kingsley, *Representative Bureaucracy*, Antioch press, Ohio, 1944, pp. 91–92. Also see B. B. Gilbert, *The Evolution of National Insurance in Great Britain*, Michael Joseph, 1966.

[25] A. V. Dicey, *Law and Public Opinion in England*, 2nd edn., 1914, paperback edn., 1963, lectures 7 and 8.

of temporary civil servants from industry and the universities. In this period the use of quantitative methods was developed. Rationing and planning schemes had to be worked out. The economic orthodoxies of the thirties finally gave way to Keynesian economics, enabling promises of full employment to be honoured, but requiring a managed economy. The so-called "positive" State was finally called into existence, replacing the old "regulatory" or "supervisory" State.

In reality the positive State may not be particularly active. In some cases "interventionist" State would be a better term. Much depends on the character and style of the Government in power. In Britain the State has entered into a partnership with other associations in its attempts to manage the economy. True, vast concerns like the railways and power industries are publicly owned, involving governments directly in industrial and technological problems. But the greater part of the economy is still privately owned, and governments often operate by suggestion and persuasion rather than by compulsion.

Enough has been said to indicate that the State is deeply involved in economic, social, and technological matters. Yet the administrative class of the civil service is overwhelmingly composed of arts graduates. Given that modern societies depend on the social and physical sciences, if they are to progress materially, can it be rightly said that the British administrative elite is unrepresentative of important "social forces", to use Mosca's term?[26]

Because the administrative class lacks certain types of knowledge and experience, and because the State is not all-powerful, a vast network of advisory committees has sprung up based on lists of the "great and the good" which the Treasury and other departments keep. Whether this amounts to undesirable patronage, extended to a restricted, unrepresentative, and largely self-interested and irresponsible circle, is a debatable point. In

[26] G. Mosca, *The Ruling Class*, McGraw-Hill, 1939, introduction, pp. xix, 65, and 144–5. By "social force" Mosca meant any human activity which has social or political significance for a given society. At any given time in a society, in Mosca's view, control of the appropriate social forces is essential to the possession and retention of power.

official quarters, such committees are considered a necessary means of consultation with affected or interested parties. Nevertheless, such committees are not elected and their advice is mostly unknown to those outside the magic circle. If specialist or technical opinion is needed, should it not come from within the civil service? Are not these committees a standing indictment of the civil service?[27]

We have seen that the administrative class is often said to consist of "amateurs", meaning people without specialized or vocational qualifications. But one should be wary of accepting criticisms without first subjecting the critics to scrutiny. Some businessmen who come into contact with senior civil servants find them naïve about industrial and commercial affairs. But this may merely indicate that the values and priorities of businessmen and civil servants differ. Academics who criticize the civil service may merely be concerned that their own specialisms should be accorded greater status and prestige. Politicians may find the civil service a convenient whipping boy for their own failings. But even if one discounts bias, a case is made out. Within the civil service itself there is concern, a feeling that the administrators cannot fully understand or control outside advisers or specialists within the departments.[28]

Some critics of the administrative class claim that the numerous and complex functions of the State call for the use of modern management techniques. In their view, the main fault of the class lies in its ignorance of scientific management. By this they

[27] See Political and economic planning, *Advisory Committees in British Government*, Allen & Unwin, 1960. Also W. L. Guttsman, *The British Political Elite*, MacGibbon & Kee, 1963, pp. 338–55.

[28] Amongst numerous criticisms see Lord Chandos, *Memoirs*, Bodley Head, 1962, p. 349; Sir Basil de Ferranti, letter in *The Times*, 9 Oct. 1965; Fabian Society, *The Administrators*, Fabian Tract, 1964. For disquiet within the civil service see summary of notes by First Division Association, representing the Administrative Class, in *The Times*, 12 Dec. 1964. Some defence of the existing pattern is offered by Enoch Powell in *Whitehall and Beyond*, BBC Publications, 1964, pp. 52–55, and by Lord Bridges, *Portrait of a Profession*, Cambridge, 1953, pp. 22–23. See also The civil service examines itself, *The Economist*, 8 Aug. 1964, and exchanges between D. N. Chester and B. Chapman concerning latter's book *British Government Observed*, Allen & Unwin, 1963, in *Public Administration*, Winter 1963.

mean a systematic approach to decision making. The administrative class, they believe, should know a great deal about such matters as the use of computers, operational research, management accounting, systems analysis, and so on. The amateur's reliance on intuition and guesswork is thereby eliminated. Sometimes management science is treated as a social science, and sometimes it is argued that the administrative class of the future will require education in both the arts or humanities *and* in scientific subjects.[29]

The argument for management training or education is often buttressed by references to the scale of modern public administration. The Government, it is pointed out, directly or indirectly, has a say in the expenditure of more than 40 per cent of the gross national product; and something like a quarter of the working population is employed in central and local government and the nationalized industries. To control these vast resources, it is argued, requires the use of the most sophisticated management techniques available.

It may be argued, however, that although the functions of the State do call for the use of such methods, they are not the main business of the administrative class. Rather are they the concern of numerous professional civil servants and senior executive class officers who have shown that they know how to make good use of them. In other words, one must distinguish between the functions of the State, the functions of the administrative class, and the functions of other classes.

The functions of the administrative class involve it in what is manifestly political work. Its members help to prepare ministerial speeches and they draft answers to politically inspired parliamentary questions. They represent their departmental minister in negotiations with interest groups. Part of their job is to calculate the power of such groups to obstruct departmental policy

[29] See, for example, J. Robertson, Whitehall: the managerial revolution, summary of evidence to Fulton Committee, *The Sunday Times*, 15 Jan. 1967. Also P. D. Nairne, Management and the administrative class, *Public Administration*, Summer 1964.

or to embarrass ministers. In all he does the administrative class official is expected to keep his minister out of political trouble. He can scarcely do this if he is not conscious of the wide domestic, and perhaps international, implications of departmental activity.

It is true that many principals, and some more senior officials, are employed on work which calls for managerial skills rather than political foresight or acumen. Even so, the young administrative class officer is selected partly with a view to his fulfilling political functions. Early in his career he may be assigned to political tasks to give him experience and to test his competence and suitability for the higher ranks of the class. The senior administrative class official must be more than a competent manager if he is to be a success.[30]

To some extent one cannot but feel that the preoccupation with science and managerial techniques is a manifestation of a desire to take public administration out of politics. In practice it seeks to substitute the values and priorities, often hidden, of one set of people for those of other people. The responsibilities of the public administrator are not equivalent to those of management, even higher management, in private enterprise concerns. The chief end of private economic enterprise is still to make profits which are regarded as satisfactory by shareholders and management a relatively restricted section of the community. If this can be reconciled with social responsibilities, good labour relations, increased managerial power, empire building, and so on, so much the better.

The ends of the State are much more complex and they are apt to change with successive governments. Resources cannot be allocated in government solely by reference to some estimated monetary return on capital expenditure. Nor can the efficiency of government be measured by, say, the rate of increase in the gross national product.

[30] See R. G. S. Brown, Organization theory and civil service reform, *Public Administration*, Autumn 1965. Also Sir Henry Self, The responsibility of administrators, in A. Dunsire (ed.), *The Making of an Administrator*, Manchester University Press, 1956, pp. 81–82.

There is no general agreement as to the yardstick which should be applied. It is at least arguable that it should be ethical rather than economic; but even economic yardsticks have an ethical content, often unrecognized or unadmitted by economists. John Stuart Mill thought that government the best which most effectively promoted the virtue and intelligence of the people, a belief with a long and respectable ancestry, though somewhat out of fashion. It is true that Mill leaves open the question of what exactly constitutes virtue.[31]

Nevertheless, with the qualifications and reservations that have been made, one may accept that it is desirable for the administrative elite to be renewed or regenerated either by an influx of more expert people or by post-entry training. In fact, efforts are already being made in both these directions.

In June 1964 a new method of entry was announced, for a limited number of posts at assistant secretary and principal level. Briefly, posts are advertised, inviting persons with suitable industrial, commerical, or other qualifications and experience, to apply. A short list is drawn up and final selection follows a two-day session of tests and interviews organized by the Civil Service Selection Board. It was originally planned that up to six principals, between the ages of 30 and 35, would be recruited. In 1965 the number actually recruited was fifteen. The civil service was then 10 per cent under strength at principal level. Six of the successful candidates in 1965 had been to Oxford or Cambridge, the remainder to other universities. In 1966 ten people between the ages of 30 and 36 were recruited as principals by this method.

A similar form of entry is through a special competition which takes in a higher age range, between 30 and 52, open to members of the armed forces and members of the overseas civil service, some of whom may have become redundant. In 1966 forty-one people were recruited as principals in this way.[32]

[31] J. S. Mill, *Representative Government*, Everyman edn., p. 193.

[32] Civil Service Commission, Annual Reports, HMSO, 1964, 1965, 1966. Also report in *The Times*, 16 March 1966.

The use of these methods may stem not so much from a desire to broaden the social background of the administrative class, or to increase its expertise, as from the failure of the normal methods of recruitment to provide suitable recruits in sufficient numbers. Ostensibly, the main aim is to bring into the civil service people with valuable experience in other fields.

Given the relatively small numbers involved, the uncertain status, prospects, and influence of the successful candidates, and the short time in which the experiment has been working, these developments will not radically transform the administrative class. And if entrants by these methods are to make a success of their careers in the civil service, in the sense of securing promotion, they must presumably adjust to civil service procedures and attitudes. If they do not so adjust they could cause friction within departments. Some friction is possible in any case since they may adversely affect the career prospects of officials recruited in the normal way, either at executive class or administrative class level.

There seems little prospect of increased mobility between the scientific officer class and the administrative class. In their earlier years, scientists tend to be promoted more rapidly than administrators. There is no incentive to transfer. In later life, the scientist, having spent his early career mainly in specialist work, finds it difficult to adapt. Moreover, it appears that posts of assistant secretary level have never been on offer to members of the scientific classes. Comparisons with private-enterprise organizations are suspect in this connection. Scientists may be regarded as potential administrators in Imperial Chemical Industries and elsewhere, but the qualities required of an administrator in these concerns, as already suggested, are different from those required of the administrator in the civil service.[33]

The diversion of good scientists, who are difficult enough to come by, to tasks for which they are not fitted, and where they have still to prove themselves, involves risks which may not be justified by the results. Sir Henry Tizard, an outstanding scientist

[33] *6th Report Estimates Committee, 1964–5*, p. xxvii, paras. 86–87.

and administrator, recognized the difficulty of finding men who combined scientific knowledge with political acumen, administrative ability, and managerial skill.[34]

But even the most intelligent layman may not fully appreciate the subtleties of specialist advice. In translating this advice for ministers he may unwittingly mislead. If, as part of his training for generalist work, he is shifted fairly frequently between departments, dealing with different subjects and services, his "amateurism" is apt to become obvious. It may be true that a man who has done five jobs in fifteen years develops confidence and the capacity for identifying the strong or weak points in any situation at short notice.[35] But it may also mean that he is not really in control of departmental matters since he will be heavily dependent on the opinions of others. It has been suggested that there should be a scientific secretary in each department on the same level as the permanent secretary, the chief administrative officer. This raises delicate questions of relationships and responsibilities.[36] Clear identification of responsibility is a good administrative principle and it is probably wiser to leave the permanent secretary unambiguously in command on the official side.

It is sometimes claimed that the higher ranks of the administrative class are not the preserve of "amateurs" to the extent usually suggested. In 1964 about a third of permanent secretaries and deputy secretaries had degrees in science, mathematics, or economics.[37] This may or may not be considered a satisfactory proportion. One would like to know when they obtained their degrees, whether economics or science subjects were merely parts of their courses, and, above all, whether they have kept up with developments in science or economic theory. Experts who are out of date can be as harmful as amateurs, assuming they can be legitimately described as experts.

[34] See R. W. Clark, *Tizard*, Methuen, 1965, pp. 369–72.

[35] Lord Bridges, *op. cit.*, pp. 22–25.

[36] In speech by Lord Todd, 254 *HL Deb.*, No. 23 (15 Jan. 1964), col. 673. See also Sir James Dunnett, The civil service administrator and the expert, *Public Administration*, Autumn 1961.

[37] N. Hunt, in *Whitehall and Beyond*, p. 34.

Lord Bridges has put in a plea for degree courses which would be less oriented to turning out specialists in particular subjects. Such courses would train men to appreciate scientific attitudes and methods of research.[38] It is difficult to envisage their introduction in British universities on any large scale. Here subject specialization is very marked; and there is no vested interest to press for such courses. As Machiavelli observed: "It must be considered that there is nothing more difficult to carry out, nor more doubtful of success, nor more dangerous to handle, than to initiate a new order of things."[39]

There remains another way of increasing the expertness of the administrative class, namely post-entry training. It is probable that there will be no dramatic change in the tendency to recruit mainly young arts graduates as direct entrants. It is also probable that the meagre interest shown in the administrative class by scientists, both outside and inside the civil service, will continue. If the character of the class changes at all over the next few years it is likely to be the result of changes in training (but see pp. 254–62).

Training in the Civil Service

Training involves various means of inducing people to think and behave in particular ways. Training may be conscious and deliberate, but it is not invariably so. It is normally related to the tasks or functions of an organization or department. It differs from education, the object of which is to make people think for themselves and to adopt critical attitudes. Education may produce "misfits" who challenge the ends of organizations and society.

A great deal of training in the civil service consists of putting new entrants under the guidance of some more experienced individual. This is sometimes described as training on the job. This method is used in the training of all classes, from assistant clerical officer to administrative class officials. Training on the

[38] Lord Bridges, in *Whitehall and Beyond*, pp. 64–65.

[39] Machiavelli, *The Prince*, World's Classics edn., Oxford, p. 24.

job is easy and cheap to organize. New recruits contribute something to the work of departments almost as soon as they arrive; they act as assistants and are soon dealing with simple duties on their own. This is not without importance in departments which are often overworked and understaffed. This type of training has an obvious appeal for those who are sceptical about the existence or value of a body of knowledge called "administration" which can be taught and studied formally. If there is an art of administration, such people claim, it can only be acquired by practical experience in the actual duties involved.[40]

Training on the job in some form is certain to remain an important part of training in general. But it has certain disadvantages as compared with other methods; at the very least it needs to be supplemented. Firstly, it lays an extra burden of instruction on experienced members of departments, distracting them from their other duties. Secondly, it is likely that traditional ways of doing things will be taught and that new or alternative methods will be neglected. Thirdly, instruction is an art, calling for qualities which are by no means common. Fourthly, its apparent cheapness may be deceptive. A great deal of time can be wasted because instruction tends to be on an individual basis, with numerous repetitions over time. And finally, it is scarcely the most exciting or interesting introduction to the work of a department.

But although other methods of training are increasingly favoured, they too raise many problems. It is possible for senior officials to obtain sabbatical leave for training or education; grants or fellowships are available for study at certain universities, for example. The number of officials who apply for fellowships, however, is small. In 1961–2 only one award was made.[41] It is probable that little incentive to further study exists in the form of improved prospects of promotion in the senior grades.

Prolonged periods of study leave are only possible when there

[40] See C. H. Sisson, *The Spirit of British Administration*, Faber, 1959, pp. 34–37 and 132–8. For an opposing view see E. N. Gladden, *Civil Service or Bureaucracy?*, Staples, 1956, ch. 5.

[41] D. Peschek, Training public officials, *New Society*, 24 Oct. 1963.

is a sufficient reserve of manpower to cope with the work normally done by those granted such leave. The burden on most departments is such that they simply cannot release people for any great length of time. And when the size of the civil service is attracting adverse comment, and governments are trying to secure economies in public expenditure, the situation is unlikely to improve. The Committee on Representational Services Overseas recommended a manpower reserve of 10 per cent to allow for training, but it is difficult enough to find suitable candidates to fill normal vacancies in the Diplomatic Service.[42]

In point of fact there are few courses geared specifically to the needs of public administration in the universities and other educational institutions. It is possible to obtain diplomas in Public Administration from some universities. There is also a Diploma in Government Administration, obtained by passing examinations arranged by the Local Government Examinations Board. The Diploma of London University is open only to graduates, which limits the number of candidates. A diploma, in Britain, is regarded as very much inferior to a degree. A small number of the more junior executive class or departmental class officers obtain diplomas in Public Administration. They do so mainly by attending evening study at technical colleges or by some form of correspondence course.

There are courses in particular subjects which are attended by civil servants. For example, the Home Office sends officers on language courses. A certain number have attended management courses at the Administrative Staff College, Henley. This is an independent institution which caters for private enterprise, the nationalized industries, and local government, as well as for the civil service. Normally only a handful of places are available for the civil service.

The precise courses for which officials are released, and the general character of training, vary from department to department. The management side of the Treasury has broad responsi-

[42] *Report of the Committee on Representational Services Overseas, 1962–3*, pp. 24–25 and ch. 5.

bility for training and education, but the departments are allowed a measure of discretion and independence. It follows that generalizations about training methods and opportunities in the civil service can be misleading. What is true of one department may not be true of another.[43]

In response to a recommendation of the Committee on the Training of Civil Servants, which reported in 1944, departmental training officers are appointed in the larger departments. They work closely with the Training and Education Division of the Treasury, set up in 1945. The Division has known periods when training was looked on as an expense rather than as an investment in efficiency. In the sixties, however, there has been something of a revival of interest in formal training. The chief reasons appear to be the boom in management courses for private enterprise, which some people hoped would speed the nation's economic recovery; the Report of the Plowden Committee on the Control of Public Expenditure, which suggested that there was insufficient appreciation of the value of management training in the public service; and publicity given to the French *École Nationale d'Administration*, ENA for short.[44]

In many ways the French civil service is even more elitist than the British. It is certainly more specialised in the higher ranks; there are a number of elites, consisting of financial experts, engineers, and so on. There is a greater degree of interchange with private enterprise concerns; senior civil servants and top administrators in private firms have often received similar sorts of education and training at the French *polytechniques*. The French civil service tends to be taken as a model by certain reformers in Britain, especially those whose main complaint is against the amateurism of the administrative class.

Candidates who are successful in competitions to enter the ENA undergo an arduous course. This is partly practical, involving

[43] See K. R. Stowe, Staff training in the National Assistance Board: problems and policies, *Public Administration*, Winter 1961; and R. J. S. Baker, The training of assistant principals in the Post Office, *ibid.*, Spring 1963.

[44] *Control of Public Expenditure*, Cmd. 1432, HMSO, 1961, paras. 44–59.

a sort of superior training on the job, and partly theoretical. The practical part of the course, however, includes experience in a private concern or a nationalized industry as well as a spell of duty in one of the French regions. At the end of their second year, students take an examination which decides the corps they will join after their third and final year of training.[45]

The ethos behind the ENA is so alien to British tradition that there have so far been no attempts to set up a counterpart. But following the Plowden Report on the Countrol of Public Expenditure new schemes were devised for the training of assistant principals, and in 1963 the Treasury Centre for Administrative Studies was opened. This may be regarded either as the minimum response which could be made in the face of pressures from reformists or critics, or it may be seen as a genuine attempt to adapt British practice to changed conditions.

The Centre for Administrative Studies provides a three-week course on the structure of government for assistant principals after they have served for about six months in a government department. When they are in their third year of service, assistant principals return to the Centre for a twenty-week course in economics, statistics, management techniques, government, and the structure of industry, Each course is planned for about thirty members; officials of the Diplomatic Service participate.

As it stands the Centre is a modest affair in comparison with the ENA, though it is a considerable innovation in British terms. The Director of the Centre is aided by two assistants. In 1965 one of these was a principal seconded from the Treasury, the other was a first secretary on loan from the Foreign Office. The directing staff organize courses. Most of the teaching is done by visiting lecturers from the universities and elsewhere. The emphasis

[45] On the École Nationale d'Administration see F. Ridley and J. Blondel, *Public Administration in France*, Routledge, 1964, ch. 2; B. Chapman, *The Profession of Government*, Allen & Unwin, 1959, paperback edn., pp. 88–94 and 115–24; G. Langrod, *Some Current Problems of Administration in France Today*, University of Puerto Rico, *passim*; and H. Parris, Twenty years of l'École Nationale d'Administration, *Public Administration*, Winter 1965.

is on economics, statistics, and quantitative methods.[46] In addition to the course for assistant principals in their third year, the Centre arranges one-day presentations of management techniques, designed to tempt senior civil servants who have little time to spare for keeping abreast of developments. Courses of up to three weeks are organized covering such matters as mathematical models, data processing, and staff management.

A few civil servants have attended short courses in management arranged by the business management schools of the universities of London and Manchester. Here civil servants have the advantage of mixing with people from the business world, nationalized industries, local government, and so on. It is possible that more use will be made of such courses following a recommendation to this effect in the report of a working party on management training.

The working party, set up by the Chancellor of the Exchequer in November 1965, submitted its report as evidence to the Fulton Committee early in 1967. It recommended that civil servants who are expected to reach what it calls middle-management level should attend, by the age of 30, two central courses providing twelve weeks of training in all. A small number of officers who show promise of reaching higher levels would be selected for three courses which, by the age of 30, would provide them with nearly a year of management training. Older civil servants would have opportunities for management training and opportunities to meet their opposite numbers in industry, commerce, and local government.

The working party was asked to report on the need for a Civil Service Staff College. Its proposal that the central management courses for those up to the age of 30 should be directed by an organization developed out of the Centre for Administrative Studies suggests that there will be no staff college in the foreseeable future, though the Centre might eventually develop into one. (But now see Chapter 8, p. 258.)

[46] See C. D. Keeling, Treasury centre for administrative studies, *Public Administration*, Summer 1965. Also see *Treasury Report on Civil Service Training, 1966–7*, HMSO, 1968, pp. 5–7, and appendix C, p. 35.

The working party report bears a close resemblance to the Treasury's own remarks on training in its submission to the Fulton Committee. This is scarcely surprising since the chairman of the working party was a Treasury official. Obviously, when the Fulton Committee reports, in 1968, the prospects of the working party's recommendations being implemented are extremely good.[47]

It is apparent from all this that management training has been "sold" to the civil service in much the same way that it has been sold to British business. No doubt it is all to the good that civil servants at various levels should be acquainted with and able to make use of management aids and techniques. On the other hand, one cannot but feel that management has been oversold, that it is regarded, in some quarters, not as an aid, but as a substitute for thinking about the ends of policies: that somehow social priorities and values can be computerized. This is not so. There is no particular virtue in quantification as such. What appears to be lacking in the education and training of managers, both private and public, are discussions about ends, as opposed to means.

It may be objected that civil servants *should* concern themselves with means, not ends. Ends, it is often suggested, are the province of the politicians. It is for them to decide what ends are to be sought or what abundance is for. But the ends–means distinction is by no means clear. If policy is concerned with *what* is to be done, ends, and administration with *how* policy objectives are to be achieved, i.e. with means, it will be found in practice that they overlap.

For example, it is the policy of both major political parties to encourage British exports. *What* is to be done is scarcely a political issue or a policy issue. But *how* the end is to be achieved is essentially a policy matter, involving values and niceties of judgement. Methods may vary from selective credit control to tax concessions and direct government participation in export

[47] Mention should also be made of the *Whitley Review of Training in the Civil Service*, issued by the Training and Education Division of the Treasury in 1964. Parts of the *Review* were published in *Public Administration*, Spring 1965. Also see T. E. Chester, Management training in the public sector, *District Bank Review*, March 1968.

industries. It is the "how" question, rather than the "what" question, which involves priorities, values, interests, powers, and responsibilities.

There are numerous other areas where the distinction between policy and administration is difficult to maintain. For example, the manner in which the social services are to be financed involves both policy and administration, and they cannot be kept in separate compartments.

Policy and administration are parts of a continuous process of decision taking carried on within hierarchical organizations. A decision to apply to enter the Common Market, taken at Cabinet level, is one which limits the discretion of decision-takers outside the Cabinet. It sets an objective or target. Such a decision is itself the culmination of a process of deliberation. But it does not put an end to all discretion lower down in the hierarchy, and it triggers off further decision taking.

Within the endless process of taking decisions, what is regarded as policy at one level, or by one set of people, may be regarded as administration at another level. Those decisions which one's subordinates are permitted to take, within the policy or rules one has laid down, tend to be regarded as administration or execution. And those decisions which come from above, or which one feels obliged to refer upwards, tend to be treated as involving policy. But, except perhaps at the very lowest level, there is always a choice amongst alternative means. The final choice of means is governed, consciously or unconsciously, by some criterion derived from further preferred ends which are bound up with value judgements.

It is tempting to believe that the social sciences and quantitative methods are value-free; it may well be that the apparent neutrality of such disciplines and methods has a special appeal for civil servants, who are supposed to be objective and impartial in the advice they offer ministers. But if there is any justification for devoting time, effort, and money to the social sciences, it is that they are intimately concerned with the values of society. By choosing some aspects of society for study or special emphasis, and neglecting other aspects, the social scientist is tacitly expressing certain values. And, ultimately, it is with the examination and exposure of values that the social sciences are concerned.[48]

The most senior ranks of the administrative class can influence policy, more or less directly, by the advice they give, the briefs they prepare, and by the information and statistics which they put at the disposal of ministers. This is not to say that officials determine policy, or that ministers are mere tools in the hands of some unified managerial group which aspires to take over their political role. But the values of officials do affect policy, and such values, like those of other people, are partly unconscious and internalized, bound up with social class and background. Values may be further wrapped up in the jargon of economics, sociology, or operational research.

If senior officials are drawn disproportionately from one section of the community, certain values, associated with other classes, tend to be overlooked. Furthermore, it is desirable that at least some members of the senior ranks of the civil service should have direct experience of the needs and problems of people with different backgrounds from their own. Intellectual ability alone is not enough. The lives of other people, outside his own immediate circle, often seem strange even to the most intelligent, sympathetic, and imaginative administrator. But it may be that the harmonious partnership of the political and administrative elites would be damaged by a change in the class character of one or the other.

The Political Elite and the Administrative Elite

In this context we shall assume that the members of the Cabinet constitute a political elite. This does not imply that all members of the Cabinet are equally important, or that certain politicians outside the Cabinet are not as important as some of those who are members of the Cabinet.

Between 1868 and 1955 about 14 per cent of Cabinet ministers were of working-class origin, 42 out of a total of 294. Of these,

[48] See C. J. Friedrich, *Man and His Government*, McGraw-Hill, 1963, ch. 2.

23 were members of the two short-lived Labour Cabinets of Ramsay MacDonald. A further 12 served under Lord Attlee between the years 1945 and 1951.[49] In Mr. Wilson's Cabinet of 1964, 11 out of 23 ministers had been to Oxford and 6 had attended one of the better-known public schools. Another 6 went to grammar schools, usually indicative of a middle-class background. Mr. Wilson's later Cabinets have not changed their character in terms of class.

As might be expected, Conservative Cabinets exhibit middle- and upper-class predominance to a greater degree. And Conservative governments have been in power more often than Labour governments. In the Eden Cabinet of 1955 two-thirds of the members had been to one of the Clarendon schools, i.e. one of the better-known public schools.[50] Half of Sir Alec Douglas-Home's Cabinet were old Etonians like himself. This is by no means untypical. Of all Conservative Cabinet ministers between 1918 and 1955, over 56 per cent had been to Eton. Yet only some 6 per cent of the total population attends any sort of public school, let alone Eton.

The social composition of Cabinets is closely connected with that of the House of Commons, which provides the majority of Cabinet ministers. After the general election of 1966 the MPs in the Commons were overwhelmingly middle and upper class. Out of a total of 630 members, 266 had attended a public school; 71 of them sat on the Labour benches. In terms of occupation white-collar jobs and the professions greatly outnumbered manual workers.[51]

From what has already been said about recruitment to the administrative class of the civil service it will be evident that its higher ranks are occupied by people with a similar social and educational background to that of the political elite. Kelsall found

[49] See W. L. Guttsman, *op. cit.*, p. 79. Guttsman defines as of working-class origin those Cabinet ministers whose fathers were manual workers, clerks, tradesmen, or in the ranks of the armed forces during the subjects' childhood (see p. 77, footnote).

[50] S. H. Beer, *Modern British Politics*, Faber, 1965, p. 382.

[51] See *The Times Guide to the House of Commons' 1966*.

that after the Second World War 61 per cent of those who entered by open competition were the sons of men in administrative, professional, or managerial occupations. This was almost five times as many as the corresponding group of the population as a whole. We have seen that the Estimate Committee's findings for 1957–63 indicate no fundamental change in this respect.

Much is made of the effect of promotees in broadening the social character of the administrative class. But the chances of former executive class officials reaching the highest ranks are less than those of the direct entrants. Moreover, there can be no doubt that the executive class is itself socially unrepresentative because few children of working-class parents are likely to obtain the requisite educational qualifications.

It is small wonder that Greaves finds the harmonious working of the political system to depend on an upper middle class occupying the chief positions in the Government, Legislature, Church, Army, and Business. It is the common class background and values of most of the leading figures which produce the readiness to compromise, and the element of unity amongst a plurality of elites, upon which stability depends.[52] No elite is completely closed to talent and ability; individuals may enter and regenerate elites, but rarely in any society does one totally new and different elite group replace an old one. But for an individual to enter the elite of the civil service, that is the higher ranks of the administrative class, he must be earmarked by his seniors for promotion. The few who move between departments, to occupy the very top posts, are subject to the approval of the Prime Minister. He is advised by that Joint Permanent Secretary at the Treasury who is designated head of the civil service. The latter will normally seek the opinion of other very senior officials.

Furthermore, most of those who aspire to the higher ranks

[52] H. R. G. Greaves, *The British Constitution*, Allen & Unwin, 3rd edn., 1955, pp. 250–1. See also R. Aron, Social structure and the ruling class, *British Journal of Sociology*, vol. 1, March 1950 and vol. 2, June 1950, for general discussion of relationship of elite structure and class structure. These articles are reprinted in L. Coser (ed.), *Political Sociology*, Harper Torchbooks, 1966.

must obtain a type of education at present available to only a small proportion of the total population. In Britain about 8 per cent of those in the appropriate age group go on to some form of higher, or further, education on a full-time basis. But only about half of this proportion are in the universities. One estimate is that white-collar workers, who make up 20 per cent of the population, produce 40 per cent of the ablest children, who go on to secure 60 per cent of sixth-form places and 80 per cent of university places. Manual workers, because of their greater numbers, produce about 60 per cent of the brightest children, who obtain about 20 per cent of university places.[53]

As Weber noted, democracy "takes an ambivalent stand in the face of specialized examinations". On the one hand, they seem to open doors to all who qualify, from all social strata. But on the other hand, when educational opportunities and motivations are different for each social class or status group, there is good reason to believe that a merit system and educational certificates will favour a privileged group.[54] Thus, even if one does not believe that the administrative class should reflect the class structure of the country, there is a considerable wastage of ability in Britain because of unequal opportunities.[55]

Inequalities in educational attainment are associated with economic inequalities. With about 10 per cent of persons over the age of 25 owning 80 per cent of private capital, and with the effects of income distribution via taxation negligible, or even, since 1949, tending to reinforce inequality, it may be doubted whether plans for comprehensive education at secondary level will do more than scratch the surface of class differences in Britain.

This is not to say that the structure of education is unimportant.

[53] See J. Vaizey, *Education for Tomorrow*, Pelican, 1966, p. 67; and A. B. Clegg, Education: wrong direction?, *New Society*, 11 Feb. 1965. The *Report of the Committee on Higher Education*, Cmd. 2154, HMSO, cites evidence that the proportion of university students from working-class families remained almost unchanged, about 25 per cent, between 1928–47 and 1961. See appendix 2(B), table 6, p. 5.

[54] M. Weber, *op. cit.*, p. 240.

[55] See evidence of D. N. Chester to Estimates Committee, *6th Report, 1964–5*, pp. 230–4.

As one American commentator notes, the English educational system presents inequality as natural and even desirable.[56]

No radical change in the social character of the higher ranks of the administrative class and Diplomatic Service is likely in the foreseeable future. And old fears that a clash might occur between the political and administrative elites when a Labour government was in power with a working majority have proved unfounded. The Parliamentary Labour Party has changed over the years. Its leadership is respectable and middle class. Those ministers who are of working-class origin, who may be described as upwardly socially mobile via a parliamentary career, follow the customary British pattern of adopting the values and outlook of the class they join.[57]

The social background of the political and administrative elites does not determine their behaviour, though it must influence it. In Britain both elites are "accessible" in varying degrees. Neither is completely closed to new entrants from all social classes. Both may be influenced by interest groups of many kinds in a political system which is pluralistic. And the political elite is subject to the influence of the electorate and the competition of an organized Opposition which presents itself as an alternative government.[58]

The professional ethics of the higher ranks of the civil service oblige its members to be as objective as possible in tendering advice to ministers. But complete freedom from bias is not humanly possible with respect to the matters with which civil servants deal. No official can isolate his professional life from the complex process of cultural assimilation which occurs through daily contact with some groups, isolation from others, and the influence of neighbourhood.

Finally, if a bureaucracy is to operate successfully in any society it must be committed to the political order of which it is part.

[56] R. Rose, *Politics in England*, Little Brown, 1964, ch. 3. Also see article The indefensible status quo, *The Economist*, 15 Jan. 1966; and article, Britain's rich and poor, *ibid.*, 26 Feb. 1966.

[57] See Guttsman, *op. cit.*, pp. 275–7.

[58] On the accessibility of elites see W. Kornhauser, *The Politics of Mass Society*, Routledge, 1960, pp. 51–60.

As Friedrich puts it, objectivity must be placed within the framework of value reference provided by a group or organization. Objectivity is not absolute, but relative to the political order.[59]

All this is of some significance in a governmental system which involves ministerial responsibility for the actions and decisions of civil servants. Given the scale and complexity of modern government the latter must be accorded a great deal of discretion. Ministers accept responsibility *for* the actions of civil servants partly because they believe they will act *in* a responsible fashion. But behaviour which is responsible in the eyes of one stratum of society may be the height of folly to another stratum.

Ministers rarely charge the civil service with irresponsibility. This is partly because the higher ranks of the civil service are largely representative of those social groups which are also dominant in the political elite. Responsible conduct is secured through an identity of outlook, closely connected with common social origins, and "internalized" or psychological controls, rather than formal institutional controls.[60]

Nevertheless, institutional controls are important. Chief amongst these is ministerial accountability to the Commons, an aspect of British government which merits close examination since it is mainly through their accountability to an elected House of Commons that governments purport to be subject to democratic control.

[59] C. J. Friedrich, *op. cit.*, p. 476.
[60] See J. D. Kingsley, *op. cit.*, pp. 278–83.

CHAPTER 3

ACCOUNTABILITY AND THE HOUSE OF COMMONS

Accountability and Party

The problem of holding accountable those who rule justifiably occupies a central place in studies of representative systems of government. John Stuart Mill observed that the moment a man, or a class of men, "find themselves with power in their hands, the man's individual interest, or the class's separate interest, acquires an entirely new degree of importance in their eyes".[1] In Britain, ministers are constitutionally accountable to Parliament, that is the House of Commons and the House of Lords, for the way in which they and their civil servants carry on the business of government. But in practice it is the situation in the Commons which really matters.

The loss of a majority in the Commons, on a matter involving major policy, would entail the resignation of the Government; a defeat in the Lords, though sometimes not without importance, e.g. in a period just prior to an election, has no such effect. The Lords will give way before the wishes of the majority in the Commons, though perhaps under protest. And it is the Commons which, legally at any rate, controls the supply of money which British governments require annually.

Party organization and discipline in the Commons render it highly improbable that the Government will be denied the funds it needs. Nor is it likely to lose its majority on a matter of policy. For these reasons the relationship of the Government and the

[1] J. S. Mill, *Representative Government*, Everyman edn., p. 252.

Commons is best described as one of accountability rather than control. Ministers are accountable in that they report past actions or future intentions, not always in any great detail, and try to justify them. The Commons attempts to elicit an account of the Government's stewardship. But in this process the Commons does not behave as a unified body.

In studying the Commons and other institutions and organizations, one should bear in mind the words of Aristotle: "As in other departments of science," he wrote, "so in politics the compound should always be resolved into the simple elements, or at least parts of the whole."[2] The Commons is manifestly divided into Opposition MPs and supporters of the Government; the latter are either politicians in the Government, or backbenchers who are members of the party which, by virtue of its majority, is entitled by convention to form the Government. So long as the Government party holds together, and only a major catastrophe could produce a serious split, it is the Cabinet which controls the Commons rather than vice versa.

But to maintain the unity of a party is no simple matter. It would be misleading to suggest that British parties in Parliament are monolithic unities, autocratically ruled by leaders who pay scant attention to the views and interests of their followers. And it would be equally misleading to imply that there are no sympathies or groupings cutting across normal party divisions. Often the two front benches, that is the leaders of the Opposition party and the leaders of the Government party in Parliament, are more in accord with each other than with their respective backbenchers. And the latter are inclined to resent the informal contacts of the Front Benches and what they regard as their collusion in organizing the business of the House.

Backbenchers of all parties occasionally make common cause on particular issues, such as capital punishment, abortion law reform, or Britain's application to join the European Economic

[2] Quoted thus in A. Lepawsky, *Administration*, Knopf, 1949, p. 231. For slightly different translation see *The Politics of Aristotle*, translated by Sir Ernest Barker, Oxford, shortened version, book 4, chs. 3 and 4, pp. 187–200.

Community. And MPs may have connections with professional or other interest groups which cut across party lines.

Nevertheless, it remains true that his party connection dominates the behaviour of the MP. There is a limit to the extent to which he will oppose his own party leadership, especially when his party is in power. The strength of modern governments *vis-à-vis* the Commons derives from the nature of political parties in Britain. For although it is customary to speak of the accountability of the executive to the Commons as if the latter were a unified body, the real situation is that of an Opposition party, which is in a minority, confronting a governing party, supported by most MPs on most issues. The behaviour of politicians is seldom characterized by a non-partisan examination of facts or administrative competence when accountability is involved. They are preoccupied with discrediting or defending the party in power, in a partial manner.

There are a number of ways in which accountability is formally attempted. Questions may be addressed to the appropriate minister, either verbally or in writing; there are debates, and discussions of "urgency" motions; financial procedure is related to accountability; and use is made of various committees. In every method, however, the influence of party is discernible.

Question Time and Debates

The first fifty minutes or so of the afternoon of a sitting day, unless it is a Friday, are reserved for Question Time. A Member must indicate whether he requires a written or an oral answer. At least forty-eight hours' notice of a question is required. In practice, however, to be reasonably certain of an oral reply on a specified day, when a large department is involved, it may be necessary to get a question down three or four weeks beforehand. There is no limit to the number of questions which can be put down for a written answer on any one day, but each Member is rationed to two questions demanding oral replies. However, the Speaker of the House allows Members to put supplementary questions.

A Member who already has two oral questions down for a particular day will sometimes draft further questions and ask colleagues to put them down in their names. He may then ask his own supplementaries when these questions are answered. The original question, whoever puts it, is often no more than a feint. It is designed to provide an opening for some devastating supplementary, the content of which is unanticipated by the minister concerned. Over 90 per cent of oral questions now lead to supplementaries; at the beginning of the century the proportion was less than 40 per cent. It is apparent that few Members are merely interested in seeking information. The growth of the supplementary indicates the political character of Question Time.[3]

When an Ulster Unionist asks the Labour Chancellor of the Exchequer to reveal the purchasing power of the pound sterling in 1967, as compared with what it was on 16 October 1964, he is not seeking information; he is hoping to draw public attention to a decline in the value of money since Labour came to power, for it can be assumed that the answer to the question is known beforehand. Equally, very detailed, but time-consuming replies by ministers are not intended to provide members of the Opposition with facts; they are designed to cut short, or prevent, supplementaries.[4]

With some assistance from their own backbenchers, ministers may exploit Question Time so as to secure favourable publicity. A Labour Minister for Social Security, for example, was asked a question about proposals to allow pensioners to earn more without adversely affecting their pensions via taxation. One may doubt whether the Labour MP who asked the question was in any way surprised by the reply given.[5]

The party political aspect of Question Time is also evident in the group efforts of some Members. Sir Gerald Nabarro is reported at one time to have written some forty versions of the

[3] See N. Johnson, Parliamentary questions and the conduct of administration, *Public Administration*, Summer 1961, p. 142.

[4] See, e.g., H. Dalton, *The Fateful Years*, Muller, 1957, pp. 394–5. Also Parliamentary Report, *The Times*, 1 Feb. 1967.

[5] Parliamentary Report, *The Times*, 7 Feb. 1967.

same basic question and circulated them to sympathetic fellow Members. A minister may answer these similar questions as if they were one, but this does not protect him from supplementaries, put to him by the numerous questioners. This tactic, amongst others, brought Sir Gerald some success in his efforts to secure changes relating to purchase tax.[6]

Groups have also been organized, by backbenchers of the governing party, to protect ministers from the effects of Opposition questioning. Mr. William Hamilton, Labour, observing that Conservative Members were tabling questions on certain matters, persuaded some Labour MPs to put down similar questions. The plan misfired when the Speaker, having heard of the plot, refrained from calling on the Labourites to ask supplementaries.

On another occasion, the resourceful Mr. Hamilton sought to protect the Labour Minister of Agriculture by flooding the Order Paper with questions addressed to another minister, in charge of a less contentious department who was due to answer before the Minister of Agriculture. It was thus hoped that Question Time would be over before the questions on agriculture were reached. Alas, the Minister of Agriculture *wanted* to decimate the Conservative questioners with his replies and the Labour Chief Whip persuaded the party backbenchers to withdraw their questions.[7]

Factional differences within the governing party sometimes come to the surface during Question Time. It is no secret that Mr. Michael Foot, Labour, disapproves of American bombing in Vietnam. When he suggested, in the course of putting a supplementary question, that the Labour Prime Minister condemn the bombing, nobody was surprised when the latter refused to do so; but the opinion of a section of the party got an airing.[8]

Certain professions are strongly represented in both parties. Questions concerning matters of professional interest may be addressed to ministers from either side of the House. They may

[6] See A manual of mischief making, *The Sunday Times*, 21 Feb. 1965.
[7] See The syndicate strikes again, *The Sunday Times*, 28 March 1965.
[8] Parliamentary Report, *The Times*, 15 Feb. 1967.

be implicitly critical even when put by a backbencher of the governing party. Dr. Shirley Summerskill, for example, put a question to the Labour Minister of Health asking if he would withdraw the oral contraceptive pill from circulation until its safety had been confirmed. Similar questions have been tabled concerning the effectiveness of anti-smoking campaigns and other matters. Such questions may provide an opening for Opposition criticism; their precise wording is therefore significant.

These "professional" questions do not bulk large in the total number asked. Most questions are fairly obviously related to straight political differences, either between the Opposition and Government, or between factions within the governing party. Occasionally, however, a case of alleged maladministration will give rise to a series of questions which appears to be unrelated to party political or factional differences. For example, the arrest of someone who was apparently a civilian by the military police, with the connivance of the civil police, gave rise to questions from both Labour and Conservative Members.[9]

One may say this was an example of the House performing its traditional function of securing speedy redress of a grievance in a non-partisan fashion. In the event, it turned out that the police, both civil and military, had ample justification for their actions, but this may be considered irrelevant. It should be noted, however, that the case had received wide publicity in the press. Most grievances are less newsworthy. And a case of arrest is perhaps simpler and more dramatic than, say, the denial of a widow's pension.

Seen in perspective, as one means amongst others of securing accountability, Question Time has its uses. But it should not be overrated. Ministers do not go in fear and trembling, for the balance of advantage lies with them. Questioners are often unable to get at the facts because they do not have access to files and documents. The minister can seldom be forced to reveal more than he wishes and he is assisted by civil servants who can anticipate likely supplementary questions. The questioner must make

[9] *Ibid.*, 14 Feb. 1967.

his own contacts and seek what aid he can, which may be precious little.

Moreover, there are many departments and ministers but only a limited amount of time for questions; therefore a rota system has to be operated. A particular minister may not be first on the rota more than once every seven weeks or so; if he is some way down his questions may not be reached. Ministers' appearances at the dispatch box to answer questions are so widely spaced that questions may lose their topicality and political impact. Nevertheless, the fact that a question may be asked in the House does affect the conduct of ministers and civil servants.

Mention should also be made of "private motion" questions. These are reserved for urgent and important matters. They are not printed on the Order Paper but require the approval of the Speaker. The Leader of the Opposition, by custom, does not put questions on the Order Paper. A reply may be sought on the afternoon of the day on which the question is accepted. On 16 November 1967 Mr. Robert Sheldon put a private-notice question to the Chancellor of the Exchequer concerning the financial situation. The latter's evasive answer, given in the knowledge that the Cabinet had decided to devalue, reinforced speculation against sterling. The decision to devalue was made public on 18 November. However, many private-notice questions are arranged by ministers to enable them to make a statement.

Members who are dissatisfied with answers to their questions may give notice of their intention to raise the matter again on the Adjournment. There are three occasions when effect might be given to such notice, assuming it is not immediately ruled out by the Speaker; for example, on the grounds that it would entail legislation.

First, there are "holiday" adjournments, held on the days before the House rises for vacation. Secondly, there are times when business on the Order Paper is completed before 10 p.m. The Government then moves the Adjournment, but this merely enables a Member who has been lucky in a ballot held for the purpose to introduce a subject which can be debated until 10 p.m. Thirdly, there are daily half-hour debates which normally follow the customary interruption of business at 10 p.m. The Speaker selects the subject for debate on Thursdays. For other days Members put down their names in the Speaker's Office, and a ballot is held once a fortnight. In November 1959 Mr. Noel-Baker, being dissatisfied with an answer given by the Minister of Transport, was able to re-open the matter by means of a half-hour Adjournment debate.[10]

Adjournment debates are not a particularly effective means of securing accountability. Their impact is slight unless the subject happens to be one which has aroused the interest of the press or some organized interest. Many Members are not in the chamber for half-hour Adjournment debates because of the lateness of the hour. If they are in the Commons, they are more likely to be in the bar than listening to the debate. The parliamentary correspondents of the press will probably be at their offices. And the time limit restricts the number of people who may speak in such debates. Usually a junior minister defends his department and he is not likely to make many concessions to critics.[11]

Until the end of the session 1966–7, a Member could seek a debate under Standing Order 9 on "a definite matter of urgent and public importance". If the Speaker was convinced that the subject fulfilled the necessary conditions, a three-hour debate took place between 7 p.m. and 10 p.m. But Speakers were bound by precedent and took a restrictive view of what was urgent and of public importance. The Member calling for the debate had to base his claim on some recent event or case and had to raise the matter at the first opportunity. He was required to show that the issue merited the immediate attention of the House and the Government. The matter raised had to deal with a particular

[10] See A. H. Hanson and H. V. Wiseman, *Parliament at Work*, Stevens, 1962, pp. 91–92. Mr. Noel-Baker put his question on 4 Nov. and secured the half-hour Adjournment motion on 10 Nov. But many dissatisfied questioners may never secure an Adjournment debate or may have to wait a long time.

[11] See report by Justice, *The Citizen and the Administration*, Stevens, 1961, paras. 85–87. Also see Hanson and Wiseman, *op. cit.*, pp. 97–99.

case and yet involve issues larger than an individual grievance.[12]

No requests for urgency debates were accepted by the Speaker in the sessions 1963–4, 1964–5, and 1965–6, although nineteen applications were made. In no session between 1930 and 1966 were more than two applications successful.[13] An example of its use occurred in 1958 when, following an urgency debate, the Home Secretary, whilst denying that his department had made a wrong decision, agreed to delay the deportation of a Spanish political refugee.[14] And, by a whim of the Speaker in 1967, the Opposition spokesman on foreign affairs, Sir Alec Douglas-Home, secured a debate on the situation in Aden.

At the beginning of the session 1967–8, the Leader of the House announced plans, subsequently implemented, to enable the Speaker to grant or refuse a debate without giving reasons based on precedent. Debates take place in the evening or the next day and must relate to subjects where ministerial responsibility is clearly involved. The terms of Standing Order 9 have also been altered. What was previously "a definite matter of public importance" has now become "a specific and important matter that should have urgent consideration". Whether the new formula will lead to more urgency debates remains to be seen.

A Private Member may try to ventilate some grievance in what is known as Private Members' time. In any session some twenty Fridays and four other half-days are set aside for Private Members business. Half the time is allotted for the introduction of bills and half for the discussion of motions. Some grievance may be wrapped up in a Private Members' motion. But attendance is likely to be sparse on a Friday, there has to be a ballot for the limited time available, and motions which do not have the support of the Government are not likely to be agreed to by the House.[15]

The debates which are most likely to attract attention are those

[12] *2nd Report Select Committee on Procedure, 1966–7*, HC 282, Dec. 1966, appendix 1.

[13] *Ibid.*, appendix 3.

[14] See Hanson and Wiseman, *op. cit.*, pp. 99–104.

[15] For examples, see Hanson and Wiseman, *op. cit.*, pp. 115–20; and P. G. Richards, *Honourable Members*, Faber, 2nd edn., 1964, pp. 212–14.

which are arranged by the two Front Benches. Some backbenchers are able to speak in these debates, but most of the time is reserved for ministers and Opposition Front Bench spokesmen. There are a number of occasions when such debates take place. For example, each session opens with a speech, read by or for the Queen, outlining the Government's policy and legislative proposals. There follows a debate, lasting about six days, on certain of these proposals.

Again, either the Opposition or the Government may put down motions calling on the House to express its opinion on some matter. A motion may be connected with a White Paper outlining government policy; or it may concern the report of a nationalized industry; it may condemn some government action, or failure to act. Debates may arise out of some ministerial statement to the House. On certain days, known as Supply Days, the Opposition has the right to select topics for debate and will naturally pick those which offer the best chance to attack government policies.[15a] There are also debates on the general principles of bills during their passage through the Commons.

Depending on the subject, the House may or may not divide on the motion. If it does, the outcome is predictable in all save very exceptional circumstances. Voting is normally on strict party lines. No amount of Opposition eloquence will induce a backbencher of the governing party to vote against the Government. A few rebels may abstain, or even vote against the Government, but not because of Opposition arguments. As one Labour backbencher put it, he is reluctant to show his distaste for the arsenic offered him by a Labour Government by swallowing the prussic acid held out by the Opposition.

But although the party political character of debates is quite plain, this is precisely what makes them significant. If accountability means anything, it is accountability to the electorate. And

[15a] At present, April 1968, there are 29 supply days. They are so called because of their historical association with the estimates submitted annually to Parliament. It would be more accurate to describe them as Opposition days, though the Opposition may, of course, choose to discuss an estimate on a supply day.

the influence of the electorate is limited to a choice between alternative governments composed of the parliamentary leaders of the two major parties. Without a series of party political debates in the Commons the electorate would be less able to judge between the two. And the Government is compelled to put up a reasoned defence of its actions.

Whether a periodical choice between two competing elites amounts to democracy is open to doubt.[16] There can be no doubt, however, that the interest of the electorate must be aroused if accountability is to be made a reality. In Britain the main responsibility for arousing interest rests with the Opposition. It is not likely to succeed unless it goes enthusiastically to work, blasting the Government with all the fire of party prejudice. At the same time it must try to convince the electorate that it can provide the nation with alternative policies and leadership.[17]

Accountability, then, is closely related to the intensity of party political conflict. The struggle for office is a vital part of the process. And if it is clear that Question Time and debates are marked by party conflict this is no less true of financial procedure.

Financial Procedure and Party Politics

Governments require the approval of the Commons for their taxation proposals. They also need annual grants of money to finance their expenditure. It is the Commons which formally exercises financial control; the House of Lords can only delay a certified money bill for a month. There is some truth in the old adage that he who pays the piper calls the tune, but in this case

[16] See J. A. Schumpeter, *Capitalism, Socialism and Democracy*, Allen & Unwin, 4th edn., 1954, chs. 21–22; and T. B. Bottomore, *Elites and Society*, Watts, 1964, chs. 6–7.

[17] Opinions differ on the tactics of Opposition. See Sir Ivor Jennings, *Parliament*, Cambridge, 2nd edn., 1957, ch. 6. Also J. Enoch Powell, 1951–9: Labour in Opposition, *Political Quarterly*, Oct.–Dec. 1959; R. H. S. Crossman, *Labour in the Affluent Society*, Fabian Society, 1960; and C. A. R. Crosland, *Can Labour Win?*, Fabian Society, 1960.

one must strike a balance between constitutional theory and political reality.

The details of financial procedure are complex but the basic outline is not difficult to grasp.[18] Money for what are known as Supply Services, granted annually, cannot be carried over from one financial year to the next. Furthermore, money is appropriated for specific purposes and governments are permitted only limited discretion to reallocate money between the various categories of expenditure.

The financial year starts in April. Estimates relating to Supply Services for the coming financial year are submitted to the Commons around the beginning of February. They set out, in some detail, the total amount of money required and the distribution of this total between and within departments. Through its party majority, however, the Government is assured of getting the funds it wants.

The Commons must also approve certain taxation proposals in the Government's annual budget. Theoretically, the budget is merely concerned with methods of raising money and not with policy. A defeat for the Government would not seem, at first sight, to be a defeat on a matter of policy. Nobody is challenging the ends in view, only the means of achieving them. But in practice the Government will not risk a defeat on the budget and will ensure that party discipline is maintained.

They will do so for at least two reasons. First, the levying of taxes and their variation are of vital interest to the electorate and organized interests. They receive a great deal of publicity. Voltaire may have exaggerated when he declared that the art of government consisted in taking away as much money as possible from one class to give to another class. Nevertheless, the annual budget does have this effect and it is thus a highly political affair. The

[18] For an up-to-date account see N. Wilding and P. Laundy, *An Encyclopaedia of Parliament*, Cassell, 1968. By tradition financial matters used to be taken in certain committees of the whole House, the committees of Supply and Ways and Means, now abolished. See report of Commons debate of 14 Dec. 1966, *Hansard*, and H. V. Wiseman, Supply and ways and means: procedural changes in 1966, *Parliamentary Affairs*, Winter 1967–8.

prospect of a government continuing in office depends in part in the character of its budgets.

Secondly, budget proposals are not merely ways of raising money. They are, or should be, an integral part of the Government's overall economic strategy. Fiscal policy should not conflict with monetary policy, though it sometimes does. As an instrument of economic policy the budget can affect total demand, business confidence, savings, investment and exports.

It was customary, up to and including the session 1966–7, to take the Finance Bill, embodying budget proposals, on the floor of the House. Thus the committee stage has been taken in a Committee of the Whole House. In the session 1967–8, however, the Government announced plans for taking the committee stage of the 1968 Finance Bill "upstairs" in a standing committee of fifty MPs. Several days, it contended, would thereby become available for the discussion of other matters. There would be a long report stage to enable non-committee members to raise constituency points. The Leader of the House assured the Commons that the Government would review the change in the following year and possibly reorganize procedure in the light of experience.

The Opposition protested that tradition should not be set aside and that all Members should retain their right to participate in the committee stage of the Finance Bill. But the Government used its party majority to get its way. The taking of the committee stage of the Finance Bill on the floor of the House has hitherto given the Opposition maximum publicity for its efforts in a popular cause, the fight against taxation. It fears that taking the committee stage "upstairs" will be to the party political advantage of the Government.

An important rule which greatly increases the control of the Government over the content of legislation in general is embodied in Standing Order 82 of the Commons. By this Order only the Crown, in effect ministers, may propose charges upon the public revenue. Thus every "money" or "financial" resolution is drafted by the Government.

In defence of the Government's monopoly of "money" resolutions it is argued that it should not be liable to meet demands for expenditure which might throw its whole financial programme out of gear. But the Government would not have to accept any such demand unless it was supported by a majority of the Commons, which would normally include most of its own backbenchers.

"Money" resolutions not only determine the total amount of money to be used in connection with some Bill; they specify the particulars of expenditure. Amendments to vary the allocation of money between items are out of order, even if the total amount of money would not be increased. It is therefore not possible to move an increase in expenditure on any parts of the proposals, even if this is matched by corresponding reductions elsewhere. The more detail the Government puts into "money" resolutions, the greater its control over Bills in all their stages in both the Commons and the Lords. It is virtually impossible to put forward constructive amendments which either do not increase expenditure in total or which do not increase the part allocated to a specific item.[19]

Furthermore, the scale of government expenditure, the detailed character of the Estimates, and the limited time available make it difficult to achieve effective parliamentary control over expenditure. For the financial year 1967–8, the Government submitted Estimates for Supply Services totalling some £9503 million. The Estimates are divided into classes and each class is split into votes. Each vote is further broken down into subheads. Thus class 1 of the Estimates relates to Central Government and Finance. Votes in this class include one designating money for the House of Commons; another is for the House of Lords. The vote for the House of Lords, for example, is distributed amongst sub-heads for travelling expenses, salaries, Lord Chancellor's Department, and so on. Bearing in mind that the Estimates are submitted around the beginning of February, it is clearly impossible to

[19] See G. Reid, *The Politics of Financial Control*, Hutchinson, paperback edn., 1966, pp. 38–45 and 84–92.

discuss the general policy implications of more than a minute part of the Estimates before the next financial year begins on 1 April.

The difficulty is not resolved by the practice of granting the Government a Vote on Account. This is a sum of money, for general use after 1 April, to cover the costs of government until the main estimates have been passed, usually around the end of July. But this does not afford the Commons much extra time to consider the Estimates.

The containment of public expenditure is a task which really falls on the Chancellor of the Exchequer and the Treasury rather than on the Commons. Treasury control over finance has been described as the precursor and concomitant of Parliamentary control.[20] It is the Treasury which vets the Estimates before they are submitted to the Commons, where approval, given the party majority of the Government, is assured. It often happens that the Government finds it needs additional funds after the Main Estimates have gone through. Supplementary Estimates are then necessary and these too will need the prior approval of the Treasury.

Supplementary Estimates may become necessary in a current financial year because of policy changes, or because of circumstances which were unforeseen when the Main Estimates were submitted. The sums involved may be considerable. In March 1960 the Committee of Supply authorized an extra amount of just under £72 million. In December of the same year an additional sum of nearly £38 million was voted for the National Health Service.[21]

It might be supposed that whatever the influence of the Treasury *before* the submission of Estimates, its hands are tied once they have been approved and money appropriated for specific purposes. But the Government may legally shift money

[20] Sir John Woods, Treasury control, in *The Civil Service in Britain and France*, W. A. Robson (ed.), Hogarth, 1956, p. 110.

[21] E. Taylor, *The House of Commons at Work*, Pelican, 6th edn., 1965, p. 205.

from one vote to another in the case of Defence Estimates and in the case of Civil Estimates the Treasury may authorize transfers of expenditure between subheads within votes. This power of Virement, as it is known, is of some consequence, given that votes may amount to £50 million or more.[22]

There also exists a Civil Contingencies Fund out of which the Treasury may authorize limited expenditure in advance of parliamentary approval, which is known to be forthcoming via the Government's party majority. Now standing at £75 million, it has been used in the past for the manufacture of atom bombs and to meet payments to farmers. It is replenished by Supplementary Estimates. Since the money has already been spent the "request" to the Commons can scarcely be denied.[23]

Parliamentary influence on certain types of expenditure is negligible once a policy decision has been taken. For example, British governments guarantee farmers the difference between a hypothetical "fair" price, agreed by the farmers' representatives and the Minister of Agriculture, and the actual market price paid by consumers for some commodity. The difference between the two prices, which must be allowed for in the Estimates, is decided by the forces of supply and demand, which may or may not be subject to monopolistic influence, the vigour of the farmers' pressure group, the bargaining skill of ministers and civil servants, and the Government's overall policy.

In 1961 mistaken forecasts of market prices were largely responsible for a Supplementary Estimate of £78 million for agricultural deficiency payments. The Estimates Committee of the Commons concluded in a report that the system meant Parliament had more or less to give a blank cheque to the Government. In subsequent years governments have played safe by including a figure in the Main Estimates which is not likely to be exceeded.[24] They are thus saved the embarrassment of submitting a large Supplementary

[22] Reid, *op. cit.*, p. 82.

[23] *Ibid.*, pp. 82–83.

[24] *2nd Report Estimates Committee, 1961–2*, HMSO. See also Agricultural Supplement, *The Times*, 7 Dec. 1964.

Estimate which is bound to lead to criticism. But it can scarcely be claimed that parliamentary control is thereby enhanced.

There are other areas where Commons influence is nullified once a policy decision is taken. Unemployment benefits and supplementary pensions vary in total with economic prosperity or lack of prosperity. And once it is decided to raise the school-leaving age to, say, 16, or to increase old age pensions, the future cost depends on the age structure of the population.

Moreover, the Government does not finance the whole of its expenditure out of money voted annually in Parliament for Supply Services. It finances a great deal of expenditure by borrowing through the issue of Government bonds and Treasury bills. The capital requirements of nationalized industries are in part met in this way; provision has also to be made for the honouring of maturing debt. Treasury management of the national debt is an important part of monetary policy.[25]

The picture so far drawn is one of only nominal control over finance. But the work of the Public Accounts Committee and the Estimates Committee affects the Government in various ways.

The Public Accounts Committee consists of fifteen MPs; its composition reflects party strength on the floor of the House. The Government therefore has a majority in the committee. The chairman, however, is an Opposition Member, if possible the MP who was Financial Secretary to the Treasury when his party was in office. The function of the committee is to consider the Appropriation Accounts kept by government departments. These accounts should show that money has been spent as authorized in Appropriation Acts passed by Parliament.

In practice, the Comptroller and Auditor-General, a servant of the Commons, examines the accounts, assisted by over 600 officials of the Exchequer and Audit Department. He will draw the attention of the Public Accounts Committee to unexplained discrepancies. He may also comment on what he regards as wasteful, uneconomic, or extravagant use of public money.

[25] See *Report of the Committee on the Working of the Monetary System*, Cmd. 827, HMSO, 1959, para. 556.

The Public Accounts Committee is small enough to conduct business expeditiously; it exhibits crossbench sympathies; the chairman is not a government sympathizer and has usually had some experience of Treasury practice from the inside; the functions and terms of reference of the committee are plain; and it is assisted by an expert official with a large and competent staff.

The Public Accounts Committee has drawn attention to such matters as the inadequacies of the costing and contracts procedure of the Ministry of Aviation and the soaring costs of developing the Anglo-French supersonic aircraft Concorde. In one of its annual reports, laid before Parliament, it noted that the army, in 1963, was still ordering 10-ton lorries on a 1957 specification, which the firm concerned regarded as obsolete. These examples are typical of its work.

Departmental officials are not anxious to be brought before the PAC to face awkward questions, especially as Treasury representatives will be present. There is thus an incentive to economize in the expenditure of public money. And there is the possibility that a report of the PAC will be debated in the Commons, with even wider and more public criticism by a reasonably informed body of MPs. In such circumstances the minister will have to defend his department as best as he can; he may feel that his officials have let him down, a cardinal sin in the civil service. The career prospects of certain officials may be adversely affected.

But even the PAC, which serves as a model for many reformers, is not without weaknesses. Because of pressure on the time of the Commons, many of its reports are not debated. In theory the PAC "educates" MPs and, through them, the public. But MPs do not always want to be educated. They are most interested in the political content of reports; when there is something which implies incompetence on the part of a minister the Opposition takes up the attack. But the reports of the PAC are supposed to be non-political, i.e. non-party. It is small wonder that attendances are usually poor when they are debated. The

House is not a firm of management consultants but a collection of politicians in search of power and office.[26]

Furthermore, in any session, the PAC is examining the expenditure of departments not for the financial year just ended, but for the year before that. This is inevitable, since time has to be allowed for the auditing of accounts. Nevertheless, there is a natural inclination on the part of MPs not to interest themselves in what, politically speaking, is ancient history. There is also some truth in the charge that the PAC shuts the gate after the horse has bolted, since waste and incompetence are discovered after the event. But the knowledge that ultimate discovery is possible must have a salutary effect on the conduct of government.

The expenditure of the nationalized industries, which is considerable, is excluded from the province of the Comptroller and Auditor-General and the PAC except when direct Government subsidies are involved. So too are large sectors of local authority expenditure.[27]

The Estimates Committee currently has thirty-six Members and is therefore considerably larger than the PAC. Until the session 1967–8 it had a membership of forty-three. It is chaired by a member of the party in power. As with the PAC and other committees, the party whips and managers effectively control membership. But the chairman of a committee normally has some influence on membership. As always, party strength on the Estimates Committee reflects that on the floor of the House.

In theory, the Estimates Committee examines some of the Estimates submitted to the Commons. But it is not normally concerned with the details of the Estimates and its work is not tied to the time-table of the financial year. The Estimates Committee is really a sort of lay efficiency team working throughout the session. Each year it sets up some half-dozen sub-committees which investigate the organization of selected departments or some general aspect of public administration. In the previous

[26] See Reid, *op. cit.*, p. 110.

[27] See E. L. Normanton, *The Accountability and Audit of Government*, Manchester University Press, 1966, *passim.*

chapter, for example, we referred to the Committee's Report on recruitment to the civil service in the session 1964–5.

In the session 1965–6 the Estimates Committee decided that each of its sub-committees would specialize on some aspect of government activity. Previously, the only specialist sub-committee was one which examined Supplementary Estimates. For example, in the session 1965–6 the sub-committee on Social Affairs was assigned to examine the Civil Estimates, Class 3, Votes 5 and 6, Police. In fact this meant that the sub-committee could make a fairly wide-ranging inquiry into police matters.[28]

Unlike the PAC, the Estimates Committee has little in the way of assistance. It is allocated a clerk from the staff of the Commons, for secretarial duties, and one or two officials are seconded from the Treasury. In the circumstances it is surprising the committee produces reports of the quality it does. Much depends on the calibre of the chairman.

The terms of reference of the Estimates Committee restrict it to recommending economies consistent with the policy implied in the Estimates. But this is less of a limitation than one might suppose. The committee may first have to decide what policy *is* implied in the Estimates; this is not always clear. Furthermore, in suggesting economies, the committee is certain to trespass on policy occasionally.[29]

For example, the committee has suggested that low duties on Danish farm produce depress market prices. The difference between market prices and certain "agreed" prices is thereby widened, with a corresponding increase in government payments to farmers. It would seem that the committee is here concerning itself with a delicate matter of policy, involving one of Britain's partners in the European Free Trade Area.

In another of its reports, the committee recommended that the Colonial Office be merged with the Commonwealth Relations Office. With more and more colonies achieving independence

[28] *1st Special Report Estimates Committee, 1965–6*, HC 21, HMSO, 1965.

[29] See N. Johnson, *Parliament and Administration*, Allen & Unwin, 1966, *passim.*

this was sensible, especially as it was hoped that some former colonies would become voluntary members of the Commonwealth. Nevertheless, a policy of winding up responsibility for the colonies was implied and the committee was rebuked by, amongst others, the then Colonial Secretary, Mr. Iain Macleod.[30] But it is not always easy for the Estimates Committee to stay clear of policy.

Unlike the PAC, the Estimates Committee is not preoccupied with past events. It is concerned with current and future activity as well as with the past. If it asks whether value for money is likely to be obtained with respect to intended expenditure it is inevitably dabbling in policy.[31] But the Estimates Committee is likely to stay clear of contentious policy matters. If its members are to work harmoniously they must avoid issues which will divide the Committee along party lines.

It follows, since the floor of the Commons is a place where party controversy is paramount, that the reports of the Estimates Committee usually arouse only limited interest. Three days in any session are set aside for debate of the reports of both the PAC and the Estimates Committee. This does not seem over-generous. However, in the course of such debates Ministers must defend their departments against reasoned criticism. Moreover, the Treasury, and other departments, produce written replies to the criticisms of the committees. It may be said that the committees "educate" departments by making them aware of possible waste and inefficiency.

Nevertheless, no report, however cogent, will have any effect unless the minister concerned is prepared to act.[32] And although the Estimates Committee does a difficult job, with few resources, it may be questioned whether MPs are the right people for

[30] *4th Report Estimates Committee, 1959–60*. Also see J. D. B. Miller, The Estimates Committee and the Colonial Office, *Public Administration*, Summer 1961; and Sir Geoffrey Nicholson, The Colonial Office and the Estimates Committee, *ibid.*, 1962.

[31] See Enoch Powell, MP, evidence to Select Committee on Procedure, *4th Report*, *1964–5*, HC 303, paras. 349 and 357.

[32] For an assessment of the general impact of the Estimates Committee see N. Johnson, *Parliament* . . ., ch. 4.

tasks which could probably be better done by cost accountants or efficiency experts, attached to the staff of the Commons. The role of the MP is not that of a lay investigator of administrative matters. He is primarily a party politician concerned with policy matters. Anything which diverts him from this role is apt to give the Government more independence and power, not less.

Commenting on financial control in general, Professor Reid justly observes that it is not a myth, though it has mythical features about it. Control is weakened by the rule that financial initiative lies with the Executive and by restrictions on amendments during debate. These bolster the power of ministers. But this does not mean that they are completely indifferent to the pressures of the Opposition and backbenchers.[33]

The PAC and Estimates Committee are useful and have some influence on government, though they can hardly be described as powerful. The PAC is unique in having the assistance of an officer with a large and expert staff at his disposal. But there are other committees of the Commons, some of them of very recent origin. These specialize on different subjects. Parliamentary reformers are continually pressing for the creation of additional specialist committees. Those which already exist therefore merit discussion.

Specialist Committees and Accountability

The Select Committee on Statutory Instruments and the Select Committee on Nationalized Industries have been in existence long enough for their effectiveness to be assessed. Two other select committees, on Agriculture and Science and Technology, only began work in 1967.

The Select Committee on Statutory Instruments dates back to 1944. A statutory instrument is a rule having the force of law which a minister is empowered to make by virtue of a parent Act of Parliament. Ministers may also have prerogative rights to make other orders having the force of law. But SIs made under

[33] Reid, *op. cit.*, pp. 163–4.

some clause in an Act form the major part of what is known as delegated legislation.

The overwhelming majority of Bills which become Acts of Parliament are drafted in government departments. It is obvious that clauses could be inserted conferring wide but vague powers on ministers to make law in the form of SIs. The practice is perfectly constitutional, for it is long established and accepted as legitimate by those who work the system. What has disturbed some observers in the twentieth century, however, has been the tendency for the number of SIs to increase in certain periods. The increase has not been continuous and indeed there are times when the number of SIs made in any one year is significantly less than in the preceding year.

A Committee on Ministers' Powers, which reported in 1932, recognized that delegated legislation involved risks of abuse. But the committee remarked that it also had positive virtues. Parliament was already overburdened and could not possibly cope with extra legislation in the form of statutes. In the view of the committee delegated legislation was an inevitable consequence of the scale and complexity of modern government, which had resulted from changes in political, social, and economic ideas.[34]

Statutory instruments are certainly necessary in a welfare state. They may deal with such matters as variations in national insurance contributions or with the standard strength of penicillin to be used in hospitals. In fact much of the concern over the use of delegated legislation has really stemmed from opposition to state social services. Moreover, there are safeguards against abuse. It is customary for departments to consult "affected" interests before drafting subordinate legislation. How far this is a satisfactory safeguard depends on how widely departments interpret "affected" interest.[35] But there are also Parliamentary checks.

[34] Committee on Ministers' Powers, Report, Cmd. 4060, HMSO, 1932, p. 4, para. 5, and pp. 51–53, para. 11.

[35] See H. Street, Delegated legislation and the public, *Public Administration*, Summer 1949.

Most SIs are laid before Parliament. Sometimes they have immediate effect and continue to do so unless a prayer for their annulment is carried by either House within forty sitting days. In other cases, SIs are not effective until both Houses have positively approved them. There are variations and refinements between these "negative" and "affirmative" types; but such checks really come too late. The time to be vigilant is when the parent Act is going through Parliament. But it is difficult for even the most alert Member to foresee the use which will be made of any clause which confers power to make SIs.

The Committee on Ministers' Powers considered the setting up of a Commons Committee to scrutinize delegated legislation. But not until 1944 did such a committee come into being. By then, there were complaints from backbenchers that the Commons could not exercise effective control over the increased volume of war-time delegated legislation. The Select Committee on Statutory Instruments, or Scrutiny Committee, has been set up in every subsequent year. The House of Lords has a similar committee, the Special Order Committee, first set up in 1925.

The Scrutiny Committee has eleven members. The chairman is a member of the Opposition. It is assisted by the Counsel to the Speaker. He provides the committee with a memorandum on the SIs which he wishes to bring to its attention. The terms of reference of the Scrutiny Committee preclude it from going into the merits of an SI. It may draw the attention of the House to an SI, on certain grounds only. These are that a charge on public funds is entailed; that the SI excludes challenge in the courts; that it makes unexpected use of powers; that it purports to have retrospective effect, without specific authorization in the parent Act; that elucidation is required; and that there has been undue delay in publication or in laying the SI before Parliament.

As the SIs brought to the attention of the committee are selected by Counsel to the Speaker, party motives are not in evidence. The committee's work is mostly confined to ensuring that the correct procedures have been followed. It is true that the committee has the responsibility of drawing the attention of the House to the unexpected use of delegated legislation. But in a political system with a long tradition of strong Executives, the greater part of delegated legislation passes without challenge from the committee.

Ministers do not appear before the committee and officials are not pressed to explain, beyond a point, why a department has made an SI in a particular form. A chairman has been known to rebuke members for concerning themselves with departmental administration. In his opinion the committee should have limited itself to deciding whether there had been a breach of practice in making or laying orders.[36]

This restrictive interpretation of the committee's role can scarcely ease the problem of finding MPs willing to serve on it. The Scrutiny Committee may have some appeal for lawyers in the Commons, but on the whole its work is somewhat uninteresting and technical.

Clearly the committee is too small and inadequately staffed for detailed examination of the 1000 or so SIs brought to its attention annually. It meets once a fortnight for a few hours only. Its comments on an SI may not reach the Commons until it has been in force for some time. And because, in certain cases, an SI can only be annulled if a prayer is successfully moved against it within forty sitting days, delay undermines the effectiveness of the committee.

In practice, prayers usually originate with the Opposition. They are moved with the intention of criticizing the Government or to delay government legislation. Both parties treat prayers seriously enough to put the whips on. It is therefore virtually impossible to move a prayer against the Government with any hopes of success.[37]

From time to time suggestions are made for extending the functions of the Scrutiny Committee. For example, that it should

[36] G. Marshall and G. C. Moodie, *Some Problems of the Constitution*, Hutchinson, 1961 edn., pp. 120–1.

[37] See J. Eaves, *Emergency Powers and the Parliamentary Watchdog: Parliament and the Executive in Great Britain, 1939–51*, Hansard Society, 1957, pp. 181–2.

act as a complaint receiving body *after* an SI has come into operation. It has also been suggested that the committee should consider the "merits" of SIs. But successive governments have rejected these and other ideas.[38] In short, it looks as though the Scrutiny Committee will continue to play its present somewhat limited role. For this reason it is seldom cited by those reformers who see committees as the solution to Parliamentary control of the Executive.

Because the Scrutiny Committee is non-partisan, and somewhat slow in reporting, Opposition MPs who wish to attack the Government, using an SI as a convenient weapon, tend to use their own initiative. Party political motives confer a degree of energy and ingenuity on their efforts which the Scrutiny Committee lacks. The best-known example is the work of the Active Backbenchers Committee of the Conservative Party in the period 1945–51.

In the Active Backbenchers Committee each member specialized on a particular type of SI, such as those relating to food subsidies, transport, fuel, industry and trade, and so on. Close contact was maintained with interest groups outside Parliament, either directly, or through specialist committees of the Conservative Party in Parliament. It is the practice of ministers to submit SIs to their relevant party committees if they are thought to be controversial. Most departments send copies of all SIs to the chairmen of party committees.[39] The Active Backbenchers Committee certainly harassed the government of the day. Whether it improved the quality of administration is another matter.

The Select Committee on Nationalized Industries attracts a great deal more attention than the Scrutiny Committee. It issued its first report in October 1957. In many cases its reports are valuable sources of information. The terms of reference of the committee are, to examine the reports and accounts of the nationalized industries established by statute whose controlling boards are appointed by ministers of the Crown and whose annual

[38] See J. E. Kersell, *Parliamentary Supervision of Delegated Legislation*, Stevens, 1960.

[39] *Ibid.*, ch. 4.

receipts are not wholly or mainly derived from moneys provided by Parliament or advanced from the Exchequer. The BBC and the Atomic Energy Authority do not come within these terms; nor do organizations owned or partly owned by the Government, such as British Petroleum Ltd. and Cable and Wireless Ltd., which are not public corporations. At the beginning of the session 1967–8 the committee pressed unsuccessfully for an investigation of the Bank of England, hitherto considered outside its jurisdiction. The committee may produce a special report on its Order of Reference in the near future.

The nationalized industries do not have the same relationship with Parliament as do government departments. In the first place they are exempt from the annual submission of Estimates to Parliament. To this extent they also escape Treasury control, but the Treasury virtually controls capital expenditure. Some undertakings—for example, certain electricity boards—are fortunate in that their activities yield a surplus, which can be used to finance at least part of their capital development. But declining industries, such as British Railways, receive subsidies from public funds and are subject to a greater degree of both Parliamentary and Treasury influence.

Secondly, ministerial responsibility for the nationalized industries is lightened, ostensibly to encourage them to be more adventurous and commercially minded. Ministers are formally responsible for policy but not for day-to-day administration. Unlike civil servants, the personnel of the nationalized industries are supposedly free to take day-to-day decisions without worrying about the political consequences for ministers.

Actually, financial autonomy, and statutory provision for diversification of activity, are probably more essential for enterprise than any formal split in responsibility. And one of the consistent findings of the Select Committee on Nationalized Industries has been that the real influence of ministers exceeds their statutory powers with respect to prices and other matters.

The prices charged by nationalized industries, and the wages they pay, cannot in practice be divorced from the government's overall economic policy. It is inevitable that ministers exert considerable pressure in such matters, although the statutes relating to nationalized industries may treat them as day-to-day administration and the province of the Board. It is the informal manner in which ministers exercise their influence that causes concern. Unless they issue a directive to a Board, in what they consider to be a matter of national interest, it is extremely difficult to pin responsibility on them. Yet there is no doubt that nationalized industries have kept their prices low, and suffered losses, in response to ministerial pressure.

A minister who has influence beyond his formal legal powers may nevertheless refuse to answer questions about matters for which he is at least partly responsible. Like the harlot, he enjoys power without responsibility. As one commentator observes, the Minister can use the Board as a screen; and the Board can excuse failures by references to ministerial interference.[40]

Yet in many ways Parliament is well informed about the nationalized industries. Ministers will answer questions on matters for which they are clearly responsible; they *may* reply to other questions, which perhaps merely seek information, making it clear that they do not thereby accept responsibility. MPs may write directly to the Boards, which will generally deal promptly with their inquiries. The annual reports and accounts of the industries may be debated in government time. And opportunities to debate the affairs of the nationalized industries occur in the normal way. In addition, there is the work of the Select Committee.

This committee, in the current session, 1967–8, has eighteen members (an increase of five over previous years). It has little in the way of assistance, other than some secretarial services provided by the staff of the Commons. It might well be thought that neither ministers nor Boards have much to fear from a small committee of laymen. Given that they are dealing with some of

[40] A. H. Hanson, *Parliament and Public Ownership*, Cassell, 1961, p. 208. Also see W. A. Robson, *Nationalized Industry and Public Ownership*, Allen & Unwin, 1960, pp. 62–69 and chs. 7 and 8.

the largest concerns in the country, and with highly technical matters, the absence of qualified staff, to offer independent and expert opinion on evidence submitted by interested parties, must handicap committee members in their work.

The committee itself considered the question of expert assistance in one of its reports. It pointed out that its inquiry into the air corporations involved the examination of sixty pages of reports and eighty pages of accounts. In addition, the reports and accounts of seven foreign airlines were considered. There were also many special memoranda and accounts to be perused. The committee was of the opinion that the comments of an economist on what to look for would have been helpful; some expert help in collating and summarizing reports and answers to questions would have been useful. But, the committee felt, an officer of the status of the Comptroller and Auditor-General would probably tend towards investigations of a type which would damage relations with the Boards. They must not feel they were subject to some grand inquisition by an outside official or body. And the seconding of a Treasury official to assist the committee might suggest that the committee was not entirely independent of the Executive. The committee left it to the House to decide what additional assistance, if any, it should receive.[41] So far, only part-time help has been provided.

The committee raised an important issue when expressing its desire to avoid a grand inquisition. It is difficult to say when the *degree* of accountability is just right. If it is excessive, if Boards and ministers are criticized for every chance which does not come off, or for every human error, then they will tend to be excessively cautious. The House may be wise to deny the Select Committee on Nationalized Industries expert help on a large scale. But to deprive it of one or two economists or accountants hardly seems justified.

The successful working of the committee depends in large measure on the ability of its members to steer clear of matters

[41] *Special Report of the Select Committee on Nationalized Industries*, HC 276, 1959. For comment see Hanson, *op. cit.*, ch. 6.

which could split it along party lines. It has generally succeeded in this, but in so doing its effectiveness is limited, for it is those aspects of the nationalized industries which give rise to party political controversy which are likely to interest the MPs on the floor of the House. The formal modification of ministerial responsibility enables members of the committee who belong to the governing party to be critical of the nationalized industries with a clear conscience; there is less conflict with party loyalty when the competence of Boards, rather than of party leaders, is in question. Ministers may conclude that backbenchers could scarcely be more innocently employed than in carrying out a layman's investigation into administrative efficiency.

Those who advocate additional specialized standing committees often point to the relative success of the Select Committee on Nationalized Industries as evidence of their value. But the unique constitutional position regarding ministerial responsibility has to be borne in mind. Furthermore, the criteria by which the efficiency of the nationalized industries may be judged differ from those which could be applied to government departments. At least in part, the nationalized industries are commercial undertakings. Rightly or wrongly, the tendency in the sixties has been to assess their performance against their ability to achieve a surplus or some agreed return on capital invested.[42] This sort of yardstick could not be applied to the work of, say, the Foreign Office.

The Select Committee on Nationalized Industries has certainly produced a great deal of information which would otherwise be unavailable. To some extent it has influenced ministerial policy and thinking; in a way it is an extra administrative aide

[42] See White Paper, *The Financial and Economic Obligations of the Nationalized Industries*, Cmd. 1337, HMSO, 1961; *Report of the Select Committee on British Railways*, HC 254–1, 1959–60. For comment on financial aspects of nationalized industries see Robson, *op. cit.*, ch. 11. Also A. H. Hanson, *Nationalization: A Book of Readings*, Allen & Unwin, 1963, ch. 6, and M. V. Posner, The financial aims of nationalized industries, *London and Cambridge Bulletin*, No. 41, March 1962. The White Paper, *Nationalized Industries: A Review of Economic and Financial Objectives*, Cmd. 3437, 1967, deals with financial criteria in a more sophisticated way than Cmd. 1337 of 1961.

for ministers, as much as a device for securing accountability. Ministers have not followed the suggestions of the committee in any slavish fashion. They have adopted an eclectic approach, taking up those suggestions which accord with their own inclinations.[43]

The Committees on Agriculture and Science and Technology have broad terms of reference. They are not specifically confined to matters of administration. The Select Committee on Agriculture is required "to consider the activities in England and Wales of the Ministry of Agriculture, Fisheries and Food and to report thereon". The Select Committee on Science and Technology is given an open invitation "to consider Science and Technology and to report thereon". The committees may sit in public and invite ministers to appear before them to answer questions. Ministers are not obliged to appear because constitutionally they are accountable to the House as a whole.

In the session 1966–7 the Agricultural Committee consisted of sixteen members; the Science Committee was fourteen strong. (In the session 1967–8 the Agricultural Committee was increased in size to twenty-five.) Neither committee had expert staff attached to it. But, as one would expect, the members tended to come from agricultural constituencies, or to have some qualifications or interest in science and technology. The chairman of the Scientific Committee was an electrical engineer, and the committee included the director of a firm of chemical manufacturers and the vice-chairman of the Conservative Parliamentary Committee on Technology. The chairman of the Agricultural Committee was a member of the Welsh Tourist and Holiday Board; there were also three MPs who were described as farmers, an official of the National Union of Agricultural Workers and a former Chairman of the Fisheries Sub-Committee of the Conservative Parliamentary Committee on Agriculture.

[43] For details see D. Coombes, *The Member of Parliament and the Administration: The Case of the Select Committee on Nationalized Industries*, Allen & Unwin, 1966, ch. 7. The influence of the committee should not be overrated. Hanson, *Parliament and Public Ownership*, puts it in perspective; e.g. see p. 160.

The Science and Technology Committee began its work by looking into the nuclear reactor programme. What sort of relationship it will develop with the Ministry of Technology remains to be seen.

Responsibility for science is rather more complicated. The Department of Education and Science is concerned with research in universities. And the universities have now to open their books and accounts to the Public Accounts Committee. There may thus be some overlap in the work of the two committees. It is not clear whether science is to include the social sciences. It is doubtful if the science side of university activity could be considered in isolation from the arts side without a distorted picture emerging. Furthermore, a great deal of scientific activity is of strategic or commercial importance, involving several departments and relations with other countries. Much of this activity is subject to strict security.

The Select Committee on Agriculture has already been involved in a certain amount of controversy. In March 1967 it proposed to visit Brussels, to study the possible effects on food prices if Britain joined the Common Market. This provoked ministerial disquiet, even though government party Whips had ensured a majority of pro-marketeers on the committee. The policy of applying to join the Common Market was a contentious one inside the Parliamentary Labour Party, and at that time negotiations had reached a delicate stage.

The proposed visit was also connected with a memorandum from the Ministry of Agriculture; some members of the committee felt this was misleading in certain respects. This memorandum, almost unchanged, was reprinted as a White Paper in May. But officials were perturbed at the prospect of a group of MPs setting a precedent by carrying out their own independent check, and perhaps complicating negotiations. At the same time, the committee was pressing for the right to examine relevant papers which had passed between the British delegation in Brussels and the Foreign Office.

Mr. Fred Mulley, then Minister of State at the Foreign Office, thought it wise to appear before the committee, to advise members on the procedure to be followed if and when they did go to Brussels. By July there was still deadlock in spite of the efforts of a new Minister of State, Lord Chalfont, to resolve the difficulty. Not until the Leader of the House and the Foreign Secretary were brought into the dispute did the committee receive a conditional go-ahead.[44] One report of the Agricultural Committee has complained of Foreign Office obstruction.[45]

Both the Agricultural Committee and the Science and Technology Committee were set up again for the session 1967–8. The latter is to be a permanent select committee. More specialist committees are planned, including one to deal with education.[45a] The idea of a select committee on the private sector of industry was floated by Mr. Richard Crossman when he was Leader of the House. This would have the advantage of giving backbenchers something interesting to do without, presumably, unduly worrying ministers and officials. It would be popular with Mr. Crossman's party and satisfy those politicians and academics who have been stridently calling for parliamentary reforms.

The Reform of the Commons

Most reformers are of the opinion that, in general, MPs have too little influence on policy and legislation. Government bills, drafted in departments after consultation with interest groups, reach the Commons in a more or less final form. And the same situation is said to prevail in policy matters. For example, in November 1966 the First Secretary of the Department

[44] See article, Crossman reforms begin to bite, *The Times*, 15 June 1967, and report on Brussels trip in *The Times*, 3 July 1967.

[45] *Report from the Select Committee on Agriculture, 1966–7*, HC 378–xvii, and *Evidence to Committee*, HC 378–xviii, 1967.

[45a] A select committee was set up, at the end of February 1968, to consider the activities of the Department of Education and Science and of the Scottish Education Department. It has seventeen members and is chaired by Mr. Fred Willey, a former Labour minister. The Agricultural Committee is confined to England and Wales, and will cease to exist after February, 1969. See Appendix (3).

of Economic Affairs presented a White Paper on incomes policy to Labour backbenchers *after* it had been discussed with representatives of the then Federation of British Industry and the Trades Union Congress.[46] However, any government which loses contact with backbench opinion is asking for trouble; it is on the unity of the party that its life depends. Situations vary according to the size of the Government's majority, the imminence of an election, the issues involved, the current standing of party leaders, the vigour of the backbenchers, and other considerations. Moreover, most backbenchers have some connection with outside pressure groups.

Secondly, the scale of modern government has vastly increased the volume of legislation. The anachronistic procedure of Parliament, the shortness of the session, and Opposition obstruction compel governments to resort to various devices to speed up the passage of legislation.[47] As a result, MPs may have very little time to discuss a Bill. During a debate a Government spokesman may move the closure which, if carried, terminates discussion; the party majority ensures that it will be carried. Standing Orders, under which business ends at a certain hour, may be suspended and the House kept sitting all night so that another stage of a Bill, or a debate, may be got out of the way. In the standing committees of the House, which consider the details of Bills, the "kangaroo" closure may be used. This is the right of the chairman to select certain amendments only for discussion. A timetable may be attached to a Bill. Under this arrangement, known as the "guillotine", discussion on each stage of the Bill is automatically terminated on a specified date.[48]

In 1966 timetable difficulties were primarily responsible for an important amendment involving a compulsory incomes freeze being added to a Bill then in its committee stage. The Opposition protested that the amendment fundamentally altered the character of the Bill and that a new one should have been introduced. They

[46] See article, Keeping the Commons out of the act, *The Times*, 11 Nov. 1966.

[47] On the stages of a Bill going through Parliament see E. Taylor, *op. cit.*, ch. 4.

[48] For an example of the "guillotine" see Hanson and Wiseman, *op. cit.*, pp. 135–49.

were supported by the press in this demand. And members of the Parliamentary Labour Party opposed to the Government's incomes policy saw the move as a device for stilling protest within the party. But with the summer recess looming up the Government refused to give way.

Thirdly, there is pressure for reform because of the complex and technical character of many of the functions of modern government. There are few MPs with a scientific or a technical background; even if there were many more, it is argued that they would need to be supported by properly trained staff. The Opposition and backbenchers of the governing party are in a weak position to challenge ministers advised by experts. It is difficult for laymen to decide which amongst many scientific projects are most worth while. And in the nature of things a scientific bureaucracy, with its own peculiar jargon, is not easily controlled.[49]

Fourthly, the Commons is often denied information. Without this it cannot exert much influence or secure accountability. Ministers are apt to claim that disclosure would not be in the public interest, security might be endangered, or delicate negotiations disrupted, or there would be a betrayal of the confidence of a foreign government. Such arguments are most plausibly advanced in the field of foreign affairs—for example, in connection with events in Aden and Rhodesia between 1964 and 1966. And relations with other countries are of increasing significance as autonomy decreases for middle-sized powers like Britain.

Fifthly, attention is drawn to the lack of facilities available to MPs. Their position is often contrasted with that of members of the United States Congress who enjoy generous research and secretarial assistance at public expense. Compelled to do his own homework, it is argued, the British MP cannot possibly offer a serious challenge to ministers backed by a vast bureaucracy.

[49] See A. Albu, The Member of Parliament, the Executive and Scientific Policy, *Minerva*, Autumn 1963; and S. A. Walkland, Science and Parliament, *Parliamentary Affairs*, Autumn 1964.

Finally, it is widely believed that party discipline is too strict. The backbencher is alleged to have little independence or influence. Discipline is said to be imposed even when no major issue of party policy is involved. For example, in a debate in the Commons in 1967 on decimal currency, a free vote was refused by the Leader of the House and the Chancellor of the Exchequer. The subject of debate was not whether Britain should or should not have a decimal currency, but merely the form such currency should take. There were differences of opinion in both parties, but although more than fifty MPs of all parties signed a motion calling for a free vote, this was of no avail.[50]

When the Labour Party took office in 1964, however, there were good prospects of reform. The party had spent thirteen frustrating years in Opposition and had ample experience of ministerial domination of the House. As Leader of the Opposition Mr. Wilson had more than once mentioned the need for reforms. Nor was there any lack of ideas or literature on the subject of reform.[51]

In December 1966 Mr. Crossman, as Leader of the House, initiated a debate on reports from a Select Committee on Procedure. He made it clear that there was no turning back to a time when the Commons made or unmade governments via cross-bench voting. Furthermore, it must be the Cabinet which dominated legislation and the party machines which managed the business of the House. As if to prove his point the Government had decided not to allow a free vote on the matters under discussion. With such a candid friend it might be supposed that reformers had no need of enemies. The Government secured a comfortable majority for its proposals to experiment with morning sittings on Mondays and Wednesdays, in spite of criticism from some members of its own party. In addition the House agreed to

[50] See Parliamentary Report, *The Times*, 3 March 1967.

[51] For example, see B. Crick, *The Reform of Parliament*, Weidenfeld & Nicholson, 1964; Hill and Whichelow, *What's Wrong With Parliament?*, Penguin, 1964; Hansard Society, *Parliamentary Reform 1933–60*, Cassell, 1961; Socialist Commentary, Three dozen parliamentary reforms, in *Socialist Commentary*, July 1964.

the setting up of the Select Committees on Agriculture and Science and Technology to which reference has already been made.[52]

The case for morning sittings, devoted to non-controversial matters, rests mainly on the belief that more time would be available later in the day to discuss contentious subjects. They would thus help to eliminate all-night sittings. Sceptics think otherwise. One argument against morning sittings is that they may drive a wedge between full-time MPs and those Members whose outside occupations and interests would prevent their attendance. In the course of the debate Mr. Crossman rejected this, but in any case, he contended, Members were increasingly full time. In his view this was right and proper. The idea that an outside occupation keeps a Member in touch with non-parliamentary opinion, and makes specialist knowledge available in the House, is probably more common on the Conservative side.

The principal speaker for the Opposition, Mr. Selwyn Lloyd, argued that unless ministers were free of Parliament in the mornings they would not be able to control their departments and officials. He thought Monday a bad choice, dictated by the preference of Members representing London constituencies. Few out-of-town MPs would be in London in time for Monday sittings. However, there is little alternative to Monday and Wednesday for morning sittings. On Tuesday and Thursday many Members work on standing committees and Friday mornings are taken up with Private Members business. Mr. Lloyd thought the main object of the Government was to gain extra time for more of its measures. His reactions were predictable; all the Conservative Members on the Select Committee on Procedure had voted against morning sittings.

The morning sitting experiment began inauspiciously on 1 February 1967. At 10 o'clock sixty members were reported to be present, including the Leader of the Opposition and seven

[52] See *1st Report Select Committee on Procedure, 1966–7*, HMSO, 1966; and Parliamentary Report, *The Times*, 15 Dec. 1966. The main recommendations in the *Report of the Select Committee on Procedure, on Financial Procedure, 1965–6*, HC 122, HMSO, 1966, were also accepted, namely abolition of committees of Supply and Ways and Means.

members of the Government Front Bench. A government order dissolving the Ministry of Aviation was down for what was considered formal approval as uncontentious business. In fact an Opposition Member spoke at such length that the order was not approved by the end of the morning.[53] A Bill relating to travel agents, introduced by a Labour backbencher, was opposed by a Conservative Member, who endeavoured to force a division on it. The Speaker pointed out that voting was ruled out between 10 a.m. and 1 p.m. The House was still sitting at 3.10 a.m. on Thursday, 2 February. It was then counted out, as lacking the necessary quorum of forty, on the initiative of a Conservative Member. The Government was thus denied a second reading of a Consolidated Fund Bill.

The Government suffered further frustration in the afternoon. During the process of being counted out in the morning the Consolidated Fund Bill had been put down as first business when the House resumed. But the Leader of the Opposition pointed out that a sessional order required the Government to give the House twenty-four hours' notice in such cases; the Speaker agreed, so the Bill was put off until the following week.[54]

During the second of the new morning sittings, the following Monday, the Government's attempt to legally wind up the Ministry of Aviation was again defeated by an Opposition filibuster. In the afternoon, however, the Leader of the House secured his revenge by announcing that a debate on the press, planned for Tuesday, would be postponed. Instead the House would consider the allegedly uncontroversial Ministry of Aviation Dissolution Order, the Ministry of Land and Natural Resources Dissolution Order, and the second reading of the Consolidated Fund Bill.

By the middle of March one Monday morning sitting was so poorly attended that it petered out after thirty-one minutes. The following Wednesday morning provided more lively fare.

[53] There are no rules restricting the length of speeches during morning sittings.

[54] Parliamentary Report, *The Times*, 3 Feb. 1967.

It was understood that ministers would not make important or controversial statements in the morning. Yet the Government chose this occasion to announce that the salary of the chairman of the newly created Steel Corporation would be £24,000, much more than the salaries received by the chairmen of other nationalized concerns; this was at a time when wages and salaries were subject to a policy of severe restraint.

The next day Mr. Heath, Leader of the Opposition, demanded to know why the Government had gone back on its word. There were also left-wingers of the Labour Party who felt the Government was indulging in sharp practice. Obviously there was a difference of opinion regarding what was controversial and important. The Leader of the House advised Mr. Heath to take up the matter through "the usual channels"; the latter said he had already done so. Mr. Crossman admitted that representations had been made to the department concerned, which took the view that the salary announcement was not a matter of major importance.[55]

In April 1967 the Leader of the House announced that, for the rest of the session, forty-eight hours' notice would be given of ministerial statements to be made during morning sittings.

Morning sittings, in the form they took in the 1966–7 session, did little to provide the Commons with extra time later in the day. All-night sittings were as frequent as ever. The fact is that the Opposition party will obstruct business in the morning if this leaves the Government free to press on with contentious legislation later. Nevertheless, some form of morning sittings is probable whilst Labour remains in power. At the beginning of the session 1967–8 new government plans for occasional morning sittings were reported. These would be arranged at short notice when a Bill was running into trouble or when it appeared likely that there would otherwise be a series of all-night sittings. But there is no reason to believe that the Opposition will not impede progress as in the past.

Some observations have already been made on existing Specialized Standing Committees. But, since more committees are

[55] Parliamentary Report, *The Times*, 17 March 1967.

the chief remedy prescribed for parliamentary ills by reformers, additional comment is called for.

Reformers argue that as members of committees develop specialist knowledge there will be more effective scrutiny of policy and legislation. They contend that with many matters referred to committees, more time will be available for debates on major issues on the floor of the House. It is held that committees are a valuable training ground for potential ministers. It is suggested that there could be more effective scrutiny of the Estimates if these were farmed out to the relevant committees. It is further suggested that additional specialist committees will inform and brief MPs and help Parliament to act as a broker of ideas, putting facts and viewpoints before the electorate. And it is denied that committees will usurp ministerial responsibility for policy or undermine accountability to the House as a whole.[56]

Reformers are divided on the question of whether specialist committees should become directly involved in the legislative process by taking over the committee stage of Bills from the present general committees. The majority are opposed, believing that party differences would split specialist committees and damage their fact-finding and educative functions. Purely investigatory committees, it is argued, would not divide along party lines, even when considering matters of major importance.[57]

The Study of Parliament Group, an association of university teachers of government and officers of both Houses of Parliament, has advocated specialist committees on the Social Services, Machinery of Government, and other subjects. The group has suggested that such committees might be developed from the specialist sub-committees of the Estimates Committee. It takes an intermediate position on legislative functions. After their second reading, Bills would go to non-specialist standing committees, as

[56] See B. Crick, *op. cit.*, pp. 161–4 and 171.

[57] See D. Coombes, *op. cit.*, p. 213. Also Hansard Society, *Parliamentary Reform, 1933–60*, pp. 42–45; and H. V. Wiseman, *Parliament and the Executive*, Routledge, 1966, paperback edn., pp. 206–13.

at present, but the nucleus of such committees might consist of MPs who were also members of specialist committees.[58]

Some advocates of specialist committees bolster their case by references to foreign experience. *The Economist*, for example, holding that party bickering is responsible for serious study of policy passing to outside bodies, has suggested that something on the lines of US Congressional committtees is called for. They would take some responsibility for policy and, in *The Economist*'s opinion, the sharp line between Government and Opposition would tend to become blurred, as in Washington.[59]

Sceptics argue that committees will undermine the prestige of the House rather than strengthen it. If ministers are hauled before committees for questioning and criticism it is not the House but the committees which will get publicity. Members will be diverted from the floor of the House. And although ministers will remain technically responsible *to* the House, they will no longer be clearly responsible *for* policy which may be influenced by committees. Who should *take* responsibility or bear the blame if things subsequently go wrong?

A further line of criticism concerns the relationship of ministers and civil servants. At present the advice of civil servants is confidential. Hence the names of senior officials are not bandied about in party controversy. It might be difficult to maintain a permanent, non-party, civil service if confidentiality were abandoned. A powerful investigating committee might well discover that a policy, or some aspect of policy, of party political interest emanated from a civil servant. This must obviously be the case in many instances for which ministers now take responsibility. Would offending civil servants be required to resign if their role received greater publicity? Or would the House, which for party reasons is interested in attacking ministers, merely be indifferent to the information dug up by committees? And would not civil servants, fearing public censure and attack to which they could

[58] Study of Parliament Group, evidence to Select Committee on Procedure, see *4th Report of the Committee, 1964–5*, HC 303, HMSO, 1965, appendix 2.

[59] Rule by Inquiry, *The Economist*, 30 Oct. 1965.

not easily reply, be excessively cautious in tendering advice to ministers?

Certainly if there were powerful committees specializing on a department's work, officials would have to take into account the status and influence of the chairmen when advising ministers. They would have to be aware of factional differences on committees and their connections, if any, with pressure groups. Relations with committees would have to be carefully cultivated. Ministers and officials would have to assess possible reaction in the Commons if a conflict should develop between a department and one or more committees. All this would enormously complicate the process of government and might bring little in the way of compensation.

The fact-finding role of committees, when ministerial responsibility is involved, is full of difficulties. It is not the custom for officials to oppose in public the policies of their ministers, even if such policies conflict with the confidential advice they have given. The information made available to committees by departments will tend to be that which justifies ministerial policy. It is improbable that a civil servant would publicize differences within a department by openly casting doubts on the wisdom of ministerial decisions before a Commons committee.

Furthermore, although very senior officials *might* be willing to risk their necks in answering questions which involved nebulous distinctions between policy and administration, more junior officials would not be so forthcoming, for fear of offending their superiors.

It is sometimes suggested that specialist committees of the Commons are a natural extension of the specialist committees of the parliamentary parties, but this is not convincing. Ministers may make concessions to their own followers because party unity is important when confronting the Opposition. Major policy is decided and fought out on a party basis. This must reduce the influence of all-party committtees of the Commons which seek to avoid splitting along party lines. Comparisons between party committees and committees of the Commons are mainly useful for highlighting differences. And the same is true of comparisons between committees operating in different political systems.

There are so many differences between the political systems of Britain and the USA that the operation of Congressional committees scarcely seems relevant. The more sophisticated advocates of committees are aware of this. But they may also be conscious of the fact that US experience is by no means entirely favourable to their case.

Chief amongst the constitutional differences is the fact that an adverse vote in the US Congress does not entail the resignation of the Government. The consequences of, say, Democratic Congressmen voting with Republicans against the proposals of a Democratic President, or participating in an attack on presidential policy, are far less serious than any cross-bench tendencies in Britain. The US President, who takes formal responsibility for all policy, is ultimately answerable to the voters who elect him. On the other hand, the legislature cannot be dissolved by the President at a time he finds convenient for an election.

Furthermore, the USA has a federal constitution and fears the concentration of too much power in the hands of the federal executive; in Britain there is a tradition of strong central government which stems from the concept of the Sovereignty of Parliament and party control of Parliament. In the USA it is not unusual for a President to be confronted with a legislature and a committee system which is controlled by a rival party. Moreover, the President faces not one elected chamber, but two, both of which can delay and obstruct in various ways.

The most important political differences are connected with parties. American parties are far less disciplined and centralized than are the British; at the national level they are less oligarchical. All this is reflected in committee behaviour. A Congressman depends on his own State or district organization, and largely raises his own funds for electoral purposes. He does not need the endorsement of a Central Office. Party labels mean less than in Britain and personality is more important.

In a sense there is a multi-party system in the USA. The Democratic organization in the State of New York bears little resemblance to the Democratic organization in, say, Virginia. Indeed, there are differences between the Democratic Party in New York City and New York State. The same applies to the Republican Party.

There is nobody who is equivalent to a British Leader of the Opposition. And the fact that a President may only serve for two terms tends to limit domination of a party by one individual for any great length of time. There are numerous other differences, relating to the selection of candidates and so on, into which it is unnecessary to go in this context.

Even if all these differences are ignored it cannot be said that the experience of US Congressional committees is completely favourable to those who wish to see additional specialized committees in Britain. Committees in the USA have held up or emasculated civil rights legislation. There is a great deal of overlap and proliferation of sub-committees. The chairmen of committees and sub-committees are sometimes reactionary, elderly, and inclined to be unduly interested in self-aggrandizement and the extension of their empires. Officials sometimes play off committees against government policies to which they are opposed. And it may be doubted whether US Congressional committees are as influential as is sometimes supposed. For example, they can only inquire after the event into such matters as US involvement in Korea, Cuba, or the Dominican Republic. But it can also be held that certain committees, such as those on Appropriations, are too powerful, in that they can obstruct executive action for purely sectional reasons.

It is certainly the case that committee work tends to empty the floor of both Houses in Congress. And the investigatory hearings of committees do not necessarily educate the public. Many are held in executive session, that is, in secret. And the object of many hearings is not to arrive at an impartial judgement; the end in view is plainly politically partisan and the evidence submitted by supposedly objective and expert staff is slanted accordingly.

If this is true of a system where parties are weak and ill disciplined, with corresponding freedom for committee members, it may not be true of a system where parties are extremely well disciplined. Nevertheless, American experience cannot be completely ignored.[60]

On a more mundane level there is always the problem of finding personnel to serve on numerous committees in a House of Commons which still includes many part-time Members. There is the further problem of deciding the committees to which a particular MP should be assigned. In Britain a "seniority" system of assigning personnel is not likely to have much appeal for party leaders. On the other hand, it is difficult to devise some satisfactory test of "merit"; but however the matter is decided, the party leaders would be firmly in control and the party whips would exercise considerable patronage.[61]

The Parliamentary Commissioner

In October 1965 the Government issued a White Paper announcing its intention to appoint a Parliamentary Commissioner for Administration.[62] This was in fulfilment of an election pledge, but the idea of a Commissioner, or British Ombudsman, had

[60] For further information on US congressional committees and parties see J. M. Burns, *The Deadlock of Democracy*, Calder, 1964; V. O. Key, *Politics, Parties and Pressure Groups*, Crowell, 1964; B. M. Gross, *The Legislative Struggle*, New York, 1953; and J. D. Lees, *The Committee System of the United States Congress*, Routledge & Kegan Paul, 1967.

[61] Those who have doubts about the value of committees are less vocal than those who favour them. For the views of some opponents see G. R. Strauss, The case against parliamentary specialist committees, *The Times*, 9 June 1966; also remarks of Michael Foot and Sir Richard Nugent, Parliamentary Report, *The Times*, 28 Oct. 1965; and evidence of Sir Laurence Helsby and Rt. Hon. Herbert Bowden to Select Committee on Procedure, *4th Report, 1964–5*, paras. 162–97 and 299–329. Also see R. Butt, *The Power of Parliament*, Constable, 1967, *passim*.

[62] Cmnd. 2767, Oct. 1965.

been canvassed for some time. An association of lawyers—Justice—had supported the idea in a semi-official report, published in 1961.[63] Justice took the view that existing means of redress were inadequate and suggested that a British version of the Ombudsman, who investigates complaints in Scandinavian countries, would be useful.

The suggestion naturally had a somewhat stronger appeal for the Opposition, at that time the Labour Party, than for the Government Front Bench. But some backbench MPs, on both sides, feared that an Ombudsman would undermine their status and deprive them of direct responsibility for investigating the complaints of their constituents. These fears were not stilled by the recommendation of Justice that the Ombudsman, or Parliamentary Commissioner, should report his findings to a select committee of one or both Houses.

In 1962 the Conservative Lord Chancellor, Lord Dilhorne, on behalf of the Government, rejected the idea of a Parliamentary Commissioner. He contended that the Commissioner would interfere with the prompt dispatch of business, that there was already adequate means of redress and that such an office would interfere with ministerial responsibility to Parliament alone.[64]

Scarcely any commentator accepted the Lord Chancellor's claim that opportunities for redress were already adequate. But some critics of the Ombudsman proposals felt that such an institution would be used to harass overworked, but generally fair-minded and competent middle-grade officials, while the big fish would escape the net by invoking such political formulas as confidentiality, security, and the public interest. In the opinion of these sceptics a Parliamentary Commissioner would at best be a minor innovation, but one which might divert attention from the more radical reforms needed to modernize Parliament and the courts.

They pointed out that in the Scandinavian countries relations

[63] Justice, *op. cit.*, ch. 14.
[64] See leading article, *The Times*, 12 Nov. 1962.

between the executive, legislature, and judicial system differed from those in Britain. There were different customs and constitutional conventions; and the populations of the Scandinavian countries were much smaller and the social and economic structure generally less complex. However, the Labour Opposition pledged itself to establish a Parliamentary Commissioner "with the right to investigate and expose any misuse of government power as it affects the citizen".[65]

Under the terms of the Labour Government's White Paper the Parliamentary Commissioner was to have the power to compel the production of documents, including departmental minutes. But documents relating to the work of the Cabinet or its committees were excluded. He would not normally pursue matters within the competence of the courts or administrative tribunals.[66] The Commissioner would not investigate complaints involving the commercial relationships of departments with customers of suppliers. Nor would he be concerned with the armed forces, the police, local government, nationalized industries, hospitals, or personnel problems within departments. Many of these areas of administration were precisely those where critics thought a Commissioner was most needed.

Furthermore, the Commissioner was not to comment on policy. He was not to investigate the exercise of discretionary powers, unless it appeared that a decision had been affected by a fault in administration. What constituted a fault in administration was not clear. Finally, in order not to deprive backbenchers

[65] *Labour Party Election Manifesto, 1964*. For pros and cons generally, see T. E. Utley, *Occasion for Ombudsman*, Christopher Johnson, 1961; W. A. Robson, *The Governors and the Governed*, Allen & Unwin, 1964; D. C. Rowat (ed.), *The Ombudsman*, Allen & Unwin, 1965; J. D. B. Mitchell, The ombudsman fallacy, *Public Law*, Spring 1962; B. Chapman, The ombudsman, *Public Administration*, Winter 1960; S. A. de Smith, Anglo-Saxon ombudsman, *Political Quarterly*, Jan.–March 1962.

[66] White Paper, *The Parliamentary Commissioner for Administration*, Cmd. 2767, HMSO, 1965. On Administrative Tribunals see J. A. G. Griffith and H. Street, *Principles of Administrative Law*, Pitman, 3rd edn., 1963, pp. 156–207. Also *Report of the Committee on Administrative Tribunals and Inquiries*, Cmd. 218, HMSO, 1957, and published evidence and memoranda submitted to the committee.

of their traditional function of investigating complaints, the Commissioner was only to act on the instance of an MP. The White Paper was not one to strike terror into the hearts of ministers or the higher civil service; this was hardly surprising, since it had been drafted in the departments.

When the Bill to create the office of Parliamentary Commissioner was introduced in the Commons it empowered ministers to forbid the disclosure of documents, or other information, when they considered security or the public interest would be prejudiced. The public interest being so vague a concept, this virtually enabled ministers to suppress the publication of evidence which supported a critical finding by the Commissioner. When the Bill received its second reading the Leader of the House admitted that the most valid criticism was that it was too timid. But he thought it better for a reformer to be chastised as a laggard than branded as an irresponsible revolutionary.

The Bill was given a mixed reception. Sir Hugh Lucas-Tooth estimated that he received about 500 complaints a year from his constituents. If this were typical it meant about 300,000 complaints to all Members. Did the Government expect the Commissioner to investigate 10 or 10,000 cases a year? Sir John Hobson thought the real crux was whether the Parliamentary Commissioner would have the authority or power to criticize ministers. Mr. A. J. Irvine suggested that the powers of investigation given the Commissioner might have been conferred on a senior MP, preferably a member of the Opposition. During the course of the debate Mr. Quintin Hogg pressed for a Commons Committee to supervise the work of the Commissioner; this was accepted by the Government.[67] The committee considers points of principle raised by the Commissioner's investigations and examines complaints from MPs who think he has failed to deal adequately with cases brought to his notice.

By the end of March 1967 the newly appointed Commissioner, Sir Edmund Compton, nominated by the Prime Minister even

[67] Parliamentary Report, *The Times*, 19 Oct. 1966.

before legislation setting up the office had gone through Parliament, was writing to MPs explaining how he would tackle complaints. He expected to handle between 6000 and 7000 cases a year. He was equipped with a staff of forty-five, drawn from the executive class of the civil service. The number could be increased to sixty-three if need be.

The Parliamentary Commissioner has no power to order a remedy for maladministration or error. If persuasion fails he must rely on MPs to press for action. In the Sachsenhausen case, concerning the denial of compensation to victims of Nazi persecution, they did so. The then Foreign Secretary argued in the Commons that attacking civil servants, rather than ministers, in Parliament amounted to a major constitutional change. But he got little support for his old-fashioned interpretation of total ministerial responsibility extending to culpability. In the majority of cases, especially those involving social service benefits, pensions and tax relief, persuasion by the Commissioner is likely to produce a remedy.[68]

Even so, it can be persuasively argued that maladministration and errors are best dealt with by administrative courts, which can build up a body of case law based on consistent principles. The model is the French *Conseil d'État*. The Council on Tribunals, which could have formed the nucleus of a system of administrative courts, is tending to be overshadowed by the activities of the Parliamentary Commissioner. Its terms of reference could have been widened. The net result is that the country now has two

[68] See *3rd Report of Parliamentary Commissioner*, HC 54, 1967–8, on Sachsenhausen. His *1st Report*, HC 6, 1967–8, shows that his staff at the end of Oct. 1967 totalled 59. Also see *4th Report*, HC 134, 1967–8, which shows that the Commissioner investigated 188 complaints between 1 April and 31 Dec. 1967. In 19 cases he found some element of maladministration but he had no criticism to make of action taken to remedy injustice caused. Of the 19 cases, 6 concerned the Inland Revenue, 5 the Ministry of Social Security, 3 the Ministry of Labour, and 2 the Ministry of Housing and Local Government. The Foreign Office, Ministry of Transport, and the Customs and Excise were involved in one case each. Altogether 1069 complaints were received from MPs, and 849 were completed by 31 Dec. Of these completed cases, 561 were held to be outside his jurisdiction and 100 were discontinued after partial investigation.

relatively weak institutions for dealing with maladministration instead of one reasonably strong one.[69]

The Commons, if it is to command widespread interest, should not be overoccupied with matters of administration. Rather should it be concerned with major issues of politics; these are inevitably fought out on party lines. For this reason, those who are critical of oligarchical tendencies in British parties are more on the right lines than those who would attempt to secure more effective accountability by tinkering with the machinery of the Commons. The force which moves the machinery is party. But it may be the oligarchical tendencies of British parties that drive some backbench MPs to find compensation in setting up shop as administrative experts or investigators of maladministration. To understand the working of the Commons one must understand parties.[70]

Accountability and the Party System

There are two related problems involved when party leaders form a government. To whom are they answerable for the policies they pursue as government ministers, and what is their relationship with members of their own party, both inside and outside Parliament?

It has been held that party leaders, when in office, are accountable not to party members but to the electors. On this view

[69] On the Conseil d'État see G. Langrod, *Some Current Problems of Administration in France Today*, pp. 41–57; and C. Freedeman, *The Conseil d'État in Modern France*, Columbia, 1961. Also see M. H. Smith, Thoughts on a British conseil d'État, *Public Administration*, Spring 1967; and J. D. B. Mitchell, Parliamentary commissioner is the wrong answer, *The Times*, 16 March 1967. For the Council on Tribunals see the Annual Reports of the Council and J. A. Griffith, The council and the chalkpit, *Public Administration*, Winter 1961. The origins of the Council and the Commissioner are connected with the celebrated Crichel Down case. On this see W. A. Robson, Some lessons of Crichel Down, *The Listener*, 27 Jan. 1955; and *Report of the Public Enquiry into the Crichel Down Case*, Cmd. 9176, HMSO, 1954.

[70] Lack of space precludes discussion of further possible reforms. See Appendix (4).

if the mass of the governing party attempted to determine policy it would cut across the chain of responsibility leading from Cabinet, to Parliament, to electorate. It follows that there is a possibility of conflict between parliamentary democracy and inner-party democracy.[71]

But the answerability of ministers to the electorate is limited. True, the electors can ultimately change the party position in the Commons, and so bring about a change of government. But the choice open to them is very restricted. The major parties have too firm a grip on the system for smaller parties to make much headway. Furthermore, the electorate is generally atomized and unlead. There are numerous organized interests in society, some of which are in a position to influence ministers, sometimes through their connections with the political parties. But they are not to be equated with the electorate. The extent of their influence is still largely unknown in spite of interesting studies of some of them. Again, the electorate is often uninformed or, worse, misinformed on political matters. This is partly owing to the indifference of voters and partly because undistorted information is difficult to obtain. On the whole the politically interested section of the electorate is found in the parties.

Unlike the mass of the electorate, parties consist of people who are organized, and relatively well informed on political matters. Because they endeavour to have a wide appeal, in the British system, parties are less restricted in the ends they pursue than are pressure groups. And it is through party organization that political leaders both attain office and control the legislature. The distribution of power and influence in parties is therefore crucial to British representative government. For if ministers are answerable to anyone, it is to their own followers in the Commons, on whom the life of the government depends, at least in the day-to-day business of government between elections. And MPs in

[71] R. T. McKenzie, *British Political Parties*, Heinemann, 2nd edn., 1963, pp. 644–5. Also see R. Miliband, Party democracy and parliamentary government, *Political Studies*, June 1958; and J. Rasmussen, Problems of democratic development in Britain: an American View, *Political Quarterly*, Oct.–Dec. 1964.

turn have a loyalty to other party members, outside the Commons, as well as to the parliamentary leaders.

The power of the leader of a British party, when he is also Prime Minister, is very great. He disposes of considerable patronage when filling Cabinet posts, though he has not got a completely free hand in this respect. Altogether there are something like a hundred ministerial jobs to be allocated amongst members of the Parliamentary Party, most of whom are eager for office.

The Prime Minister may threaten to dissolve Parliament in order to bring recalcitrant followers to heel. Such a threat is unlikely because no party leader wants an election when his party is too openly divided. But the right to decide the appropriate moment for an election, within the statutory limit of five years, does enhance the power of the Prime Minister.

Moreover, a party's electoral prospects are bound up with the mysterious business of party images. And the image of a party is at least partly determined by the personality of its Parliamentary leader. Leaders cannot be attacked or denigrated by members of their own party without the whole party suffering.

Finally, although the selection of candidates rests mainly with local parties and associations, the Parliamentary leader can bring pressure and influence to bear. Candidates need the endorsement of central offices or headquarters which are largely under the control of the parliamentary leaders, especially in the case of the Conservative Party.

A Labour MP who is rebellious might eventually be suspended or expelled from the PLP on the initiative of the leader and chief whip; but the final decision on punishment rests with a liaison committee, which links the front and back benches. The Conservative Party in Parliament is more tolerant. The leadership last expelled a rebel, Captain Cunningham-Reid, in 1942, but he was also at odds with his local association, which had requested his resignation. The Conservative rule is to leave rebels to be dealt with by their local constituency association. These are often dominated by people well to the right of the parliamentary leadership.

Nevertheless, it does not pay the leaders of parties to frequently discipline or ignore backbenchers since they are representative of interests and opinion in the constituencies. Moreover, there are independent journals which will support dissident backbenchers. If leaders appear to emerge victorious in their skirmishes with rebels this is often because they have taken careful soundings of opinion in the Parliamentary Party and made concessions where necessary. Before battle, with the assistance of the whips, they prepare their ground and strategy.

Also offsetting and modifying oligarchical tendencies is the institutionalization of the role of party leader in Britain. That is to say, there is a pattern of behaviour, derived from tradition and practice, which leaders are expected to observe. And expected behaviour includes consultation with followers and some give and take. In addition there are always rivals waiting to step into the leader's shoes. The history of British parties includes many instances of leaders who have been openly dropped or discreetly removed. There are also many examples of revolts by back-bench MPs.[72]

It is over-concentration on formal organization, rather than the actual process of decision-making in parties, which makes the "iron law of oligarchy" such an apparently self-evident affair. At the very least one can say that there are numerous elites and oligarchies involved in parties as large and complex as those in Britain; and these various groupings are not always agreed and united.[73]

But, given these qualifications, there remain distinct oligarchical

[72] See, *passim*, McKenzie, *op. cit.*, and S. H. Beer, *Modern British Politics*, Faber, 1965. N. Nicolson, *People and Parliament*, Weidenfeld & Nicolson, is an informative account by a Conservative Suez rebel.

[73] See S. C. Ghosh, Decision-making and power in the Conservative Party, *Political Studies*, 1965, pp. 198–212. The classic exposition of the law of oligarchy is R. Michel's, *Political Parties*. For comment see essay by S. Neumann in *Modern Political Parties*, Chicago, 1956; also essay by H. Daalder, in *Political Parties and Political Development*, La Palombra and Weiner (eds.), Princeton, 1966.

and autocratic features. Evidence of *some* dispersion of power and influence does not necessarily mean that they are distributed in the best possible way. It is certainly unfortunate that British MPs should have to hazard their seats and careers when they oppose their leaders on matters about which they feel strongly. On the floor of the Commons they will seldom carry their opposition beyond verbal dissent and occasional abstention in the lobbies. But the abstention of a few rebels is not a powerful weapon. Much depends on the size of the Government's majority. And a combination of fierce verbal attacks and weak action tends to bring the House into disrepute as an instrument of accountability.

It is possible to think of changes which might reduce the power of party leaders. For example, there could be experiments with primary elections, whereby registered party voters could influence the selection of the parliamentary leader. A statutory limit might be set to the length of time any one man could serve as Prime Minister. His power to decide when to hold an election might be curbed, by ensuring that the life of Parliament must last the statutory limit. But American experience shows that all these arrangements have disadvantages. Electoral reforms, such as the use of the alternative vote, might encourage the smaller parties.[74]

In any case, these suggestions are utopian so long as the present system works to the advantage of the leaders of the two major political parties; it is they who primarily initiate change. It is some consolation to know that the influence of backbenchers is somewhat greater than is popularly supposed. And if the overall impact of the Commons on policy is less marked than in certain past periods, it remains true that ministerial accountability to Parliament affects the process of public administration and the organization of departments.

[74] See E. Lakeman and J. D. Lambert, *Voting in Democracies*, Faber, 1955, and M. Duverger, *Political Parties*, Methuen, 1959, book 1, ch. 3, book 2, ch. 1. On United States primaries see A. Leiserson, *Parties and Politics*, Knopf, 1958, pp. 242–54.

Accountability and Government Departments

Accountability to Parliament affects departments in various ways. It has been said that since ministers may be asked questions in the Commons about the work of their departments, there is a reluctance to delegate; any departmental decision may have political repercussions or put the minister in an embarrassing position. As a result, it is claimed, there is a tendency towards over-centralization. Civil servants, mindful of their duty to keep their minister out of trouble, allegedly clear even relatively trivial matters with their immediate seniors, who in turn pass them up the hierarchy of the department. Those at the top are overburdened with matters of detail and unable to concentrate on policy and forward planning.

In addition, it is asserted, records are kept in meticulous detail and stored for an inordinate length of time in case some matter should be raised in Parliament. Furthermore, the preparation of answers to parliamentary questions may entail consultation with other departments, communication with representatives or bases overseas, or call for specialist advice at short notice. Priority may have to be given to preparing an answer to a question asked out of mere curiosity or for party political advantage. The questioner's motive may be to obtain a little personal publicity. In the meantime more urgent matters have to be neglected. There may well remain some truth in Beatrice Webb's observation that the civil servant's greatest contempt is reserved for parliamentary institutions.[75]

Accountability to Parliament nevertheless offers advantages to departments. Attention is called to wrong decisions and failings which might otherwise go undiscovered. It also provides some guide to opinion about a department's work and an opportunity to deal with criticisms and misunderstanding. An absence of questions may indicate that a department is functioning satisfactorily; equally, of course, it may suggest that the department is doing little that is exciting or interesting. A series of questions, or some other

[75] B. Webb, *Diaries 1912–24*, M. Cole (ed.), London, 1952.

manifestation of disquiet in Parliament, may bring about the rethinking of policy or some change in administrative procedure. And departmentally inspired questions are a simple and relatively effective way of informing and educating the public.[76]

The charge that accountability to Parliament is a prime cause of overcentralization is difficult to substantiate. Centralization is not necessarily to be condemned and it is difficult to decide when a department is *overcentralized.* There are rough and ready guides, such as the time taken to arrive at decisions of a given type, but this often involves comparisons between departments or countries which are not always valid. Even comparisons within one department at different periods of time can be misleading. The functions of a department may have increased in number or complexity, or its relations with other departments have become more complicated. It is possible that overcentralization adversely affects the morale of those who are low down in the hierarchy or who are geographically remote from the central decision-taking point. But morale has been little studied in connection with centralization so far as the civil service is concerned.

Even if one accepts the unproven statement that centralization is on balance a bad thing, any tendencies in that direction cannot be attributed solely or mainly to accountability to Parliament. For, although departments are subject to the same degree of accountability, they vary in the extent to which they are centralized. The functions and size of a department are as important as accountability. Thus the Treasury, small in numbers, and concerned with the management of the national currency and the running of the civil service, has no regional organization, and decision taking appears to be concentrated in a few hands. The much larger Ministry of Social Security, however, charged with assessing needs and paying benefits, has many local offices headed by officials who exercise some discretionary powers.[77]

[76] D. N. Chester and N. Bowring, *Questions in Parliament*, Oxford, 1962, pp. 251–68. Also see evidence of effect of accountability on Post Office in *1st Report Select Committee on Nationalized Industries, 1966–67*, HC 340–1, vol. 2, paras. 26–33.

[77] See Chapters 4 and 6.

It is doubtful whether it is wise to consider departments in isolation when discussing matters affecting centralization. It is one thing to suggest that the Treasury is centralized. It is quite another to conclude from this that responsibility for economic policy is centralized. In fact, there are several departments and numerous semi-official bodies involved.

It is clear, however, that the dominant position of the Treasury in Whitehall is connected with the annual submission of Estimates to Parliament. These must have the prior approval of the Treasury. It therefore has a legitimate interest in the work of all other departments. This interest takes in all policy matters. And "policy" is interpreted very broadly. When Treasury officials were asked by the Estimates Committee whether a decision by the Admiralty to fire intermediate range ballistic missiles from surface vessels, as opposed to submarines, was considered policy, or merely the implementation of policy, they replied it was a policy matter because expenditure was affected.[78]

This does not mean that all other departments are wholly subordinate to the Treasury. The scale of government expenditure obliges the Treasury to grant them considerable freedom to draw up their own Estimates. But new projects which entail expenditure in excess of specified sums require the sanction of the Treasury. Moreover, the Treasury has an interest in expenditure previously authorized, in financial matters delegated to departments and in a department's methods of financial control. It plays the major role in deciding total annual expenditure and attempts to secure a reasonable balance between services.

Government accountability to the Commons for financial matters may lead to the abolition of a department and a reallocation of its functions. Departments may be merged or drastically reorganized. We saw earlier that the Estimates Committee was at least partially responsible for the merger of the Colonial Office and the Commonwealth Office. The Treasury itself was reorganized at the end of a long process which started with the same committee. The Estimates Committee was instrumental in

[78] See *6th Report of the Estimates Committee*, *1957–8*, HC 254–1.

the setting up of the Plowden Committee on the Control of Public Expenditure.

But the reorganization of the Treasury was also an expression of dissatisfaction with the machinery for handling economic policy generally. This aspect of public administration merits close examination because the success of modern governments is largely judged in terms of economic performance.

CHAPTER 4

THE GOVERNMENT AND ECONOMIC AFFAIRS

Governments and the Economy

There are numerous reasons why governments, irrespective of their party political complexion, are certain to be deeply involved in economic affairs. *Laissez-faire* is a myth, though, like other myths, it is not without importance.

In the first place, the Government is ultimately responsible for the management of the national currency. Banks and other private institutions play an important part in the system but no government can abdicate final responsibility for monetary matters.

Secondly, economic affairs are intimately connected with international relations, especially for Britain. The State, as the most inclusive association, represents the nation in its dealings with other nations. The Government is therefore responsible for arrangements which influence international trade, and these profoundly affect domestic economic activity. The development of communications and the extension of world trade enhance the role of government in economic affairs. Regional economic associations, such as the European Free Trade Area and the European Economic Community, are clearly the creations of governments.

Strategic and political considerations affect the direction of overseas trade and in part determine the source of imported goods and materials. Profitable markets may be cut off for ideological reasons. Governments may encourage or discourage investment in different parts of the world. The State's responsibility for defence makes demands on capital and labour which could be put to alternative uses. And the defence burden varies according to the Government's view of the nation's proper role in world affairs. It is also affected by the general international situation. The stationing of troops overseas and the purchase of equipment and weapons from abroad affect the balance of payments. In short, political and economic considerations are inextricably mixed.

Governments decide the level of tariffs on imported goods, they negotiate agreements relating to the movement of aircraft and shipping, and they regulate the employment of foreign labour.

A third reason why governments are deeply involved in economic affairs derives from their traditional function of enforcing the law. There is a vast body of law relating to such matters as taxation, company organization, and the employment of labour. Economic and political developments are continually extending the range of such laws. The growth of monopolistic enterprises and the virtual abandonment of the belief that consumers are automatically protected by market forces lead to further regulation and control by governments.

Fourthly, in a country as highly industrialized and densely populated as Britain, physical planning is necessary for both economic and social reasons. An adequate system of transport on a national scale is required. Physical controls enable governments to influence the location of industry and to deal with the problem of localized unemployment. Such controls greatly affect the value of land and property.

A stock of houses is needed if the working population is to be mobile in an economy whose structure is always subject to change. And because the distribution of wealth and income is such that large sections of the population cannot afford to buy their own homes, the central government and local authorities must provide rented and subsidized accommodation.

Fifthly, economic prosperity depends on the existence of an educated and skilled labour force. Since the last quarter of the nineteenth century in Britain the State has been responsible for the provision of education for the vast majority of the people.

Furthermore, the State provides many facilities for vocational, scientific, and technical training.

Finally, political pressures compel the State to intervene in economic matters. The vast majority of voters, for example, are workers interested in full employment. In 1944 the then Coalition Government pledged itself to maintain full employment; Keynesian economic theory has provided the means by showing how governments can regulate total demand. No government would now willingly enter an election campaign at a time when unemployment was considered high in contemporary terms, though it may deliberately put people out of work at some point in between elections.

Clearly the ability to regulate total demand places immense power in the hands of the Government. Variations in total demand affect all sectors of the economy and have repercussions on business confidence and capital investment, on which future productivity depends. Rightly or wrongly, governments are now held to be primarily responsible for general economic prosperity. If prices rise or economic growth, however defined, is thought to be unsatisfactory, it is the Government which is blamed. There is a widespread belief that the Government is omnipotent in economic matters.

Political parties reinforce this belief by claiming that they will run the economy more efficiently than their competitors once they become the governing party. It is true that right-wing parties usually claim they will do so by stimulating private enterprise. But this will not absolve them from blame if things go wrong. Even the freest free enterprise economy, these days, is subject to government control and influence.[1]

Economic pressure groups continually seek government aid and assistance. They often complain of unfair practices by overseas competitors. They may hope to obtain capital from some government-backed financial institution on favourable terms.

[1] See F. Oules, *Economic Planning and Democracy*, Penguin, 1966, especially section on Western Germany, pp. 317–36. On the USA see M. Dimock, *Business and Government*, Holt, Rinehart & Winston, 4th edn., 1961.

Such pressure groups have their connections in the parties and in Parliament and they try to influence policy and legislation to their particular advantage.[2]

In Britain the State is a major purchaser of goods and services. It employs far more people than even the largest private concern. It operates vast industrial and commercial enterprises, using enormous quantities of capital. It controls the sources of power on which industry in general depends and which vitally affect costs of production. It encourages and finances research and development. If it so wishes, it can resort to physical controls.

Government intervention in economic matters is a foregone conclusion. But governments differ on what is the proper degree of intervention and what methods to use. If we take the period since 1945 it is possible to distinguish various phases in each of which some particular view on the proper role of government in economic affairs has prevailed. In the period 1945–51 there was a predilection for planning of a certain type. For the greater part of the period 1951–61 the tendency was to restrict government intervention to monetary and fiscal measures, designed to remedy an adverse balance of payments. The move away from planning was partly the consequence of a change from a Labour to a Conservative administration, but the shift was evident before the Conservatives took over. By 1961, with the Conservatives still in power, another reaction had set in and tentative experiments with a different type of planning began. When Labour was returned to office in 1964 it was publicly committed to pursue a more vigorous policy of planning. Each of these periods will now be separately discussed.

[2] See S. E. Finer, *Anonymous Empire*, Pall Mall, revised edn., 1966. Also J. D. Stewart, *British Pressure Groups; Their Role in Relation to the House of Commons*, Oxford, 1958; H. H. Wilson, *Pressure Group: the Campaign for Commercial Television*, Secker & Warburg, 1961; P. Self and H. Storing, *The State and the Farmer*, Allen & Unwin, 1962, and *Political Quarterly*, Jan.–Mar. 1958, Special Number on Pressure Groups.

Economic Planning, 1945–51

The word "planning" is used in various senses and it is easy to shift from one meaning of the word to another without really being aware of it. It may be so broadly defined that virtually any period can be described as one of planning. Henri Fayol equated planning with prevision. By this he meant looking ahead so as to have a clear idea of what is to be done.[3] So defined, planning is a characteristic common to prudent housewives and large-scale organizations. Again, planning may be thought of as long-term forecasting, and the "long term" may be as short as five years.[4]

It would be tedious, though not unrewarding, to compare the various definitions of planning put forward by such pioneers of administrative theory as Gulick and Urwick oı Chester Barnard.[5] Since we are concerned with economic planning by a central government it is convenient to accept the view of Lord Franks, advanced during the period under discussion. Central planning and control, in his opinion, meant positive intervention by governments in the management and direction of industry and trade, in accordance with general policy objectives.[6]

If removing the allocation of resources from market forces entails planning, in the sense defined, then it was more or less inevitable in the period 1945–51. This is so even though a different party might have been in power. British planning at this time had its roots in shortages of foreign currency, food and raw materials. There had to be conscious thought on the part of politicians and

[3] M. Dimock, G. O. Dimock, and L. W. Koenig, *Public Administration*, Rinehart, revised edn., 1958. In Fayol's view there are four other steps in administration which follow planning. These are organization, command, coordination, and control.

[4] See J. Mitchell, *Groundwork to Economic Planning*, Secker & Warburg, 1966, pp. 123–4.

[5] See L. Gulick and L. Urwick, *Papers on the Science of Administration*, New York, 3rd edn., 1954; and C. Barnard, *The Functions of the Executive*, Havard, 1938. On the development of administrative thought see B. M. Gross, *The Managing of Organisations*, Collier–Macmillan, 1964, vol. 1, part 2.

[6] Lord Franks, then Sir Oliver Franks, *Central Planning and Control in War and Peace*, London School of Economics and Political Science, 1947, p. 7.

officials about resource allocation, and hence a view on social and economic priorities and the national interest. Wartime rationing had made government intervention seem more natural and acceptable. The Conservative Opposition, however, attacked planning as an unnecessary restraint on liberty and enterprise, brought about by doctrinaire socialism and bureaucrats greedy for power.[7]

But official pronouncements showed little confidence in the ability of the Government to control the economy and little enthusiasm for making the attempt. In 1948 a White Paper stressed the difficulties of reconciling "coercive" planning with democracy. The powers of the Government were, and ought to be, limited. Only planning based on the voluntary co-operation of private associations was compatible with democracy. Such a view would now be identified with what is termed "persuasive" planning. In addition it was held that British planners faced special difficulties. A country so dependent on foreign trade was largely at the mercy of events overseas which she could not control. It was not possible to formulate plans which would bind the nation to a predetermined course of action even for a period as short as eighteen months.[8]

A description of the administrative arrangements designed to serve this type of planning must begin with the Cabinet and certain of its committees. In the immediate post-war years the Lord President's Committee was responsible for economic planning. By 1947, however, an Economic Policy Committee, chaired by the Prime Minister, was dealing with economic policy and supervising economic planning. In addition there was a Production Committee presided over by Sir Stafford Cripps, who for a time bore the title of Minister for Economic Affairs. Sir Stafford shortly became Chancellor of the Exchequer, following the resignation of Hugh Dalton over a budget leak, and the Ministry of Economic Affairs was absorbed by the Treasury.

[7] On this period generally see B. W. Lewis, *British Planning and Nationalization*, Allen & Unwin, 1952.
[8] White Paper on European Cooperation, Cmd. 7572, HMSO, 1948.

The Cabinet and its committees were served by two sections of the Cabinet Office—the Economic Section and the Central Statistical Office.

The Economic Section, established in 1941 to meet wartime needs, was absorbed by the Treasury in 1953. For about twelve years, however, it was to some extent independent of the Treasury. Consisting of half a dozen economists, recruited on a temporary basis, and a small number of career civil servants, seconded from departments, its functions were to make general studies of the economic situation and to attempt to forecast trends. But it is doubtful if it played more than a minor role in the formulation of policy. Its personnel were continually changing, they were relatively junior, their career prospects lay elsewhere, they were too few to constitute an effective planning staff, and they were not really in a position to play off the Cabinet Office against the Treasury.

In 1947 a Chief Planning Officer was appointed and an Economic Planning Staff set up. Both had purely advisory functions. The Cabinet and its committees, and ministers and their departments, were responsible for final decisions and their implementation.[9]

The Chief Planning Officer, Sir Edwin Plowden, now Lord Plowden, has been described by one writer as an able and public-spirited businessman. Another states he has a dislike of and disbelief in planning.[10] Lord Plowden had had no formal training as an economist but he had been Chief Executive in the Ministry of Aircraft Production during the war and was familiar with Whitehall procedure and practice. Since he had direct access to a powerful minister, the Chancellor of the Exchequer, he was at least potentially influential.

The Economic Planning Staff were initially part of the Lord President's Office but they moved rapidly through the short-lived Ministry of Economic Affairs and into the Treasury with Sir Stafford Cripps.

[9] Central Office of Information, *Post-war Britain, 1948–49*, HMSO, p. 54.

[10] Morrison, *op. cit.*, p. 308; and T. Balogh, *Planning for Progress*, Fabian Society, 1963, p. 5, fn. 3.

Lord Morrison described the Planning Staff as a mixture of businessmen, statisticians and economists, but the majority were administrative class officials who remained in close contact with the departments from which they were seconded.[11] The prime task of the Economic Planning Staff was to draw up a long-term plan for the use of the nation's economic resources. But it was soon acting as an agent of the Treasury, guiding and reconciling departmental programmes.

The Government had announced a long-term economic programme covering the years 1948–52. The main object of the programme was to remedy Britain's adverse balance of payments situation and in particular to overcome a shortage of dollars by stimulating exports to the USA. The programme, after some mention in the annual *Economic Survey* for 1949, received little publicity. This is not to say that the policies implicit in the programme were not put into effect. On the contrary, they were acted upon with some success. But the long-term programme of that time scarcely merited the description of a national economic plan.[12]

The Economic Planning Staff had a separate life of about five and a half years in the Treasury. It was then merged with another section to form the Home and Overseas Planning Staff. This section of the Treasury was mainly concerned with departmental co-ordination and served two interdepartmental committees.

Also in 1947, a year of some significance for economic administration, an Economic Planning Board was set up. This was officially recognized as the chief consultative body on which private interests were represented. The ubiquitous Lord Plowden was chairman. Other members included representatives of the Federation of British Industries and the Trades Union Congress. On the official side the permanent secretaries of the Board of Trade, Ministry of Labour, and Ministry of Supply were members, as was the Director of the Economic Section of the Treasury. The Economic Planning Staff was also represented.

[11] See J. W. Grove, *Government and Industry*, Longmans, 1962, p. 437.
[12] See J. Mitchell, *op. cit.*, ch. 4.

The Planning Board, which survived until 1962, had a purely advisory role. It was not a planning body in the sense of having responsibility for drawing up national plans and seeing to their implementation. Its role was officially described as one of advising the Government on the best use of economic resources. The Planning Board had no staff; it has been described as a "useless" body because it was not in a position to commission independent surveys and investigations.[13] But the members of the Board presumably found it a convenient means of influencing policy and official thinking.

In addition to the Economic Planning Board, the Government was advised by the National Production Advisory Council on Industry. This had been in existence since 1941. The Council consisted of representatives of employers, trade unions, nationalized industries, and the chairmen of eleven separate Regional Boards for Industry. There were no civil service members. The members of the regional boards were appointed by the Chancellor of the Exchequer after the usual consultation with recognized bodies.

The Treasury had little direct contact with industry. But other economic departments maintained a fairly close relationship with certain industries because they operated a system of allocating raw materials. Although there was a gradual running down of the system, as post-war shortages eased, departments continued to "sponsor" certain industries. An industry or sector of the economy was assigned to a particular department which considered its claims and problems and represented them in official discussions. Thus the Board of Trade was responsible for consumer goods industries, the Ministry of Supply for industries making capital equipment, and the Ministry of Transport for railways, roads, and shipping.[14]

The main object was to ration scarce raw materials, but

[13] P. D. Henderson, *Economic Growth in Britain*, Weidenfeld & Nicolson, 1966, p. 217.

[14] See *Political and Economic Planning, Government and Industry*, PEP, 1952, chs. 5 and 6.

industries were open to coercion by the threat of cutting off their supplies. It was also necessary to obtain licences to export certain goods and materials. And licences were needed for permission to build. There were further controls over the raising of capital. But many of these arrangements were operated in partnership with trade associations and similar bodies. It was by no means certain that the Government was the senior partner.

Ministers and civil servants, as well as the representatives of industry, were anxious to end shortages and to abandon controls. By 1951 these aims were clearly accepted in principle by the Government. The return of the Conservative Party to office, in 1951, ensured the continuance of a trend already evident.

It is now possible to comment generally on the period 1945–51. In the first place, the impact of the war was still very evident. This compelled the Government to intervene in the running of the economy to an extent that would have been less acceptable to industry in "normal" times. Secondly, in spite of government intervention, there was a marked reluctance in official circles to accept positive State direction as compatible with democracy. Weak words like "persuasion" and "advice" abound in official pronouncements and documents. Little was heard of "direction" and "control", words which would have been unpalatable to interested parties.

Thirdly, there was a marked tendency to create bodies and offices with important-sounding titles but little in the way of powers. And their functions often overlapped. The Economic Section "advised" the Cabinet. The Economic Planning Staff tried to "harmonize" and "co-ordinate" the policies and programmes of the separate departments. A Chief Planning Officer was appointed, but with advisory functions only.

Fourthly, in this period certain industries and services were taken into public ownership, including coal, gas, electricity, and the railways. This was less politically controversial than is sometimes supposed. There is little reason to believe that the Conservative Party in Parliament was opposed to the nationalization of such declining industries as coal. And it has not proposed the denationalization of such "natural" monopolies as gas and electricity. But it has consistently opposed the public ownership of steel and road haulage services, where there are profits to be made.

But clearly nationalization gave the Government control over the prices and capital investment programmes of large-scale basic industries. Such control has repercussions on the private sector because it affects the capital market and costs of production.

Fifthly, businessmen were drawn into Government, or the process of government, through numerous advisory committees, trade associations, and pressure groups. Before the war there had been disquiet about the business-in-government aspects of Conservative administrations. The Public Accounts Committee was especially critical of what it called the "dual allegiance" aspects of the system. In 1941 *The Economist* was complaining that officials were reluctant to control industry; they preferred to abdicate in favour of private monopolists.[15] In the post-war period this attitude was still in evidence and the harmony of private and public interests was largely taken for granted.

There was a somewhat touching faith in the impartiality of businessmen and trade union leaders in their role as government counsellors. The association of interested parties with the process of planning is not the most satisfactory protection against possible abuse of power by a strong central government. The best safeguard may be a disinterested and representative Parliament, as Mannheim contends. But this leaves open the thorny question of what is meant by "representative" in this context.[16]

Lord Morrison was singularly prescient when he asserted, in the thirties, that attempts to control, influence, or regulate private industry would invite numerous pressures on departments and entail an extension of bureaucracy in the sense of petty inter-

[15] See A. Rogow, *Labour Government and British Industry*, Blackwell, 1955, p. 60.

[16] K. Mannheim, *Freedom, Power and Democratic Planning*, Routledge, 1951, p. 112.

ference, form filling and inspection.[17] There is no doubt that ministers and officials were kept very busy in the period 1945–51 and were probably overworked.

Sixthly, partly because they were overworked, ministers and officials showed little enthusiasm for physical controls, though these were an essential part of governmental power. For example, the Government could pressurize the car industry because of its control over the allocation of sheet metal.[18]

Seventhly, there was some justification for doubts about the possibility of long-term planning in Britain because of the influence of events overseas which she could not control. Nevertheless, external influences can be allowed for in the formulation of plans. The long-term programme of 1948–52 was bound up with the policy of the USA and dollar aid to Europe. British planning arrangements were part of the machinery supporting the efforts of the European planners of the Organization for European Economic Co-operation.[19]

Finally, the period is marked by the dominance of the Treasury in economic matters, subject only to ultimate Cabinet control. The Treasury absorbed the Economic Section of the Cabinet by 1953, but such independent influence as the latter had was declining long before that year. The Treasury acquired the Economic Planning Staff. The influence of the chief planning officer depended on the Chancellor of the Exchequer. With the run down of physical controls other departments lost much of their influence and power. Economic policy was dominated by the persistence of an adverse balance of payments, and the desire to avoid a repetition of the devaluation of the pound which had occurred in 1949. Such matters were primarily the concern of the Treasury.

[17] H. Morrison, *Socialisation and Transport*, Constable, 1933. At the time Lord Morrison favoured outright public ownership, at least in the case of transport.

[18] See A. Shonfield, *British Economic Policy Since the War*, Penguin, 1958, p. 168.

[19] J. Mitchell, *op. cit.*, p. 77.

Economic Affairs, 1951–61

It is reported that Sir Winston Churchill wished to tame the Treasury when the Conservatives came to power.[20] If so, he did not succeed. With the abandonment of physical controls it was inevitable that greater use would be made of monetary weapons, such as the manipulation of bank rate, which had been put in cold storage by Labour chancellors. However, the distinction between physical and monetary controls is not as sharp as one might suppose. Restricting and rationing credit may be thought of as a less detailed form of physical control, since those who are denied funds cannot obtain the materials and supplies which they require.

By restricting credit, in response to government pressure, the banks and other monetary institutions are acting as agents of the Treasury. But they are unlikely to be willing agents because a restriction of credit will adversely affect their profits. And it is by no means certain that the men who allocate credit will be as conscious of national needs and priorities as the civil servants who operate physical controls.

The reluctance to use other forms of control compelled governments in the fifties to resort to what has been described as "backstairs intervention"—for example, dropping hints to banks that the Government would prefer not to see money advanced to finance the import of certain goods.[21] But financial institutions are not the only source of credit. Firms, including overseas firms, may extend credit to customers. Trade credit can offset a financial squeeze and is much more difficult to control, assuming it can be controlled at all.[22]

Any attempt to impose a general squeeze on credit is unsatisfactory for a variety of reasons. Socially desirable and economic-

[20] See H. Daalder, *Cabinet Reform in Britain 1914–63*, pp. 224–6. Also S. Brittan, *The Treasury Under the Tories*, Penguin, 1964, pp. 164–6.

[21] See G. N. Worswick and P. H. Ady, *The British Economy, 1950–1959*, Oxford, 1962, pp. 72–73 and 89.

[22] See the somewhat indefinite comments in the *Report of the Committee on the Working of the Monetary System*, Cmd. 827, 1959, paras. 297–320.

ally profitable ventures are affected adversely. And large firms or organizations, which can finance developments out of their own resources, have a distinct advantage over small but enterprising concerns. There is less risk involved in lending to large or monopolistic firms and they can afford to pay higher rates of interest.

In the fifties, and in later periods, the overriding objectives of the Treasury were to maintain the exchange value of the pound sterling and to preserve its role as an international reserve currency. To achieve these objectives adequate reserves of gold and dollars are necessary. An adverse balance of payments position cannot be tolerated for very long, even if this means holding up industrial expansion and investment.

The priorities of the Treasury have been blamed for the "stop–go" characteristics of the economy and held to be largely responsible for Britain's unsatisfactory rate of economic growth. In the last analysis, however, it is the politicians, and particularly those in the Cabinet, who must bear the responsibility for policy.

At the risk of oversimplification the stop–go cycle may be described as follows. When the balance of payments position is favourable and pressure on the pound is eased, rates of interest are lowered and credit restrictions removed. This may be accompanied by changes in taxation designed to stimulate demand. A brief expansion occurs; the "go" stage is in being. The time lag between the stimulus of demand and an increase in supply causes prices to rise. Businessmen are optimistic; there is an increase in capital investment and a demand for labour. Soon, however, the import of raw materials and machinery, unaccompanied by an immediate equivalent sale of British goods to foreigners, adversely affects the balance of payments. There is also an increase in the import of consumer goods, to meet demands which cannot be satisfied by home producers in the short run. The reserves begin to fall. Foreign holders of sterling, fearing devaluation, switch to dollars or gold. Money invested in London is reinvested in New York or elsewhere. The British authorities then implement the stop phase, raising interest rates and restricting credit. Unemployment rises, as the demand for labour drops off, and capital investment falls, prejudicing future productivity.[23]

Political events must be brought into the picture because they affect the balance of payments. Trouble with Rhodesia sends up the price of copper. A sudden outbreak of war between Israel and the Arab countries cuts off oil supplies, and a more expensive source has to be found in the USA or elsewhere. Foreign countries may deliberately encourage speculation against the pound for political ends. British property and investments overseas may be seized by the government of some emergent African state. In the circumstances it is unfortunate that the subject of political economy has been largely abandoned in the mistaken belief that politics and economics are more usefully studied as separate disciplines.

In its defence of the pound the Treasury will be assisted by various interested parties. The USA will not be anxious to see the dollar occupying the most exposed trench should sterling be abandoned as an international reserve currency. The American department of the Foreign Office will doubtless make its voice heard in the Cabinet and elsewhere. The Foreign Office will be anxious to placate foreign holders of sterling. The Bank of England and other financial institutions, which have links with the Treasury, will tend to give the department general support.

It is possible, indeed probable, that the Treasury tends to identify the national interest with the interests of the organizations and groups with which it has most contact. In a way these are its clients. Their advice is likely to favour the retention of sterling as an international trading and reserve currency. It has been justly observed that in nine cases out of ten, "men come easily to believe that arrangements agreeable to themselves are beneficial to

[23] On the international role of sterling see C. McMahon, *Sterling in the Sixties*, Oxford, 1964. Also see S. Strange, *The Sterling Problem and the Six*, Chatham House, 1967; and *Report of the Committee on the Working of the Monetary System*, ch. 8.

others".[24] But in any case, the position of sterling is certain to be in the forefront of political controversy.

Doubtless the electorate has but the haziest notion of matters of high finance, but it is of some advantage to the Treasury to be dealing with issues which are easily dramatized and which are bound to be seized on by party politicians and the press. A run on the pound will always make the headlines. And no self-respecting Opposition spokesman will fail to proclaim that the country faces ruin if remedial action is not taken. If the pound takes precedence over productivity, the electors, the press, and, above all, the politicians are as much to blame as the Treasury.

Furthermore, although it is customary to speak and write of *the* Treasury, this department, like any other, is not an indivisible unity but is made up of various groups and sub-groups. When it is suggested that the Treasury advocated this, or opposed that, what is really meant is that those persons in the Treasury who were most powerful or influential were able to present their views to the outside world as though they had the support of all or most of the department.

But, given all these qualifications, the Treasury, as the major economic department, must bear a major part of the responsibility for Britain's economic difficulties. The stop–go cycle of the fifties and the tendency for Britain to occupy a place at or near the bottom of tables comparing Western European rates of economic growth were certainly laid at the door of the Treasury by critics of government policy.

It was said that Treasury officials were typical civil service amateurs, ignorant of economic theory. There is no reason to suppose they were as ill informed as some writers implied, but their priorities were different from those of certain economists.[25] There was criticism of the lack of trained economists of senior rank in the civil service generally, and in the Treasury in

[24] A. V. Dicey, *Law and Public Opinion in England in the Nineteenth Century*, paperback edn., 1963, pp. 14–15.

[25] For example, see essay by Lord Balogh in *Crisis in the Civil Service*, H. Thomas (ed.), Blond, 1968.

particular.[26] Whether economics is the exact science some of its practitioners apparently believe is open to doubt. One eminent economist has noted that queasiness is often ascribed to economists and suggests it derives from personal judgements being involved in arguments.[27]

Apart from criticisms of personnel, there were others relating to the overall functions of the Treasury. Some critics thought the department should be relieved of the management of the civil service, and that the final preparation of the annual estimates might be carried out by a new organization modelled on the US Bureau of the Budget. It was felt that one department should not be responsible for tackling both day-to-day economic problems and long-term planning.[28]

The discussion of these matters was partly responsible for the investigation of Treasury Control by the Estimates Committee in the session 1957–8 which led to the setting up of the Plowden Committee on the Control of Public Expenditure. The Plowden Committee first met in October 1959. When it reported, in 1961, the committee put the development of long-term surveys at the core of its proposals. There was no doubt, the committee stated, that chopping and changing in government expenditure policy, which was the result of the stop–go cycle, frustrated efficiency and economy in the running of the public services. But long-term surveys, if they were to be meaningful, implied a greater degree of planning of the economy as a whole.[29]

[26] See P. D. Henderson, *The Use of Economists in British Administration*, Oxford Economic Papers, 1961. Also see R. Opie and D. Seers in Thomas, *op. cit.*, and Sir Eric Roll, Economists in Government, *The Economist*, 16 Mar. 1968.

[27] J. Robinson, *Economic Philosophy*, Pelican edn., pp. 26–27; also see pp. 71–93, 117–37.

[28] For general discussion of these topics see S. Beer, *Treasury Control*, 2nd edn., Oxford, 1957.

[29] *Report on the Control of Public Expenditure*, Cmd. 1432, 1961, paras. 18–24. On various aspects of the Plowden Report see special issue of *Public Administration*, Spring 1963. For one example of the way stop–go produces frustrations and raises costs see E. Layton, *Building by Local Authorities*, Allen & Unwin, 1961, ch. 2.

One other aspect of this period needs to be mentioned. There was an attempt to influence prices and incomes by setting up a Council on Prices, Productivity, and Incomes in 1957. The council, which consisted of three members, was required to produce an annual report. Its powers were nil and its influence negligible. At best it was hoped that the publicity given to its pronouncements would have a moderating effect and prepare the public for deflationary measures. All that was thought necessary was a rational presentation of the "facts" and an appeal to good sense. But the "publicly responsible" course tended to get overlooked by trade unionists and businessmen. As one commentator has put it, people kept noticing the unstated political assumptions behind the economic arguments of the council.[30] In the event, incomes continued to rise faster than productivity and the inflationary trend persisted. It was clear that the Treasury's methods had failed to bring the situation under control.

There was no sudden conversion of Conservative governments to strong State intervention at the end of the fifties. But there was disillusion with what has been called "persuasive postures" and with monetary and fiscal measures as effective means of controlling the economy.

Economic Affairs, 1961–4

In the autumn of 1960 a special budget was necessary to halt a run on sterling; Britain was in another stop phase and the stagnation of the economy was in marked contrast to the continuing boom in some countries in Western Europe. The following year the Government decided that the time had come for Britain to apply to join the Common Market.

It was argued by the Government that British manufacturers would reap the benefits of economies of scale associated with a large and expanding market. This would enable costs and prices to be lowered. British industry would also have to face the competition of highly efficient German and French firms. Monopolistic and

[30] A. Shonfield, *Modern Capitalism*, Oxford, 1965, p. 155.

restrictive practices, which the combined efforts of the Board of Trade, Monopolies Commission, and Restrictive Practices Court, had failed to stop, would yield to the onslaught of market forces.[31] Such arguments had considerable appeal for Conservatives committed to an ideology of competition and *laissez-faire*.

But the decision also had attractions for those who advocated firmer State intervention in the running of the economy. The achievements of the French, at that time, were widely attributed to economic planning. France has a system of planning, combining State intervention with private ownership, which is compatible with the ideologies of both the major political parties in Britain. And the very decision to apply for membership of the Common Market forced the British Government to consider the diversity of principles which underlay its taxation and social security policies, its agricultural policy, its industrial location policy, its transport policy, its incomes policy, and many other matters. An attempt had to be made to co-ordinate economic policy and machinery and bring them into line with Continental practice.

The setting up of the National Economic Development Council, which bore a faint resemblance to the French *Conseil Supérieur du Plan*, probably owed something to the Common Market application. This was one of the two most notable developments relating to economic administration in this period. The other was the reorganization of the Treasury which originated in the Plowden Report on the Control of Public Expenditure. We shall deal with the Treasury reorganization first.

The reorganization, which came into effect early in 1962, divided the Treasury into two sides, the Financial and Economic Policy Side and the Management of the Civil Service Side. Two joint permanent secretaries were appointed. Sir William Armstrong took over the Financial and Economic Policy Side; Sir Laurence

[31] On the Monopolies Commission and the Restrictive Practices Court see M. Hall, The consumer sector, in Worswick and Ady, *op. cit.*, ch. 12. Also see P. H. Guenault and J. M. Jackson, *The Control of Monopoly in the United Kingdom*, Longmans, 1960.

Helsby headed the Management Side and became the official head of the civil service.[32] His predecessor in the latter role, the late Lord Normanbrook, had combined it with the office of Secretary of the Cabinet. This position was now considered to need the undivided attention of one man because of the heavy duties involved. As a result Sir Burke Trend became Secretary of the Cabinet.

The two sides of the Treasury were split into five functional groups. The Economic and Financial Side was divided into the Public Sector Group, the National Economy Group, and the Finance Group. When the Department of Economic Affairs came into being, with the advent of a Labour government, the National Economy Group was moved into it. But an Economic Section remains at the Treasury. The Management Side was divided into the Pay and Conditions of Service Group and the Management Group.

It was hoped that reorganization on a functional basis would produce more effective control over government expenditure. The Treasury had hitherto been split into divisions, many of which dealt with a group of related departments for expenditure purposes. A Social Services division, for example, handled the estimates and expenditure of the Ministries of Health, Education, Housing and Local Government, and other departments. Expenditure relating to establishments had been dealt with by four separate divisions; there were also certain "mixed" divisions, which were responsible for both the establishment and other types of expenditure of some departments.

The functional principle was advocated on various grounds. It was thought that Treasury officials would be more conscious of total government expenditure and less inclined to limit their interest to the expenditure or affairs of a few departments only. It was intended that they should become aware of the best methods used by departments over the whole field of government. They

[32] Sir Laurence retired at the end of April 1968 and Sir William Armstrong became the new head of the home civil service. Sir Douglas Allen took over the Financial and Economic Policy Side. See Appendix (5).

could then disseminate information about such methods throughout the service. And because government was becoming increasingly complex it was considered desirable to encourage specialization on the functional principle.

The function of the Public Sector Group is to try to contain public expenditure and to get the best value for money. The Plowden Report on the Control of Public Expenditure had pointed out, in 1961, that Supply Expenditure was running at some 22 per cent of the Gross National Product. Total public expenditure, including that of the nationalized industries and the local authorities, represented about 42 per cent of GNP. And the public sector as a whole was employing approximately 25 per cent of the labour force of the country.[33]

The Plowden Report emphasized that too many past decisions had been taken in a piecemeal fashion without regard to national resources. It advocated surveys of public expenditure and resources to cover five-year periods. The idea of five-year forward looks implied at least intelligent guesses as to the future state of the economy and a minimum degree of government intervention. For when forward looks are taken it is but one step further to try to keep the economy on the course foreseen.

The function of the Finance Group is to implement monetary and fiscal policy, including the management of the national debt. It is responsible for both home and overseas finance. Given the priority accorded sterling in the Treasury, this group is possibly the most influential in the department.

When the National Economy Group was in the Treasury it was split into two divisions. One division was responsible for making economic forecasts. In addition to making short-term predictions concerning the national income, balance of payments and other economic indicators, the division attempted to make a five-year forecast each spring. These forecasts are still essayed by the Treasury and the Department of Economic Affairs. They are tentative in character and subject to continual modification.

[33] *Report on the Control of Public Expenditure*, Cmd. 1432, 1962, para. 10.

Most members of the forecasting division were professional economists and came under the Head of the Government Economic Service, who controls the Economic Section. If any Treasury officials favoured expansion, even when sterling came under attack, it was the members of this division. But they can hardly have presented a serious challenge to stop–go policies. Their removal to the Department of Economic Affairs, however, probably made the Treasury less growth-conscious.

The other division of the National Economy Group dealt with such matters as incomes policy, labour mobility, and regional planning. It was the Treasury's main channel of communication with industry and bodies like the National Economic Development Council.

The National Economy Group attempted to reconcile short-term stability and long-term economic growth. It was supposed to co-ordinate the activities of the Finance Group and the Public Sector Group. In practice the Public Sector Group was, and is, the centre of Treasury operations. Seniority and rank are a reasonable guide, and it is pertinent to note that the National Economy Group commanded the services of only 7 administrative class officials at a time when there were 48 in the Public Sector Group and 45 in the Finance Group.[34]

The functions of the Management Side of the Treasury are fairly obvious. As we saw when discussing the civil service generally, management has been taken more seriously since the appearance of the Plowden Report. The complexity and scale of public administration do call for the use of modern techniques. The Management Side deals with such matters as pay, complements, postings, gradings, training, organization and methods, and mechanization.[35]

The Treasury has hitherto turned a deaf ear to suggestions that it should be relieved of control over the civil service, to enable it

[34] S. Brittan, *op. cit.*, p. 78.

[35] See *5th Report Estimates Committee, 1963–4*, on Treasury Control of Establishments, HC 228, 1964. Also see article by W. W. Morton, *Public Administration*, Spring 1963, and Quarterly Notes, *Public Administration* Autumn 1966. See Appendix (6).

to concentrate its energies on economic planning and the management of the economy. Its control over personnel and training, as well as its control over finance, enables the Treasury to dominate other departments. No one is likely to become a Permanent Secretary, or attain high rank, who is not acceptable to the Treasury (see Chapter 8, p. 255). Those members of the administrative class who find their way into the Treasury are regarded as an elite within an elite. No other department, with the possible exception of the Foreign Office, is so well placed to get its way.

The reorganization of the Treasury changed nothing fundamental. The same sort of people remained in control and traditional ideas prevailed. The reorganization was a necessary concession made in the face of criticism and mounting pressure. The logic behind the separation of the Finance Group and the National Economy Group was difficult to discern. No doubt there were sectional battles and personality conflicts involved. The magic word "co-ordination" was invoked to bring the work of the separate groups into some sort of relationship and compatibility. But this was a burden laid on a joint permanent secretary already saddled with checking the expenditure of departments. Furthermore, there was confusion of function and responsibility between the Treasury and the National Economic Development Council. The National Economy Group had special responsibility for the private sector, but so had the NEDC.

NEDC was conceived in 1961. In July of that year, during a debate on a balance of payments crisis, the Chancellor of the Exchequer, Mr. Selwyn Lloyd, revealed that he was not afraid of the word planning. It may be assumed that he meant planning of the "persuasive" or "indicative" type and not the Soviet variety. The best-known example of "persuasive" planning at that time was the French version.

In the French system a *Conseil Supérieur du Plan*, consisting of ministers, employers, trade unionists, and others, was originally intended to act as a senior body which would give its approval to the National Plan. Since 1958, however, a *Conseil Économique et Social*, has tended to appropriate the role designated for the

Conseil Supérieur. In addition there are a number of *Commissions de Modernisation*. Some of the *Commissions* are "horizontal" and deal with problems or aspects of planning common to industry as a whole. They are concerned with such matters as manpower, research, and regional planning. Other *commissions* concentrate on particular branches of industry or on a social service. There are *commissions* for chemicals, sources of power, education, housing, and so on. Numerous working parties are set up whose main task is to fix a target of probable expansion for a particular industry.

At the centre of the planning system, however, is the *Commissariat Général du Plan*. This is an office of economic technocrats who draw up a National Plan. The *Commissions de Modernisation* and working parties adjust their targets to fit in with the overall plan. The Plan indicates the relative shares of increased output which the Government thinks ought to go to different income groups. The *Counseil Économique et Social* considers the claims of social investment and private consumption and may suggest changes in the proposed balance.[36]

This very elaborate and complicated machinery has been built up over a long period. In 1961 the French had more than a dozen years of planning behind them. There are good reasons for believing that the special conditions which have made the system reasonably successful in France do not prevail elsewhere; and particularly not in Britain.

A serious attempt to introduce the French system into Britain would entail a transformation of the relationship of the State and private interest groups, a radical shake-up of the permanent civil service, and the downgrading of the Treasury. In short, it would involve many changes which are unlikely to occur unless a firm initiative is taken at Cabinet level.

The early French Plans were largely concerned with post-war reconstruction in a country which was recovering from wartime

[36] See P. Bauchet, *Economic Planning: The French Experience*, Heinemann, 1964, and J. and A. M. Hackett, *Economic Planning in France*, Allen & Unwin, 1963.

devastation and foreign occupation. Strong State leadership was unavoidable. Moreover, France is a country where the *étatiste* tradition can be traced back to the seventeenth century. In Britain there is far less readiness to accept State intervention as "normal" or as essential to economic progress.

Again, the particular skill of the British civil servant lies not so much in taking a positive lead, as in securing compromise and the reconciliation of conflicting interests. They are adherents of the Benthamite view; that is to say, they believe that the public interest lies in giving each group in society the maximum of what it is after, providing that this is consistent with what other groups are after. Everybody gets a prize because all are winners.[37]

In France the public interest is differently conceived. It is more than the sum of reconciled sectional interests and something which transcends them. The technocrats of the French civil service are inclined to think that they represent the public interest or general will. And they do not doubt that their knowledge and experience are as good as those of any businessman. They are trained specialists and their prestige is high. Because France has suffered from unstable political régimes there has been greater reliance on bureaucratic competence.[38]

In this context it does not matter whether French planners have in fact been mainly responsible for the progress of the French economy in the fifties and early sixties.[39] But it is relevant to point out the futility of the belief that planning on the French model will produce similar results when British habits, behaviour, and traditions are totally different.

A tentative approach to planning in Britain was initiated with the setting up of the National Economic Development Council in 1962. When it was first constituted NEDC consisted of twenty

[37] See S. E. Finer, *op. cit.*, pp. 108–9.

[38] See A. H. Hanson, Planning and the politicians: some reflections on economic planning in western Europe, *International Review of Administrative Science*, No. 4, 1966, pp. 281–2. Also see A. Shonfield, *Modern Capitalism*, pp. 71–72.

[39] For a sceptical view of French planning see C. Kindleberger in *France: Change and Tradition*, Gollancz, 1963.

members. The Chancellor of the Exchequer acted as the chairman. The other members were the President of the Board of Trade, the Minister of Labour, two chairmen of the boards of nationalized industries, six representatives from the trade unions, six representatives of employers' organizations, two independents, and the Director-General of the NEDC staff. The Council later included the First Secretary of State for Economic Affairs, who took over the chairmanship for a time, the Minister of Technology, the chairman of the Prices and Incomes Board, and a representative of financial institutions of the City of London.[40]

The terms of reference of NEDC were to seek ways of increasing the rate of economic growth. Initially NEDC relied on its staff to produce reports on the economy, as a prelude to drawing up an economic programme. Under its first Director-General, Sir Robert Shone, the staff was split into two divisions. One of these was concerned with general economic problems; the other was responsible for making contacts with industry. In contrast to the *Commissariat Général du Plan*, the members of the staff are not permanent officials in the public service. The majority were on temporary loan from the universities and industry or business. The staff produced two reports on economic growth soon after NEDC was set up. The Council ultimately suggested that an annual growth rate of 4 per cent was possible for Britain. Between 1956 and 1961 the actual growth rate had been under 3 per cent, so the "target" was apparently ambitious.

Associated with NEDC are a number of Development Councils for particular industries and services. These are popularly known as little Neddies, just as NEDC itself has come to be called Neddy. In 1963 there were nine little Neddies in existence; by the end of

[40] NEDC replaced the largely moribund Economic Planning Board which dated back to 1947; associated bodies, such as the National Production Advisory Council and the old Regional Boards for Industry, were also dispensed with. By Dec. 1967, NEDC had 24 members and the Prime Minister had taken over the chairmanship. Its full-time staff, NEDO, rose from 61, in Nov 1962 to 171 in Nov. 1967. See B. Taylor, NEDC after six years, *Westminster Bank Review*, Feb. 1968.

1967 there were twenty-three. Membership follows the usual pattern. The chairman is normally a businessman of standing in the industry in question, and there are representatives of trade associations, trade unions, and government. The little Neddies collect information, brood over the general problems of the industry or service involved and produce reports. They also serve as a channel of communication with government departments.

NEDC has never been much more than a propagandist body advocating growth. Since everybody is in favour of growth it offends nobody. It has no powers and its pronouncements commit nobody. When the Department of Economic Affairs came into existence it appropriated many of the staff of NEDC. But the staff have never been particularly influential. There is a fairly rapid turnover of personnel and one may doubt whether many members of the National Economic Development Office feel their careers and reputations are bound up with the success or failure of NEDC.

Since 1964 NEDC has been overshadowed by the newly created Department of Economic Affairs, which appropriated some of its functions as well as some of its staff. But NEDC has never been at the centre of policy making. Conservative governments did not make it privy to their plans and it has no right of access to official documents.

Mr. H. F. R. Catherwood, a former managing director of British Aluminium and one-time Chief Industrial Adviser in the Department of Economic Affairs, became Director-General of NEDC following the resignation of Sir Robert Shone. Since July 1966 the Director-General has had the unenviable task of persuading industry to be more growth-conscious at a time when the Government has been enforcing a policy of severe deflation.

In August 1967 the Prime Minister temporarily took on direct personal responsibility for overall economic policy and in so doing became chairman of NEDC. The Chancellor of the Exchequer deputizes in the absence of the Prime Minister.

Deflationary policies have also taken much of the drive and

rationale out of the work of the little Neddies. In October 1966, Sir Joseph Latham, then deputy chairman of AEI, resigned from the chairmanship of two little Neddies. In his opinion, key people were giving too much time to activities which did not make a direct contribution to production and profits. Little Neddies had already lost the services of Mr. Joseph Rank, the miller, and Mr. Arnold Weinstock and Sir Arnold Lindley, from the upper regions of electrical engineering.[41]

To a certain extent new organizations like the Ministry of Technology and the Industrial Reorganization Corporation impinge on and overlap and duplicate the functions of the little Neddies. In addition, a host of interdepartmental committees may ultimately be concerned with some issue originating with a little Neddy.

It is scarcely surprising that some impatience has been expressed in little Neddies. Administrative arrangements are cumbersome and time-consuming and policy and machinery are fundamentally out of line. It is no good setting up bodies to stimulate growth and then following anti-growth policies.

Economic Affairs Since 1964

In January 1964 Mr. Wilson, then Leader of the Opposition, made one of his most effective speeches on economic policy. Speaking in Swansea to a Labour audience, he put the emphasis on production. On production, he argued, depended Labour's social policies and Britain's standing in the world. The Labour Party, he claimed, had an economic plan, unlike the Conservative Government. If and when Labour was returned to power there would be a policy of sustained growth. There would be an incomes policy, but it would be one based on rising production. There would be no faith-breaking interference with collective

[41] See report in *The Times*, 28 Oct. 1966, and article Little Neds at sea, *The Sunday Times*, 30 Oct. 1966. On NEDC and NEDO generally see Sir Robert Shone The National Economic Development Council, *Public Administration*, Spring 1966; H. Phelps Brown, The National Development Organization, *Public Administration*, Autumn 1963; and B. Taylor, *op. cit.*

bargaining and no wage freeze forced on the country through a stagnant economy. Unlike the Conservatives the Labour Party would not look to the Common Market to solve the nation's economic problems. In October Mr. Wilson led his party to its first electoral victory for thirteen years.

Almost his first act as Prime Minister was to set up the Department of Economic Affairs, the long-awaited ministry which was intended to galvanize industry and challenge the Treasury and its priorities. The DEA itself later gave birth to new Regional Economic Councils and Boards, and a Prices and Incomes Board.

The arch critic of the Treasury, Dr. Balogh, now Lord Balogh, was transported from Oxford to act as economic adviser to the Cabinet, initially on a full-time basis. To protect the Chancellor of the Exchequer from possible departmental brainwashing, and to provide new and stimulating ideas, Mr. Nicholas Kaldor was brought in from Cambridge as a part-time adviser.

To reinforce the efforts of the little Neddies, in case they failed to persuade industry to take advantage of the latest technological developments, a Ministry of Technology was set up. This was given responsibility for the sponsorship of such "gadget" industries as machine tools, electronics, telecommunications, and computers.

Undoubtedly the centrepiece of the new machinery was the Department of Economic Affairs, initially headed by Mr. George Brown who bore the title of First Secretary of State and Secretary of State for Economic Affairs. In the hierarchy of the Parliamentary Labour Party Mr. Brown was then second only to Mr. Wilson. His appointment as Secretary of State for Economic Affairs might therefore be taken as evidence of the importance attached to the DEA by the Prime Minister. The First Secretary's status seemed further enhanced when he took over the chairmanship of NEDC.

The first permanent secretary of the DEA, Sir Eric Roll, was a former economics professor at Hull University who had entered the public service during the Second World War. Sir Eric is reported to have been the driving force in the British delegation concerned with Britain's first application to join EEC.[42]

In terms of numbers the DEA was, and is, a small department. In April 1965 the DEA had 488 people in posts. The Estimates for 1967–8 show a figure of 569. By way of contrast, the Treasury, generally considered amongst the smallest of the departments, has a complement of 1755 for 1967–8, but only 70 are classified as senior staff.

Of the 488 people in the DEA in April 1965, 8 were industrial advisers, 23 were economists, and 60 were administrative class officials. The remainder were mostly executive class officers, clerks, typists, and messengers. All of the industrial advisers and 22 of the 23 economists were recruited on a temporary basis. About half the economists were taken over from the National Economic Development Office; most of the remainder came from the universities.[43] It is possible that there will be a smaller proportion of temporary economists in all departments, including the DEA, as the Government Economic Service, set up in March 1965, grows in numbers.

The use of temporary industrial advisers, on loan from their firms, was thought necessary because of the lack of experience in industry of full-time senior civil servants. The opinions of such advisers presumably carry some weight with other industrialists. The relatively large number of economists originally in the DEA forestalled the charge that insufficient expert opinion was brought to bear on economic policy. And the fact that many of them were not full-time civil servants, cast in the Treasury mould, might have been considered a further advantage.

The functions of the DEA have been described as essentially related to co-ordination. It has no executive functions. Mr. Wilson regards this as desirable. He is on record as saying that

[42] N. Beloff, *The General Says No*, Penguin, 1963, p. 115.

[43] See *6th Report Estimates Committee*, Session 1964–5, HC 308, evidence of Sir Eric Roll and Mr. I. F. Hudson, paras. 708–37.

if the DEA were responsible for executive action it would not be able to fulfil its role as a Central Economic Planning Department.[44]

The idea of a planning, co-ordinating department, relieved of executive responsibilities, has its attractions. In theory, such a department is not burdened with day-to-day chores; there is time to sit back and think and it is not identified with particular interests or subject to their pressures. But there is at least some truth in the contention that he who has the execution of policy is its master. And there are distinct advantages in having the support of powerful interest groups which have influential connections in Whitehall and Westminster.

Furthermore, a co-ordinating department may itself be strong or weak. It is much easier to persuade people to behave in a certain way when one has something to bargain with. The Treasury is a strong co-ordinating department because of its control over government funds and the civil service. But a co-ordinating department which can only argue may be kept very busy indeed, persuading and cajoling in numerous meetings and negotiations. In the short history of the DEA there have been occasions when one was reminded of the famous Ouida gaffe, "all rowed fast but none rowed faster than stroke". And the outcome of furious activity may be nothing more than verbal assurances of goodwill or vague statements of intent.

It has been claimed that the DEA represents only the national interest. As a disinterested body, it is said, the DEA can develop close relations with both sides of industry.[45] But it is difficult to see how a "disinterested" department can compete with "interested" departments, like the Ministry of Agriculture and Ministry of Technology, in developing *close* relations. The friend of all is nobody's special friend. Because it devotes its energies to solving the problems of the whole economy the DEA cannot easily develop special relationships.

[44] See conversation with Norman Hunt reprinted in *The Listener*, 6 April 1967, p. 449.

[45] See DEA Progress Report No. 12, HMSO, 1965, and Sir Eric Roll, The Department of Economic Affairs, *Public Administration*, Spring 1966, pp. 7 and 11.

But it is difficult to accept the proposition that the DEA *is* totally disinterested. Every government department is an interest in its own right. The power of any one affects that of other departments. The status and standing of ministers and officials are associated with influence of the department in which they serve. The DEA has an interest in the prestige of economists in the public service. It had an interest in the National Plan. And it has an interest in preserving the existence of the little Neddies which are associated with its work.

Within the DEA there is a General Planning Group, an Industrial, Prices, and Incomes Group,[46] an External Policies Group, and a Regional Planning Group. The DEA works in association with the Treasury on such matters as general economic policy, forecasting, and public expenditure. The functions of the External Policies Group clearly impinge on those of the Treasury and Board of Trade. The Industrial Group works closely with the Board of Trade, Department of Employment and Productivity, and Ministry of Technology, as well as with the Industrial Reorganization Corporation and the Prices and Incomes Board. With the possible exception of regional planning there is scarcely any economic sphere where the DEA is the dominant party.

The Regional Planning Group supervises and assists the regional economic planning councils and boards which have been set up. There are 11 of these, 8 for England and 1 each for Scotland, Wales, and Northern Ireland. The Scottish Region is primarily the responsibility of the Scottish Office, though the DEA is represented on the regional board by a senior official.

The general role and functions of the DEA were not significantly altered when the Prime Minister took on personal responsibility for economic policy. It was stressed that the Board of Trade would have the leading part in overseas trade but there

[46] Following the reconstruction of the Cabinet in April 1968, major responsibility for prices and incomes policy passed to the First Secretary and Secretary of State for Employment and Productivity, Mrs. Barbara Castle, who took over the Ministry of Labour, now renamed the Department of Employment and Productivity. A few days later the Prime Minister announced he had given up his personal overlordship of economic affairs.

were no fundamental changes. In practice, however, the position of the DEA appeared to be transformed. It lost its reputation as an independent department and seemed to become an outpost of the Cabinet Office or Prime Minister's Office. Superficially this might be thought to enhance the position of the DEA in Whitehall, but this depends on the will of the Prime Minister. In reality the change was not remarkable, for the influence of the DEA has always depended, ultimately, on the support of the Prime Minister and this is by no means guaranteed.

One can only speculate as to the future of the DEA; it would not appear to be bright. It is more rewarding to study its past. There is much that can be learnt from the methods used in drawing up the first National Plan. This experience has profoundly affected the Labour Government's attitude to planning. The structure and functions of the regional boards and councils also call for further discussion, as does the role and position of the Prices and Incomes Board.

The National Plan

Mr. Michael Stewart, who succeeded Mr. Brown at the DEA, once wrote that there was no doubt that, at least until the end of the decade, decisions on what to produce and how to produce it would be taken by the controllers of private firms and by nobody else.[47] The type of planning instituted by Labour governments in the 1960's clearly reflects this belief.

The National Plan, published in September 1965, was indicative rather than directional. In an indicative plan there is no positive direction by a State planning department or commission. Instead, possible growth rates are worked out by government economists and these are put to firms for comment. On the basis of answers received, and later discussion, a growth rate is selected as possible or feasible.

The co-operation of private industry is essential in this sort

[47] M. Stewart, Planning and persuasion in a mixed economy, *Political Quarterly*, April–June 1964.

of exercise. Co-operation is not easy to obtain when a government has the reputation of being socialist. In the opinion of one economist, Labour governments have had to establish a reputation as reluctant nationalizers before indicative or feasible planning could be undertaken.[48]

The actual process of drawing up the Plan was as follows. On the basis of general assumptions long-term targets were worked out in the DEA. This was followed by an industrial survey, based on questionnaires sent out to industry. Various sectors of industry, through little Neddies or trade associations, were asked their probable plans and demands for capital and labour up to 1970. Questionnaires sent out in February 1965 began to reach the DEA in April and May.

The DEA then attempted to fit the answers into a coherent pattern. It finally decided that a 4 per cent growth rate was possible. This entailed an average annual increase of 3·8 per cent between 1964 and 1970. The DEA could scarcely have settled for less than NEDC had suggested as possible when the Conservatives were in power.

As was to be expected, the Plan encountered criticism when it appeared. *The Economist* described it as a Pale try. It pointed out that the little Neddies, which were given a key role in the implementation of the Plan, met infrequently. They would probably indulge in mutual backscratching with other committees. It might also have observed that the little Neddies have no powers and cannot persuade firms to do anything they regard as unprofitable. But what is profitable for a firm is not necessarily in the public interest.

The Government, *The Economist* charged, had got responsibility without power, the prerogative of the cuckold down the ages. Real power, it stated prophetically, lay with foreign bankers. The Government could not do the things it would like to do because of its fears for sterling.[49]

Clearly the DEA relied very much on information supplied

[48] See A. Shonfield, In Labour Britain, *The Listener*, 3 March 1966.

[49] *The Economist*, 18 Sept. 1965, pp. 1071–3, 1115–18, 1121–3.

by firms. Just how seriously its questionnaires were taken is unknown. It is quite likely that the information supplied to the DEA was almost valueless. The intentions of firms can change very quickly and the reputations of individuals working for private enterprise were not at stake in this type of forecasting. Moreover, questions were put to firms in a somewhat misleading form.[50]

Firms weıe asked to answer questionnaires on the *assumption* that a growth rate in excess of past and current trends would occur. Available evidence showed the improbability of the suggested growth rate. The returns put in by firms were in answer to a hypothetical question, not expressions of intent. No assumption should have been made without first finding out what firms intended to do in the absence of any new or unexpected turn of events.[51] But the production of a National Plan may itself alter business expectations by removing some uncertainties about future government policy. In the case of the 1965 Plan, however, what has been termed the "confidence trick" of planning did not work.[52]

Even before the deflationary measures of July 1966 administered the death blow, there were inconsistencies between the objectives of the Plan and actual government policies. High interest rates were not consistent with the desire to encourage an increased rate of growth. But they probably helped to protect sterling by attracting foreign capital to London. High interest rates and cuts in both central and local government expenditure can scarcely have stimulated the building industry, singled out by NEDC as having insufficient capacity to cope with growth at the rate predicted.

Furthermore, it became apparent that economic forecasting, in anything more than the most general terms, was an extremely hazardous undertaking. For example, manpower losses in coal-mining soon exceeded those envisaged in the Plan and threatened

[50] See J. Brunner, What use is the Plan?, *New Society*, 25 March 1965.
[51] See *The National Plan: Its Contribution to Growth*, PEP, 1965, pp. 338 and 346.
[52] See S. Brittan, *Inquest on Planning in Britain*, PEP, 1965, p. 18.

an increased bill for imported oil which one estimate put at £200 million by 1970. In March 1966 *The Times* reported that there was little prospect of the main objectives of the Plan being achieved.[53]

The Plan could have been modified or even drastically revised. But in July 1966 the political decision was taken to abandon it. There were no ministerial resignations over this decision though the Secretary of State of Economic Affairs was reported to have wanted to go. Instead, in a Cabinet reshuffle, he went to the Foreign Office and Mr. Michael Stewart took over the DEA. In August 1967 Mr. Stewart handed over to Mr. Peter Shore, with the Prime Minister taking final personal responsibility for economic policy.[54] During a life of less than three years, therefore, the DEA was headed by three different ministers and also acquired a temporary overlord.

The DEA has experienced some difficulty in holding on to key personnel apart from ministers. In October 1966 the Permanent Secretary, Sir Eric Roll, left to take up an appointment in private business. He was succeeded by Sir Douglas Allen.[55] The tendency of the department to rely on people seconded from industry and the universities weakens its position in Whitehall. For example, after a relatively short period with the DEA one industrial policy co-ordinator returned to private business and journalism. And an industrial adviser, loaned to the DEA in 1966, quitted this post in September 1967 to take up an appointment as chairman of the Upper Clyde shipping group. A rapid turnover of personnel at the top is scarcely conducive to good morale and continuity of policy.

It is unlikely that the DEA will ever attempt another National Plan on the 1965 model. But at least the July 1966 measures show that although British governments have had little success in stimulating growth, they can certainly achieve striking results

[53] See *The Sunday Times*, 24 April 1966, on manpower losses in mining, and an article on the National Plan in *The Times*, 18 March 1966.

[54] In April 1968 he disembarrassed himself of this responsibility.

[55] Sir Douglas has since been assigned to the Treasury, as Joint Permanent Secretary in charge of the Financial and Economic Policy side. Sir William Nield became, April 1968, Permanent Secretary of the DEA. See Appendix (5).

in the other direction. It is worth while specifying the weapons used to bring about a business recession.

On 14 July 1966 the Government raised bank rate by one point to 7 per cent, the second time it had reached what is normally regarded as a crisis level in under two years. On top of this, the lending powers of banks were reduced by the use of a device known as special deposits. In effect, these freeze some of the liquid assets of banks and prevent them making advances to borrowers on a scale they would otherwise prefer. Hire-purchase controls were strengthened, particularly in connection with the purchase of motor vehicles.

Planned public expenditure at home was reduced by some £300 million. A 10 per cent surcharge was imposed on all rates of purchase tax and on duties on beer and spirits. Control over office building was extended and the cost limit above which buildings were controlled was reduced from £100,000 to £50,000.

As an original contribution to these traditional weapons of the stop–go armoury, the government called for a six-month standstill on incomes and prices. This was to be followed by a further six months of severe restraint. It proved necessary to back up the freeze with statutory powers.

These measures certainly worked in reducing investment and productivity. Business confidence was undermined, unemployment rose, and many firms were soon operating well below capacity.

By the end of 1966 the overall balance of payments was showing a surplus, but this did not indicate any fundamental improvement in Britain's economic position. It was a temporary and fleeting achievement. The official index of industrial production fell by nearly 4 per cent between July and November 1966. At the same time the retail price index rose by 4 per cent, partly because of a selective employment tax which had come into effect in September.[56]

The July 1966 measures are a clear indication of the power of governments to influence the economy in a negative way. It appears

[56] See Annual monetary survey, *Midland Bank Review*, May 1967.

to be much more difficult to achieve a situation which will encourage growth. The so-called "go" phase of the stop–go cycle is in essence nothing more than the removal of restraints previously imposed.

The impact of this deflationary policy varied from one part of the country to another. The work of the regional boards and councils was thus affected. As the regional organizations were not consulted they were taken somewhat unawares by the sudden change of direction on the economic front. The result was to produce a certain amount of disillusionment with regional planning as well as with National Plans.

Regional Boards and Councils

The main objective of the Regional Planning Group of the DEA is to secure a more balanced use of economic resources. It encourages the employment of manpower and capital in areas of high unemployment and it tries to ensure a more even distribution of prosperity to counteract the inflationary tendencies of excess demand in more active regions.

Soon after the Labour Party took office in 1964, the Government announced the setting up of the regional economic planning councils and boards. These were to assist the DEA in its efforts to stimulate economic growth.

The regional councils are purely advisory bodies. Each council consists of some twenty-six persons, appointed by the Secretary of State for Economic Affairs. Most of the members are drawn from both sides of industry, the local authorities and the universities. Their functions are to assist in the formulation of regional policies and to comment on the regional implications of national economic policy.

The regional boards are composed of from fifteen to twenty officials drawn from government departments. They take the initiative in suggesting plans for the regions. The boards, which are chaired by an official of the DEA, are expected to work closely with local authorities in the regions and to co-ordinate the work of central government departments. As far as possible they are housed in the same building in cities designated as regional capitals.

The regional councils are particular examples of the numerous advisory committees which form part of the British system of public administration. Since they are composed of persons already burdened with other duties, who meet infrequently for relatively short periods, the influence of councils on thinking in Whitehall is probably limited. Much depends on the drive and determination of the chairman, who has the unusual right to attend meetings of the corresponding regional board.

In comparison with local authorities, regional councils and advisory committees, generally, are undemocratic. The members of local authorities, with the exception of aldermen, are directly elected. They are responsible to the extent that they can be turned out of office by the local electorate. The members of regional councils represent nobody but themselves and are chosen on the advice of officials who consult interested bodies.

However, many members of the regional councils are drawn from the local authorities. They are mostly elected representatives but may include local officials. It is a reasonable assumption that they have more knowledge and experience of local problems than the civil servants who sit on the boards. They constitute a useful link with local planning bodies, physical planning being one of the functions of certain local authorities. For example, the Region for North-west England embraces twenty-four planning authorities, whose responsibilities impinge in various ways on regional economic problems.[57]

The regional boards, too, are nothing new. They are in essence a form of interdepartmental committee. The power delegated to officers by their respective departments varies. The regional controllers of the Board of Trade, which has a long-established regional organization, are permitted considerable discretion, including the granting of industrial development certificates

[57] See article Regional Men, *The Economist*, 24 April 1965. Also *Economic Planning in the Regions*, HMSO, 1966.

for buildings up to 50,000 square feet. The principal regional officers of the Ministry of Health, however, are reported to have no executive powers and virtually no staff. Some departments have no representatives permanently stationed in the regions. They dispatch an official from London to attend meetings.[58]

The autonomy of the regional boards is clearly limited. The members are drawn from an administrative elite which has centralist inclinations. Each regional policy must fit into a national policy for which the Cabinet and particular ministers have responsibility. The most powerful economic department, the Treasury, has no regional organization and is not represented on the boards. Furthermore, the boards are inadequately staffed to perform their functions of gathering information, preparing briefs, staffing meetings, and conducting research.

These generalizations must be qualified to take into account varying circumstances. Some regions appear to be more rational than others from the economic point of view. The Region for South-west England stretches for over 300 miles and takes in some pretty diverse territory and interests. The Scottish Region, on the other hand, although it is too large, has long been recognized as a problem area, is well represented in the Commons, and is assisted by a separate department in Whitehall.

There have been complaints from councils that they are being treated in an off-hand fashion. The chairman of the South-west Council was infuriated by the decision of the Ministry of Transport to build a new liner port at Bristol without consulting the council. The South-east Council has complained that it was not consulted over the Government's original plan to build a third London airport at Stansted. The chairman of the Northern Council has expressed disappointment over the lack of response to its study entitled *Challenge of the Changing North*. The Government replied that it had to bear in mind the national economic situation and the aspirations of other regions. It would seem that

[58] T. E. Chester and I. R. Gough, Regionalism in the balance: Whitehall and Townhall at the crossroads?, *District Bank Review*, March 1966.

regional councils and boards play a subordinate role in the formulation of economic policy.[59]

It remains to consider the position of the National Board for Prices and Incomes and to refer briefly to the functions of other economic departments.

The Prices and Incomes Board and Other Economic Departments

In December 1964, after strenuous efforts on the part of the Secretary of State for Economic Affairs, the Government, employers' representatives, and unions issued a joint statement of intent on prices, productivity, and incomes. Amongst other things, it was agreed that incomes should be kept in line with productivity. In February 1965 a White Paper was published on the Machinery of a Prices and Incomes Policy.[60] The ineffective National Incomes Commission was wound up, and the watch on incomes and prices split between NEDC and the new Prices and Incomes Board. NEDC was to keep general movements under review and the PIB was to investigate particular cases referred to it by the Government.

The next month Mr. Aubrey Jones, a Conservative MP who was also an industrialist and former minister, was appointed chairman of the PIB for a five-year period at a salary of £15,000 a year. Plans were soon announced for keeping incomes from rising more than 3½ per cent a year. The reaction of the trade unions was far from enthusiastic, to say the least. But since they are closely tied to the Labour Party most unions felt obliged to give the Government support. The main opposition came from

[59] See *The Times*, 29 July 1966, 18 May 1967, and 5 Sept. 1967. The vice-chairman of the South-west Council resigned in March 1968, claiming that Whitehall pre-empted councils by taking decisions regardless of their recommendations. The chairman of the South-west Council was due to leave the following month on taking up a post in London. See report and letter in *The Times*, 27 March 1968. For various meanings of "regionalism" see B. C. Smith, *Regionalism in England*, Acton Society, 1964–5.

[60] Cmd. 2577, 1965.

the Transport and General Workers' Union. At the annual conference of trade unions in September 1965 the General Secretary of the TUC was able to secure a majority for a wage review plan to be operated through the TUC, but there was a big minority vote against the plan.

In November another White Paper appeared, outlining proposals for what was termed "an early warning" system.[61] After some difficulties, legislative effect was given to these proposals. The result of this legislation was that the Government could hold up a price or income increase for a month while it decided whether to refer it to the PIB. There could then be a further three months' delay until the PIB reported. By July 1966 even the 3½ per cent limit was abandoned in favour of a nil norm, to be followed by a period of severe restraint. Under later legislation, passed in 1967, the PIB was empowered to recommend the delay of an income or price increase for a six-month period.[62]

Now on any view this is a remarkable example of positive intervention by a government in the management and direction of the economy. But in practice the scale of the task defeats the objective. By December 1965 sixteen references had been made to the PIB and it had reported on six of them. During the period of the nil norm its task was eased, since this applied throughout the economy. But the Board's capacity to tackle numerous references is limited by the smallness of its staff, many of whom work on a part-time basis.

The chairman is seeking to extend the role of the PIB. He has stated that the PIB should concentrate on the long-term rather

[61] *Prices and Incomes Policy: An Early Warning System*, Cmd. 2808, HMSO, 1965.

[62] *White Paper Prices and Incomes Standstill*, Cmd. 3073, HMSO, 1966. In March 1968, following a deflationary budget, the 3½ per cent norm was back in favour and the Government announced plans to extend its power to delay pay and price increases, scheduled to expire in August. The new maximum period of delay would be 12 months. The power would only be exercised on the recommendation of the PIB, which would be strengthened. See Parliamentary Report in *The Times*, 22 Mar. 1968, and White Paper, *Productivity, Prices and Incomes in 1968 and 1969*, Cmd. 3590, HMSO, April 1968.

than on the solution of short-term crises.[63] But the Government necessarily looks for short-term results from the PIB, because unexpected problems arise which call for immediate action. One example is the decision to refer the affairs of nationalized industries to the PIB.

This decision followed an outcry when a substantial rise in electricity prices was announced in September 1967. It was taken without reference to the chairman of the PIB, but it was certain to give rise to many conflicts and problems. In the first place, the PIB was already fully occupied and had to farm out work to private firms of management consultants.[64]

In the second place, the PIB, an arm of the executive, is now invading the territory of the Select Committee on Nationalized Industries. If there is to be some sort of efficiency audit of the nationalized industries, whoever is responsible should be answerable to the Committee and the Commons.[65]

The PIB is also treading on the toes of departments which are responsible for the nationalized industries, including the Ministry of Transport, Ministry of Power, and the Treasury.[66]

In 1965, for example, the DEA refused the Welsh Gas Board permission to raise its prices. But the Board had been requested to raise prices by the Ministry of Power, which had sought guidance from the Treasury. The Treasury was anxious that the Board should achieve a surplus of 10 per cent, a target agreed in 1961. If it failed to do so extra capital would have to be found out of general taxation. The Secretary of State for Economic Affairs passed the matter to the PIB and the issue was ultimately

[63] See article, The progress of Aubrey Jones, *The Sunday Times*, 25 July 1965; also article, Progress report on Prices Board, *The Times*, 2 Dec. 1965.

[64] Article, Lifting the veil round the Prices and Incomes Board, *The Times*, 29 Aug. 1967.

[65] See letter from Nigel Birch, MP, *The Times*, 13 Sept. 1967.

[66] The PIB has complained that some departments shelter the industries they sponsor. The industries may be privately or publicly owned. See *2nd Annual Report of the Prices and Incomes Board*, Cmd. 3394, HMSO, 1967. In March 1968 the PIB, in addition to one on public transport in London, produced three reports on nationalized enterprises, namely, the Post Office, Cmd. 3574, the Gas Industry, Cmd. 3575, and the Central Electricity Generating Board, Cmd. 3576.

resolved.[67] But it is still not clear whether a nationalized industry should conform to a general policy of price restraint, or whether it must pursue the financial objectives agreed with the Treasury.

In so far as its work overlaps that of other bodies, the PIB is in the same position as the DEA. A résumé of some of the functions of other government departments will demonstrate the point.

The Board of Trade, after losing responsibility for regional planning and the sponsorship of certain industries, has recently enjoyed a revival of fortune. It has taken over responsibility for relations with Europe from the DEA, and its Minister, Mr. Crosland, stands high in the Labour Party hierarchy. The department is responsible for tariff policy and combats monopolies and restrictive practices. It has executive duties in connection with the location of industry which make it rather more influential than the DEA with respect to regional planning. The PIB depends on its co-operation in its attempts to control prices.

The DEA is said to have no executive responsibilities. But any pay claim may bring it into conflict with other departments, especially if it leads to a dispute. During a threatened rail strike, in February 1966, the negotiating machinery of the Ministry of Labour was bypassed because of the existence of the DEA. And the Ministry of Transport was also naturally involved. The Prime Minister finally intervened personally, which blurred responsibilities still further. In April 1966 the Prime Minister announced that in future the DEA would be responsible for general strategy on incomes and prices; the Board of Trade and Ministry of Labour were to have executive responsibility for prices and incomes respectively. But this edict did little to clarify the position. In April 1968 incomes policy was made the responsibility of the Department of Employment and Productivity, formerly the Ministry of Labour.

This by no means exhausts the complications. The Foreign Office plays a vital part in international trade and finance. The Ministry of Agriculture, Fisheries, and Food supervises an important sector of the economy where prices are of great significance.

[67] See *The Sunday Times*, 7 Nov. 1965.

The Ministry of Technology exhorts industry to make use of modern techniques and equipment in much the same way as the DEA and little Neddies. It also sponsors machine tools, electronics, and the shipbuilding and aerospace industries.

Given all these economic departments, plus the Cabinet and its committees, there is clearly room for pruning. As it is, it is difficult to pin responsibility on one department or minister when things go wrong. A judicious reallocation of its functions to the Board of Trade and Ministry of Technology could well render the DEA superfluous. In the last analysis, however, responsibility for economic policy rests with the Cabinet, and in particular with the Prime Minister, whether the latter is formally an economic overlord or not.

The value of administrative tinkering is limited if there is no corresponding change of policy. But something is to be gained from a rationalization which would reduce complications and produce a clearer identification of responsibility. As Bacon observed, "Above all things, order, and distribution, and singling out of parts is the life of dispatch; so as the distribution be not too subtle: for he that doth not divide will never enter well into business; and he that divideth too much will never come out of it clearly."[68]

[68] Bacon's *Essays*, Everyman edn., p. 77.

CHAPTER 5

FOREIGN AFFAIRS AND DEFENCE

Participation and Accountability

In economic affairs British governments share power with numerous groups. The latter are involved in a pluralistic system which engages not only government departments, but numerous advisory committees and interest groups. But power and influence vary and participation tends to be restricted to elites claiming to represent major corporate interests.

Pluralism is less apparent in the case of foreign affairs and defence. Relatively speaking, the State here enjoys a monistic position; there are several reasons for this. First, the State alone is competent to deal with other states, because it is the most inclusive association of society. Secondly, the State controls an elaborate system of diplomatic communication. Thirdly, the State recruits and trains the officials who represent the nation in its dealings with other nations. Fourthly, in foreign affairs and defence there is little time to seek unofficial advice and opinion, even when it is wanted. Fifthly, legislation is not required to the same extent as in other areas of government activity. Hence there is less need to consult interests affected by bills drafted in departments. Sixthly, security is involved; therefore information tends to be restricted to a narrow circle. Finally, the interrelationship of domestic and foreign affairs has not always been appreciated. The Government has been left to get on with what was widely regarded as its job.[1]

[1] See J. Frankel, *The Making of Foreign Policy*, Oxford, 1963, p. 84.

Ministers and officials responsible for foreign affairs have therefore traditionally had a very free hand. Parliament is frequently denied information until it is too late to influence events. Ostensibly this is because security might be endangered or delicate negotiations upset. Accountability is further undermined by a tendency towards bipartisanship in foreign policy, so far as the two Front Benches are concerned. Opposition is somewhat unreal in these circumstances.

It is reported that backbenchers can often acquire information about British policy more easily via Washington, or at Nato, than in Westminster.[2]

All officials are inclined to monopolize vital information. Amongst other reasons, it enhances their status. And they are aided and abetted by ministers and the Official Secrets Act. As Weber noted, bureaucracy "seeks to increase the power of the professionally informed by keeping their knowledge and intentions secret".[3] The fact that the higher ranks of the Diplomatic Service are mainly occupied by individuals drawn from a narrow social stratum reinforces this professional tendency.[4] Social exclusiveness is not conducive to democratic accountability via an elected chamber.

In official quarters the Commons has sometimes been confused with outside influences generally. A former Permanent Secretary of the Foreign Office, in order to isolate his department from outside influences, not only avoided talking about foreign affairs at his club but also gave up reading *Hansard*, the official report of parliamentary speeches. Apart from official telegrams he relied on his own reactions and a careful reading of *The Times*.[5] Another former Permanent Secretary has expressed the view that satisfactory information services are impossible in peacetime.

[2] P. Richards, *Parliament and Foreign Affairs*, Allen & Unwin, 1967, p. 153. On bipartisanship see D. G. Bishop, *The Administration of British Foreign Policy*, Syracuse University Press, 1961, ch. 6.

[3] Gerth and Mills (ed.), *From Max Weber*, Routledge, 1948, p. 233.

[4] See *Report of Committee on Representational Services Overseas*, Cmd. 2276.

[5] See J. Mackintosh, *The British Cabinet*, Stevens, 1966, p. 459, fn. 12.

He refers gloomily to the "invincible ignorance" of the public.[6]

It is not surprising that the Commons Select Committee on Agriculture had difficulty in gaining access to correspondence in the keeping of the Foreign Office. If the public is ignorant, it is partly because information is withheld. But the Commons is not the sole source of information about foreign affairs. There is the press, there is television, and there are learned societies.

British newspapers usually give prominence to foreign affairs, but diplomatic correspondents rely heavily on official sources of information. They must maintain reasonably good relations with the executive, which presents a highly united front. The position of British newspapers is sometimes contrasted with the power of the press in the USA.[7] But the separation of the executive from the legislature, the absence of a unified elite of career officials, and a long-established tradition of inspired leaks render the situation in Washington very different from what it is in London.

The Official Secrets Act inhibits reporting because correspondents fear they may lay themselves open to prosecution if they reveal more than a fractional part of what they know or suspect. They are inclined to censor their own work for this reason. Moreover, the Government exercises control through D notices. These warn papers that they risk prosecution if they publish certain information. The system extends to broadcasting and television.[8]

The independent television companies are more or less in the same position as the press. The BBC, as a public corporation, might be thought to be even more open to official influence. In the last resort the Postmaster-General is responsible for its

[6] Sir Ivone Kirkpatrick, *The Inner Circle*, Macmillan, 1959, pp. 199–200. Sir Ivone found it necessary to remind staff that although MPs were often ignorant they were not to be regarded as hostile snoopers (see p. 209).

[7] For example, see A. Howard, Washington and Whitehall, *The Listener*, 21 July 1966.

[8] See *Report of Committee of Privy Councillors Appointed to Inquire into D Notice Matters*, HMSO, June 1967, and White Paper on *D Notice System*, HMSO, June 1967. Also see H. Street, *Freedom, the Individual and the Law*, Penguin, 1963, pp. 207–16.

policy. But official influence is not crudely exerted. It operates, mainly, by appointing the "right" people to fill key positions.[9]

Learned societies, such as the Royal Institute of International Affairs, have a small membership and an even smaller audience. In Britain they do not enjoy the status and influence of, say, the Brookings Institute or Rand Corporation in the USA. In official circles they tend to be looked on as the harmless preoccupation of academics and intellectuals. And intellectuals are regarded as somewhat naïve people, unfamiliar with power politics.[10]

The conduct of foreign affairs, then, is not markedly subject to public opinion or manifest private pressure. But this is not to say that ministers and officials operate in a completely closed system. A public mood exists which sets some limitation on what they can do.[11] But the will of the general public is not explicit enough to be continuously effective. In general the professionals are left to get on with the job.

It may be contended that this will produce efficiency. But efficiency in public administration is not susceptible to measurement, except in certain restricted areas. Systems of government are best judged by the effect they have on the character of the general body of citizens.[12]

Again, the absence of formal consultative machinery should not be taken to imply that there are no back doors leading into the Foreign Office and Ministry of Defence. Nor does it indicate that Whitehall and Westminster are free of the lobbying of numerous interested groups. There is a complicated system of informal organization. Furthermore, the major departments concerned with foreign policy and defence must work in co-operation with other departments. And other departments have

[9] On the BBC see A. Briggs, *History of Broadcasting in the United Kingdom*, Oxford, vol. 1, 1961, vol. 2, 1965. Also see account of abortive attempt of Sir Anthony Eden to put pressure on BBC at time of Suez invasion, in H. Grisewood, *One Thing at a Time*, Hutchinson, 1968.

[10] See E. H. Carr, *The Twenty Years Crisis, 1919–1939*, Macmillan, 1946, p. 16.

[11] See Frankel, *op. cit.*, pp. 70–71.

[12] See G. C. Field, *Political Theory*, Methuen, 1956, chs. 7 and 8. Also Rousseau, *The Social Contract*, Everyman edn., ch. 15, pp. 77–80.

numerous outside connections which are thus drawn into overseas affairs.

The main reason for interdepartmental activity is the close connection of foreign policy with economic and social problems. Economic activity in particular is increasingly internationalized and the dividing line between domestic and foreign policies, never very distinct, is difficult to discern.

From the economic point of view, Britain cannot isolate herself from events, political and economic, in other parts of the world. If the USA runs into balance of payments difficulties and raises interest rates to attract foreign capital, Britain may have to follow suit. She may use diplomacy and try to persuade the USA to solve its problem in some other way. A recession in Germany may adversely affect the demand for British exports. Efforts may have to be made to deter Germany from imposing import restrictions on British goods. No competent modern diplomat can afford to be ignorant of the economic aspects of his work.

But political motives may predominate over economic; in most cases the two are inextricably mixed. All countries do things which are economically damaging to themselves in order to create even greater difficulties for other countries whose policies they dislike. Sometimes these manœuvres have the advantage of distracting attention from domestic politics. Thus Arab countries, for a time, at least, may deny oil to Britain. Britain may refuse to sell arms to South Africa. And France is suspected of encouraging speculation against sterling at various times.[13] It follows that international relations are of interest to government economic departments, the Bank of England and numerous private financial and industrial concerns.

Some departments and industries are affected by international relations because they deal with technological matters. For example, the Ministry of Technology and the aircraft industry are responsible for co-operative projects like the Anglo-French Concorde.

[13] See *The Sun*, 19 July 1966. Also article, France overplaying the gold hand, *The Times*, 1 Sept. 1966, and letter from Paul Einzig, *The Listener*, 9 Feb. 1967.

The Post Office develops communications by satellite, which entails international agreement; or it may be embroiled in some conflict of international interest.[14] Every armaments and equipment manufacturer is anxious to get a share of contracts to supply international defence organizations like Nato. Home Office policy on immigration affects foreign relations. So may Ministry of Labour decisions regarding the employment of foreign labour.

In short, the Foreign Office does not monopolize international relations, though it has the leading role. It has to collaborate with other departments and appreciate the interests of British firms and industries. In the circumstances one may question the wisdom of having separate Home and Diplomatic Services. The possibility of integration is apparently remote; the answer therefore appears to lie in greater movement and secondment between the two services.

The relative decline in Britain's position as an independent economic and military power compels her to rely more on diplomacy to achieve objectives. The effectiveness of diplomacy depends in part on the organization of the Foreign Office. This is based on both geographical and functional principles, but political influences prevail.

The Organization of the Foreign Office[14a]

Foreign Office officials are charged with the task of advising the Foreign Secretary on the political situation in various parts of the world. Their work is intensely political and this is the distinguishing feature of the department. Its organization should reflect political realities and facilitate the analysis of events in a world which is in a constant state of flux. Because events move swiftly, the organization of the Foreign Office is under constant pressure.

[14] For example, see report on systems of colour television involving the Post Office, BBC, ITV, the British Radio Equipment Manufacturers' Association, and interests in France and West Germany, *The Times*, 20 July 1966.

[14a] See Appendix (7).

The Office, as it is known in Whitehall, is divided into a number of divisions, somewhat confusingly called departments. The departments are assigned to one of several categories, namely Geographical, Economic, Functional, and Information.

The Geographical Group comprises some nine or ten departments; the number varies from time to time. Efforts are made not to overburden any one department, even when this means splitting a geographical area which would normally be considered a political and economic entity. For example, in 1965 the Geographical Departments included the following: American; Arabian; Eastern; North and East African; West and Central African; Far East; South-east Asia; Western; Northern; and Central.[15]

Since 1965 geographical niceties have generally been subordinated to political realities. The Western Department is responsible for United Kingdom relations with France, Italy, Belgium, the Netherlands, Luxembourg, West Germany, and East Germany. It thus takes in all the Common Market countries. The inclusion of East Germany appears something of a political and economic anomaly, but its affairs can hardly be isolated from those of West Germany.

At one time a separate Southern Department existed. This handled relations with Italy, Hungary, Romania, Yugoslavia, and Bulgaria. Italy was thus separated from the department which dealt with the other Common Market countries and lumped in with several members of the communist bloc. When the Southern Department was broken up all its other responsibilities went to the Northern Department, which was already responsible for Albania, Czechoslovakia, Poland, and the USSR. The so-called Geographical Departments are therefore mainly organized on the basis of political alignments and régimes. They are sometimes referred to as the Political Departments. This is clearly a more

[15] For latest details see *The Diplomatic Service List*, HMSO, published annually. Also see *Her Majesty's Ministers and Heads of Public Departments*, HMSO, issued five times each year. See Appendix (8).

sensible basis of organization than any slavish adherence to the geographical principle.

The Northern Department has lost responsibility for such countries as Sweden and Denmark. These now come under the Central Department, which handles relations with the members of the European Free Trade Area and a few countries which do not clearly fit into any political or economic association. For example, the Central Department's responsibilities include Finland, the Irish Republic, and Spain.

It is essential that the work of the political departments is co-ordinated, for no political relationship is purely bilateral. The American Department is responsible for relations between the USA and Britain, but this affects the latter's relations with other countries, which may be the concern of, say, the Western Department—France, for example.

A failure of communication between departments can have serious repercussions. If the American Department enters into some understanding with the USA without informing or consulting other departments, which can assess the implication for other countries, relations with the latter are apt to become strained and complications ensue. Yet the possibility of a failure of communication is always present.

There is a natural tendency for the officials of any one department to see things from the point of view of the representatives of the countries for which they are responsible and with whom they have most contact. They may fail to appreciate that an issue which seems relatively minor in one part of the world may be differently regarded in an area which is the concern of another department.

Specialization on the politics of particular areas can produce conflicting attitudes in the Office. At the time of the Suez operation, in 1956, the Permanent Secretary is reported to have had little interest in Middle East affairs and to have merely questioned the wisdom of having any understanding with the French. On the other hand, a group of under-Secretaries, anxious to maintain Britain's real or imaginary special relationship with the USA, which was opposed to the venture, signed a round-robin opposing the operation.[16]

There are other possibilities of internal conflict stemming from Middle East policies. The Eastern Department, for instance, handles relations with Israel, and the North and East African Department is responsible for relations with Egypt. Since it is clearly difficult to follow Middle Eastern policies which satisfy both Egypt and Israel, a certain amount of tension could develop between the two departments in the Office.

Complete harmony in any organization, even the most simple, is seldom possible for any great length of time. Some degree of conflict is desirable as a means of stimulating activity and change, providing it is kept under control.[17] In any case, the political departments need to keep conflict within bounds and to maintain formal and informal channels of communication. To succeed, they must agree on the ultimate goals of the larger organization of which they are part. In effect, the members of the Foreign Office must share the same values.

The activities of the political departments cannot be isolated from those of the economic and functional departments. The Economic Group includes the Economic Relations Department, the European Economic Organizations Department, and the Oil Department.

The Functional Group includes the Permanent Secretary's Department, the General Department, the Atomic Energy and Disarmament Department, and the Legal Department. The title "Functional" is somewhat misleading. The group is best regarded as one which comprises those departments which are not political or economic. The Functional Group includes certain departments which are responsible for relations with particular institutions. For example, there is the United Nations (Political) Department, the United Nations (Economic and Social) Depart-

[16] H. Thomas, *The Suez Affair*, Weidenfeld & Nicolson, 1966, pp. 38 and 139.

[17] See B. Gross, *The Managing of Organizations*, Collier–Macmillan, 1964, vol. 1, pp. 265–79.

ment, and the Western Organizations and Co-ordination Department.

In most cases the titles of these departments indicate their functions. The Permanent Secretary's Department briefs ministers and official representatives at international gatherings. It contacts other government departments about matters which affect the Office, even though it may not have the major responsibility. The General Department is concerned with such matters as civil aviation, shipping, telecommunications, and exchange control. The Western Organizations and Co-ordination Department is responsible for relations with bodies like Nato, the Council of Europe, and Western European Union. The Economic Relations Department co-ordinates the economic work of the Foreign Office and conveys its views to other departments in Whitehall.

The existence of the Economic Group does not mean that the political departments ignore economic matters. In general, political departments are responsible for those aspects of economic affairs which are thought to be of bilateral interest only, but there are few such cases. It is therefore essential that, say, Western Department works closely with the European Economic Organizations Department and the Western Organizations and Co-ordination Department. Britain's attempts to join the Common Market are the concern of all these departments, and are of interest to others, such as the American Department.

The political departments responsible for Egypt and Iran maintain close contact with the Oil Department. But the Oil Department will also be in touch with the American Department, since oil may come from the USA, particularly when there is political upheaval in the Middle East. In fact, the work of the political and economic departments is so intimately related that the advantages of having separate economic departments is questionable.

It is possible that relieving the political departments of certain economic responsibilities lightens their already heavy load. It may be that the Foreign Office does not wish its scarce economic expertise to be spread too thinly throughout several political departments. Furthermore, although the political departments contain some economists, they are mainly the preserve of generalists, who might not welcome an influx of economists. Finally, the existence of separate economic departments helps to counter criticism that the Office does not appreciate the economic implications of diplomacy.[18]

Amongst the departments in the Information Group are those dealing with cultural relations and news. The News Department is particularly important.

The presentation and timing of news calls for political judgement and experience. This is signified by the fact that the News Department is under the direct supervision of the Permanent Secretary. The position of the Foreign Secretary in Parliament and the country is affected by its work. It is the duty of the News Department to advise the Foreign Secretary, and other members of the Office, of trends in public opinion relating to foreign policy. It maintains close contact with the diplomatic correspondents of both the British and foreign press.[19]

The Foreign Office, in common with other departments, is anxious to decide for itself what the outside world shall know or not know about its activities.[20] There is always the possibility of information leaking out via one of the other departments in Whitehall. In particular, the Office has had to collaborate with the Commonwealth Office on many matters, but the two departments have now been merged.

Before the merger, the Commonwealth Office had major responsibility for relations with Commonwealth countries.

[18] On the interrelationship of political and economic work see *Report of the Committee on Representational Services Overseas*, Cmd. 2276, paras. 206–11. Also see paras. 233–55 on commercial functions and interchange of staff with industry.

[19] See Lord Strang, *The Diplomatic Career*, Deutsch, 1962, pp. 88–89.

[20] Secrecy appeals to politicians as well as to officials. When Sir Robert, later Lord, Vansittart, then Permanent Secretary at the Foreign Office, told Neville Chamberlain he might stand for Parliament, the Prime Minister told him he could not do so because he knew too much. See I. Colvin, *Vansittart in Office*, Gollancz, 1965, p. 171.

Since August 1966, when the Colonial Office was wound up, it had also looked after the affairs of dependent territories.

Whether there are any substantial advantages for the United Kingdom in the continued existence of the Commonwealth is debatable. It may be going too far to describe the Commonwealth as a "gigantic farce", as one anonymous writer has done.[21] But such countries as Australia, New Zealand, and Canada are increasingly tied to the USA in various ways; and certain African states in the Commonwealth are something less than friendly towards Britain. For those who believe Britain's future lies in closer links with Europe, the Commonwealth is an anachronism and a nuisance.[22]

There is bound to be some confusion when there is a separate Commonwealth Office. Pakistan, for example, is allied to non-Commonwealth countries, such as the USA, Iran, and Turkey, through membership of the Central Treaty Organization and the South-east Asia Treaty Organization. But the Commonwealth Office has been the main link with Pakistan, although the Foreign Office has responsibility for Cento and Seato.

Again, the analysis of problems relating to West Africa has not been simplified by the existence of two overseas departments. Liberia, the Ivory Coast, Toga, and the Cameroons, for instance, have always been the concern of the Foreign Office; but Ghana, Nigeria, and Sierra Leone have hitherto been the responsibility of the Commonwealth Office.

It is often impossible to isolate the affairs of a Commonwealth country from those of interested non-Commonwealth countries. Cyprus is a case in point. As a member of the Commonwealth it came within the ambit of the Commonwealth Office. But political tension on the island is mainly the result of conflict between the Greek and Turkish communities which look to Greece and Turkey respectively. These countries are the province of the

[21] A Conservative, Patriotism based on reality not on dreams, article in *The Times*, 2 April 1964.

[22] See K. Younger, *Changing Perspectives in British Foreign Policy*, Oxford, *passim*.

Foreign Office; they are also members of Nato, and other Nato countries, such as the USA, have an interest in preserving peace in Cyprus.[23]

It has clearly been important that the Commonwealth Office and the Foreign Office should have worked harmoniously together. Since the creation of a single Diplomatic Service they have tended to do so, but logic supports the idea of a single overseas department.

The proposed merger of the two departments was announced in March 1968; it is expected to be complete by the autumn. The Foreign Secretary will then be responsible for both foreign and Commonwealth affairs. In making an announcement in the Commons, the Prime Minister asserted that the amalgamation implied no change of attitude or approach to the Commonwealth connection. No other Commonwealth government, he said, now had a separate department dealing with Commonwealth relations. He was asking the Foreign Secretary to bear in mind the importance of making arrangements to ensure that the interests of dependent territories received close and sympathetic attention.

For the Opposition, Mr. Maudling pointed out that from time to time there might be conflict between the claims of foreign policy and the needs or wishes of dependent territories, such as Gibraltar or the Falkland Islands. Was it satisfactory, he asked, that disputes should be resolved in one department rather than at Cabinet level, with representation of both points of view?[24]

So far as the internal organization of the Foreign Office is concerned, it will be even more necessary that there should be good communication and co-ordination between its departments. The possibility of conflict and misunderstanding is partially avoided by fairly frequent reallocations of responsibilities which take account of changed circumstances. In addition,

[23] See Royal Institute of International Affairs, *Cyprus: The Dispute and the Settlement*, Oxford, revised edn., 1958.

[24] Parliamentary Report, *The Times*, 29 March 1968. The case *for* a Commonwealth department is argued by K. E. Robinson in *Public Administration*, Winter 1964. See Appendix (7) and (8).

superintending under-secretaries co-ordinate the work of related departments. Officials who head separate departments which have interrelated functions or responsibilities thus answer to the same superintending under-secretary. One under-secretary, for example, supervises the Western Department and the Western Organizations and Co-ordination Department. Another oversees the West and Central African Department, North and East African Department, Arabian Department, and the Oil Department.

A co-ordinating Permanent Secretary's Committee exists, specifically intended to encourage under-secretaries to give thought to areas other than those for which they are directly responsible. A unified Office view on long-term policy is thus more likely.[25]

Procedure is also designed to assist co-ordination. Routine methods have been developed over the years which ensure the circulation of documents and material to interested parties. A file or paper entering the Office will first reach the hands of someone fairly low down in the hierarchy of a department. If he feels it is beyond his competence to deal with it he immediately passes it on to a more senior official. At each level notes or suggestions may be added. When the subject is of interest to more than one department the file or paper will be circulated accordingly.

This routine is assisted by the small number of people at the top of the hierarchy, and by their propinquity, since they occupy the same building. A common outlook, derived from similar educational and social backgrounds, also assists communication.

Mobility between departments is encouraged to broaden experience and understanding, but it is limited by linguistic, subject and area specialization. There may be some advantage in broadening the experience of a Chinese speaker by assigning him to Western Department. But since there are so few people who speak Chinese, the disadvantages probably outweigh the advantages.

[25] Lord Strang, *op. cit.*, pp. 110–11.

Frequently another department in Whitehall will have to be consulted. In such cases a Foreign Office official will contact the appropriate person in whatever department is concerned. For example, someone in the General Department of the Foreign Office dealing with telecommunications will inform or consult his "opposite" number in the Post Office, and vice versa. Usually they will confer by phone, but they will also sit together on interdepartmental committees and occasionally attend the same conferences.

These procedures sound unexciting and old-fashioned but they apparently work reasonably well. It is not easy to glamorize routine, though it is an essential part of departmental control. To enable the procedures to work effectively the Foreign Office official has got to be a rapid reader, as well as a discerning one, and he must be able to write succinctly and clearly. He must also endure numerous committee meetings with whatever fortitude he can muster.

Common service sections may also help to secure co-ordination. These provide a service for all, or most, of the other sections in a department. The Legal Department of the Foreign Office, for example, serves all other departments of the Office which seek legal opinion or advice. A typing pool is a more humble illustration of an internal common service arrangement. Common services may also be provided by an independent organization, outside the user department. Thus the Central Office of Information may handle publicity for another department, such as the Post Office or Ministry of Social Security. A Diplomatic Service Administration Office has hitherto served both the Commonwealth Office and the Foreign Office with respect to personnel and other matters.

The advantages of using a common service department or section are mainly economic. A single, fully employed legal department or typing pool is cheaper to run than two or more such departments or pools, using similar but under-utilized staff and equipment. A fully employed section, serving other sections, will tend to have a volume of work which will permit it to operate on a large scale and make use of specialization and division of labour, usually considered conducive to increased output.

But administrative complications may offset economic benefits, especially when the common service is provided by an external department rather than by an internal unit. The user department loses some of its autonomy and control. It may find that priority is not being given to its urgent requirements, or that the standard of service is not satisfactory. In either case it may prove difficult to rectify the matter.

The relationship of the common service department and the user department varies according to the nature of the service. A user department will be more inclined to challenge the competence of a publicity or information department than of a legal department. Lawyers are rightly thought to be specially qualified to give legal advice and laymen hesitate to dispute their professional opinion. On the other hand, the standards of some common services are easy to judge, and when remedies are needed they are not difficult to obtain. Most people feel they can tell when they are getting satisfactory service from a typing pool.[26]

This account of Foreign Office organization is far from complete. Space precludes consideration of a number of other important departments, such as the Defence Department, the Scientific Relations Department, the Planning Staff, and the Passport Control Office. In general, however, it can be said that the organization of the Office compares reasonably well with that of other Whitehall departments, partly because the recommendations of the Committee on Representational Services Overseas were acted upon.

If there are doubts, they are connected with the size and character of the Diplomatic Service rather than with organization. There is a dearth of people with scientific, technical, or industrial training and experience. And, in spite of efforts to remedy the situation, the Service remains socially unrepresentative. The

[26] See Sir Robert Fraser, The virtues and vices of common services, in *Common Service in Public Administration*, Royal Institute of Public Administration (no date).

social origins and sympathies of politicians and officials in certain foreign governments are very different from those of their British counterparts. This must make mutual understanding difficult and produce a lack of rapport.

The relative smallness of the Diplomatic Service, less than 20,000, places great strain on its members, because they have to maintain relations with states throughout the world. Since they do a variety of jobs conscientiously they tend to be overworked. Yet they can expect little sympathy when the inevitable mistakes occur. The more cynical amongst them might endorse the remark quoted by Sir Henry Taylor, "You may write off the first joint of your finger for the Government, and then you may write off the second joint, and all they will say of you is, what a remarkably short-fingered man."[27]

By way of contrast, the Ministry of Defence has a headquarters staff almost as large as the entire Diplomatic Service and it disposes of vast sums of money. The Defence Estimates for 1967–8 amounted to £2205 million, about 23 per cent of total government expenditure for the year. The Civil Estimates show a mere £255 million for all types of expenditure on Commonwealth and Foreign Services. This includes money designated for the Ministry of Overseas Development and the British Council.

Although the Foreign Office and Ministry of Defence work closely with one another on Cabinet committees and intelligence committees, their organizational problems are very different. This is partly because of variations in size and function and partly because the people who staff the Ministry of Defence are much less homogeneous than those who are in the Diplomatic Service. The contrast between the two departments illustrates the difficulty of making generalizations about organization with respect to public administration.

Formal organization for defence has undergone considerable change since 1945. Its evolution may be traced through various phases, each of which will be separately considered.

[27] Sir Henry Taylor, *Autobiography*, London, vol. 1, ch. 23, 1874; vol. 2, 1877.

The Ministry of Defence, 1945–56

In this period the Ministry of Defence was conceived as a small department, responsible for overall defence policy. Its main function was to co-ordinate the activities of the War Office, Admiralty, and Air Ministry, which existed as separate departments. A single ministry which would absorb the Service departments was regarded as unsound and impracticable.

Also rejected was any suggestion of a Combined General Staff, working in isolation from the Service departments at the Ministry of Defence. Instead, following hallowed British tradition, the senior professional heads of the forces, the Chief of the Imperial General Staff, the Chief of Naval Staff, and the Chief of Air Staff, were to make up a Joint Staff, and remain the operational heads of their respective Services.

The Joint Staff advised the Minister of Defence on policy, and its members were responsible for the execution of policy. The allegedly fatal divorce between policy and execution, thought proven by an examination of the captured archives of the German Combined Staff, the *Oberkommando der Wehrmacht*, was thus avoided. It was contended that the Ministry of Defence, properly advised by the Joint Staff, would be free to concentrate on planning and long-term policy. The details of day-to-day administration could be left to the Service departments.

These principles were embodied in a White Paper on Defence in 1946.[28] The Prime Minister assumed ultimate responsibility for defence, aided by the Minister of Defence. A Defence Committee of the Cabinet, chaired by the Prime Minister, was to consider general strategy and co-ordinate all departmental activity for war purposes. The Defence Committee thus had executive authority. The Minister of Defence and the three political heads of the Service departments were members of the Committee, but only the Minister of Defence was a member of the full

[28] Cmd. 6923.

Cabinet. The Chiefs of Staff advised the Defence Committee and attended its meetings. They also had direct access to the Prime Minister if they so desired.

In practice the Minister of Defence was in a weak position *vis-à-vis* the Service departments. What influence he had was the result of persuasion and suggestion. His department was not only small, but it also lacked independent specialist and technical advice. It was largely confined to providing secretarial services for numerous interdepartmental and other committees concerned with defence.

In these circumstances, the control of the Minister of Defence over the distribution of resources was, to say the least, somewhat unreal. He was not in a position to judge the merits of rival Service bids. But he faced unpopularity with two Services whenever he made a decision favourable to the third. If he was to appear "neutral" in the matter of Service rivalry he could not deny any one Service a reasonable share, however irrelevant its role in modern warfare.

In his deliberations the Minister of Defence was assisted by a Joint Intelligence Staff, consisting of the directors of intelligence of the three Services, plus representatives of the Foreign Office and security organizations. But the loyalties of the directors of intelligence really lay with their respective Services. The same was true of the Joint Planning Staff, made up of the directors of plans of the three Services.

On the Defence Committee of the Cabinet the Minister of Defence confronted the three Service ministers and the Chiefs of Staff. Each Service minister was briefed by a department which was bigger and better informed than the Ministry of Defence. Any Service minister could appeal to the Prime Minister or Cabinet against the proposals of either the Committee or the Minister of Defence.

Furthermore, there were no pressure groups operating on behalf of the Ministry of Defence. In Parliament and Whitehall the Service departments were supported by such bodies as the Navy League, the Army League, the RAF Association, and the Retired Officers' Association. And there were senior ministers and officials with sentimental attachments to particular Services.

The industrial lobby, directly or indirectly interested in the supply of armaments and equipment, did not deal with the Ministry of Defence but with the Service departments and the Ministry of Supply.[29] Until it was dismantled, in 1959, the Ministry of Supply undermined the control of the Ministry of Defence over the Service departments.

Matters were not helped by the rapid turnover of Defence Ministers. There were seven in the twelve years between 1945 and 1957. The Service ministers occupied their posts somewhat longer on average. This strengthened their position *vis-à-vis* the Minister of Defence. Without the backing of the Prime Minister, which could not be guaranteed, the Minister of Defence was relatively impotent.

In 1955 the Prime Minister, Sir Anthony Eden, now Lord Avon, attempted to strengthen the Ministry of Defence in two ways. In a statement to the Commons he announced that in future the Minister of Defence would be responsible not only for the apportionment of resources *between* the Services, but also for ensuring that their distribution *within* each Service was in line with the policy approved by the Defence Committee. In practice, however, the Minister of Defence lacked the staff and technical advice to enable him to exercise effective control. But the new arrangements did give him the formal right to intervene in the affairs of any one Service. Previously he was inclined to act only in matters concerning relations between the Services.

In addition a chairman of the Chiefs of Staff Committee was appointed. His main function was to advise the Cabinet and the Defence Committee, particularly when the Chiefs of Staff could not reach agreement. He was also to represent Britain at international conferences, connected with Nato and other bodies.

[29] See W. P. Snyder, *The Politics of British Defence 1945–62*, Benn, 1964, ch. 5.

The Chiefs of Staff were thus partially excluded, and their influence on policy correspondingly reduced.[30]

The appointment of a chairman indicated dissatisfaction with the way the Chiefs of Staff Committee operated. Hitherto the Cabinet and the Minister of Defence had relied on the Chief Staff Officer of the Ministry of Defence for information about what went on at meetings of the Chiefs of Staff Committee. The Chief Staff Officer was also Deputy Secretary of the Cabinet. In spite of his impressive titles, however, he gave the Chiefs of Staff little trouble. He attended meetings of the Chiefs of Staff Committee in a non-voting capacity but was usually discreet in his revelations. In 1947, however, he had incurred the displeasure of his brother officers by giving the Prime Minister and Minister of Defence copies of a Chiefs of Staff document on defence cuts.[31]

Because of the Korean War, defence expenditure had risen from around 7 per cent of the gross national product, in the late forties, to a figure which was nearer 11 per cent in 1952. This took some of the heat out of inter-Service rivalry for funds. However, a subsequent cutback in defence expenditure revived competition. But even with this reduction, defence expenditure was only just under 9 per cent of GNP in 1956.

Clashes of temperament and inter-Service rivalry scarcely made the Chiefs of Staff Committee an ideal instrument of administration, but the introduction of a chairman did little to remedy matters. The first occupant, Sir William Dickson, a former Chief of Air Staff, had no independent assistance. He has been described as a go-between, with no power to overcome the deals and log-rolling of the Chiefs of Staff, who could always meet informally without his presence.[32]

Little might have been done to change defence organization had not the Suez operation exposed its inadequacies. During that episode the Minister of Defence, who shortly before had been

[30] See F. A. Johnson, Politico-military organization in the United Kingdom, *Journal of Politics*, May 1965, pp. 342–3.

[31] See General Sir Leslie Hollis, *One Marine's Tale*, Deutsch, 1956, pp. 147–54.

[32] Daalder, *British Cabinet Reform 1914–63*, p. 188.

Secretary of State for War, is alleged to have concealed unpleasant facts from the Prime Minister. Similar charges have been laid against the chairman of the Chiefs of Staff Committee. Political leadership, which should have been provided by the Defence Committee, was wavering and uncertain. The economic consequences of the operation were underestimated. A sterling crisis was sparked off, the worst since 1945 up to that time. And it could not be solved without devaluation or the assistance of the USA, which was opposed to the invasion. The whole affair has been justly described as "a gross failure of administrative co-ordination".[33]

The experience showed that the defence machinery creaked and was in need of an overhaul. Suez ushered in the Macmillan–Sandys era of defence organization, the first stage in the transformation of the Ministry of Defence from a weak co-ordinating department into one of the strongest in Whitehall.

The Ministry of Defence, 1957–63

Mr. Macmillan, who succeeded Eden as Prime Minister, had served at the Ministry of Defence during the premiership of Sir Winston Churchill. He was aware of the weakness of the department. And as Chancellor of the Exchequer in the Eden administration he had experienced the difficulty of containing defence expenditure and Service rivalry for funds.

One of the principal aims of the new government was to restore confidence in British military prowess. Mr. Duncan Sandys, who served as Minister of Defence from January 1957 to October 1959, could therefore generally rely on the support of the Prime Minister in any conflicts he might have with the Service ministers and the Chiefs of Staff.

In a statement to the Commons, in January 1957, Mr. Macmillan made it clear that the Minister of Defence had formal authority

[33] See P. Abrams, The late profession of arms, *European Journal of Sociology*, 1965, no. 2, p. 255. Also see Daalder, *op. cit.*, p. 189, and P. Calvocoressi, Suez—ten years after, *The Listener*, 21 July 1966, p. 78.

to decide all matters of policy affecting the size, shape, disposition, organization, and supply of the armed forces. Policy relating to defence research and development was also his responsibility. But all this was subject to the approval of the Cabinet and the Defence Committee. And the Treasury was naturally to be consulted on the financial aspects of defence policy.

There remained some ambiguity about the relationship of the Minister of Defence and the Service ministers because they outnumbered him on the Defence Committee; and in the last analysis the Committee had greater authority than the Minister of Defence.

There is evidence that Mr. Sandys wished to create a single Armed Service by merging the Army, Navy, and Air Force.[34] But the Service ministers and Chiefs of Staff, who retained their right of direct access to the Prime Minister and Cabinet, were understandably opposed to any such plan. In July 1957 the Prime Minister scotched rumours of Service integration in another statement in the Commons.

One change which did occur was the combining of the posts of Chairman of the Chiefs of Staff Committee and Chief of Staff to the Minister of Defence. But far more important than this was a shift of emphasis towards reliance on nuclear rather than on conventional weapons. This was indicated in a White Paper issued soon after Mr. Sandys became Minister of Defence.

The White Paper also formally strengthened the control exercised by the Ministry of Defence. Financial planning was to be put on a five-year basis. Service manpower was to be reduced from around 700,000 to under 400,000 in the period 1957–62. Conscription was to be ended by 1960 if sufficient volunteers came forward. Commitments for the defence of Europe were to be cut and some units were to be abolished. A mobile Central Reserve of Land, Sea and Air Forces, stationed in the United Kingdom, was to be held ready to meet obligations in the Commonwealth and Far East.[35]

[34] Johnson, *op. cit.*, p. 344.
[35] *Outline of Future Policy*, Cmd. 124, 1957.

The next year yet another White Paper reaffirmed the authority of the Minister of Defence. The only significant modification of the Prime Ministerial statements made in the Commons was the announcement that the Minister of Defence would be responsible for *major* policy, as opposed to policy in general. What constituted major policy was a matter of conjecture, so the change was something of a concession to the Service departments.

In addition, the posts of Chairman of the Chiefs of Staff Committee and Chief of Staff to the Ministry of Defence, already combined in the person of Sir William Dickson, were replaced by the single office of Chief of the Defence Staff. The incumbent was still to chair meetings of the Chiefs of Staff Committee. Formally, the Joint Planning Staff was responsible to him and he issued operational orders. Service ministers retained their right of access to the Prime Minister and Cabinet. The White Paper also announced the setting up of a Defence Board, with vague co-ordinating functions, but this merely replaced a long-standing Service Ministers Committee.[36]

The economic situation was the main cause of the move towards tighter central control. The Government had come to the conclusion that with an unsatisfactory balance of payments position, the country could not afford to spend nearly 9 per cent of GNP on defence. Only France and the USA amongst Britain's Nato allies were spending a greater proportion. The USA could afford to do so. France was embroiled in an expensive colonial war in Algeria. The object of the British Government was to reduce defence expenditure to 7 per cent of GNP and hold it at that level. Even this proportion was high for a country in economic difficulty. West Germany was spending only 4·3 per cent of GNP on defence in 1956.[37]

The Service ministers and their allies the Chiefs of Staff viewed the prospects of economies and tighter central control with something less than enthusiasm. They believed that the planned

[36] Cmd. 476, 1958.

[37] See F. Mulley, *The Politics of Western Defence*, Thames & Hudson, 1962, appendix C, pp. 264–5.

conventional forces were inadequate for the type of operation in which Britain was likely to be involved. They were sceptical about the cost and effectiveness of nuclear missiles. No doubt many officers, unfamiliar with modern weapons technology, felt insecure. Promotion prospects and career structures were adversely affected by the proposed manpower cuts and there was the unwelcome spectre of early retirement. On top of all this was the fear of still further centralization in the future and the eventual disappearance of the Services as separate entities. These human reactions were apparently not sufficiently appreciated by the Minister of Defence. Service resistance to change stiffened.

In 1957, following the White Paper of that year, the Admiralty had organized a conference at Greenwich, ostensibly to make a general survey of defence problems. But the real object was to stress the essential role of the Royal Navy. Amongst the invited guests were three influential Conservative peers interested in shipbuilding and defence matters. One was a former Secretary of State for the Colonies, another was chairman of the Commonwealth Development Finance Company. The Navy's part in the defence of the Commonwealth scarcely needed to be pointed out.

The Admiralty also made certain that plans to cut back the Navy were not overlooked by Commonwealth governments. During his tour of Asia in 1957, Commonwealth representatives several times reminded the Minister of Defence of the vital role of the Navy. And at the Commonwealth Conference, in August, the Prime Minister was urged to reconsider the cuts. The Foreign Office and Colonial Office were also pressing for another look at defence proposals.[38] When the 1958 White Paper appeared the Navy was allocated a larger share of resources than had originally been contemplated and more attention was devoted to the area east of Suez.

The RAF also went on the offensive. In May 1958 it organized a conference to which 300 guests were invited. The policy outlined at the conference bore little resemblance to that of the Minister of Defence. Guided missiles were compared unfavourably with

[38] Snyder, *op. cit.*, pp. 167–9.

the manned bomber and fighter plane. Pilots were said to possess a discretion which guided missiles could not match. Publicity was given to the use of helicopters and the transportation functions of the RAF.[39]

The Army was relatively quiescent. But late in 1959, shortly after Mr. Harold Watkinson, now Lord Watkinson, had replaced Mr. Sandys as Minister of Defence, a senior officer attacked official policy in a speech at the United Services Institution.[40] In Britain such criticism is normally reserved for memoirs published after retirement. It was rumoured that the Secretary of State for War tacitly approved of this public assault on the Ministry of Defence. Questions were asked in the Commons about the speech, and the new Minister of Defence announced that in future he would personally "clear" such speeches.

It is unlikely that these Service forays seriously perturbed the Minister of Defence. Opposition to change was inevitable and the Services were past masters of the art. But the Service ministers and Chiefs were far from united; rivalry for resources was still apparent. Many of the rising generation of younger officers were ready, and even eager, for innovation, including the emergence of a single defence Service.

In fact, however, subsequent events showed that nuclear weapons were useless in "bushfire" operations, such as Britain was involved in in Malaysia. Conventional weapons and forces on an adequate scale were essential. To this extent it could be said that the analysis of the Chiefs of Staff and Service ministers was correct and that of the Ministry of Defence mistaken. Moreover, the threat of a major nuclear war receded as the cold war atmosphere thawed. Drastic defence reforms now seemed less urgent. And those who had doubts about nuclear weapons had the additional satisfaction of seeing many projects come to grief. It was difficult to argue that economies were being secured as examples of abortive expenditure on nuclear weapons came to light. Skybolt, Blue Steel, Blue Streak, Chieftain, and Sea-

[39] See The Air Force shows its shopping list, *The Economist*, 10 May 1958.
[40] See The case of General Cowley, *The Economist*, 14 Nov. 1959.

slug, all came to grief at some stage. Even those weapons which reached the testing stage were of doubtful utility and quickly became obsolete.

In 1959 the creation of the Ministry of Aviation introduced new complications. Mr. Sandys had left Defence to become the first Minister of Aviation. In this capacity he was responsible for all aspects of missile and aircraft development. The Ministry of Defence gained little or no advantage from the demise of the Ministry of Supply and the reallocation of the functions of the old Ministry of Transport and Civil Aviation. In effect the Ministry of Defence remained something of a White Paper tiger. The department may not have been as weak as a former Minister of Defence has suggested, but it was far from powerful.[41]

In general it may be said that there was little fundamental change in defence organization between 1957 and 1963, but the seeds of future change were sown during this period. Expenditure on defence did fall from 8·8 per cent of GNP in 1956 to 7·1 per cent in 1960. But thereafter it rose again, standing at over 8 per cent in 1963. Efforts to peg defence expenditure at £1500 million a year failed. In 1963–4 the defence budget exceeded £2000 million for the first time, but since the Commons was denied essential information it could not tell whether value for money was being obtained. There was a widespread feeling that the Government was in no better position.[42]

The scale of expenditure was partly attributed to the failure of the Ministry of Defence to secure economies by rationalization and the ending of Service rivalry. But given the dispersion of responsibility for defence procurement, and the numerous powerful industrial interests involved, this was an oversimplification. And Service rivalry was bound up with wider political considerations.

British governments in the early sixties believed their standing,

[41] Rt. Hon. Peter Thorneycroft, Defence reforms that would check service rivalries, *The Times*, 23 June 1966.

[42] See R. Fletcher, *£60 a Second on Defence*, MacGibbon & Kee, 1963, *passim*.

internationally and at home, depended on the possession of an independent nuclear deterrent. Skybolt, promised by the USA in 1960, was seized on as just such a weapon since it could be delivered by Britain's ageing force of V-bombers, which were given a new lease of life, thus pleasing the RAF. But two years later the Air Force lobby in Washington failed to save Skybolt from the Congressional axe. Britain was forced to switch to Polaris missiles and nuclear submarines, a change which was welcome to the Royal Navy.[43]

By 1962 the time was ripe for another look at defence organization. Prominent amongst the advocates of a stronger Ministry of Defence was Lord Mountbatten, who had replaced Sir William Dickson as Chief of Defence Staff in 1959. He had built up a staff at the Ministry, consisting of officers seconded to him and to some extent free from attachment to their individual Services. A review of problems was set on foot by Mr. Peter Thorneycroft, now Lord Thorneycroft, soon after he became Minister of Defence in July 1962. The results were submitted to two eminent defence experts, Lord Ismay and Sir Ian Jacob, in January 1963.

The review suggested a strong Ministry of Defence, with subordinate departments organized on functional lines, i.e. on the basis of tasks to be performed. For example, it was proposed that there should be Departments of Personnel and Supply covering the whole of the forces. Lord Ismay and Sir Ian Jacob, it seems, advised against this.

The review plan also suggested that the Chiefs of Staff and their Directors of Plans, Operations and Intelligence should be fully integrated in the Ministry of Defence. They were to have no responsibility for the management of the Services. This would be the concern of separate commanders-in-chief. Lord Ismay and Sir Ian Jacob partially endorsed these proposals. They recommended bringing together the principal policy-making functions of the Service departments, such as the formula-

[43] Lee R. M. Schlesinger, *A Thousand Days*, Deutsch, 1965, pp. 730–9. Also H. Brandon, *The Sunday Times*, 8 Dec. 1963.

tion of strategic plans and the collation and dissemination of intelligence. But day-to-day administration was to remain with smaller versions of the Service departments.[44] These schemes naturally provoked disquiet in the Service departments; but their days were numbered.

The Ministry of Defence Since 1964

In 1963 a White Paper on Defence outlined an entirely new structure, which was to come into force in April of the following year.[45] The separate Service departments were to be abolished and their responsibilities taken over by the Ministry of Defence.

The Ministry was thus transformed from a small co-ordinating department into a large-scale organization, handling a budget of £2000 million annually, and responsible for some 400,000 servicemen and about the same number of civilians. But although the White Paper gave the Secretary of State for Defence complete control over administration, and major responsibility for policy, it remained to translate these intentions into fact.

Under the new arrangements a Cabinet Committee on Defence and Oversea Policy, chaired by the Prime Minister, replaced the old Defence Committee. Subject to Cabinet approval, it decides broad issues of policy. Besides the Prime Minister, the members include the Minister of Defence, the Foreign Secretary, the Secretary of State for Commonwealth Affairs, the Chancellor of the Exchequer and the Home Secretary. The Home Secretary is responsible for civil defence. Other ministers are invited to attend meetings when necessary. The main difference from the former Defence Committee is the disappearance of the Service ministers. The position of the Minister of Defence is correspondingly enhanced. The Defence and Oversea Committee is supported by a committee of officials drawn from the Cabinet Office and government departments.

Formal organization for defence is still basically modelled

[44] See article, Defence organization, *The Times*, 24 April 1963.
[45] *Central Organization for Defence*, Cmnd. 2097, July 1963.

on the 1963 White Paper. But important changes followed another review, undertaken when Labour took office in 1964. These changes have all been intended to strengthen central control and the hand of the Minister of Defence and to inculcate a "Defence" rather than a "Service" outlook.

The Secretary of State for Defence naturally occupies the topmost position in the hierarchy. Since early in 1967 the second tier has consisted of a Minister of Defence (Administration) and a Minister of Defence (Equipment). They deal with aspects of administration affecting all three Services. Below them in the formal organization are three parliamentary under-secretaries of State for Defence, each responsible for a particular Service. They suffered a decline in rank and status when the Ministers of Defence for Administration and Equipment were appointed.

To counteract any centrifugal tendencies which might arise from attachment to a particular Service each parliamentary under-secretary is given "defence" or "functional" responsibilities which cut across Service lines. Under Mr. Healey, Secretary of State for Defence since Labour took office, the Parliamentary Under-Secretary for the Army is responsible for relations with Britain's allies on matters affecting all three Services. The Parliamentary Under-Secretary for the Navy was at one time responsible for dealing with the personnel and administrative problems of all the Services. The Parliamentary Under-Secretary for the RAF looked after the procurement systems of all Services. The appointment of Ministers of Defence for Administration and Equipment entailed some reallocation of functions, but did not imply abandonment of the principle of assigning inter-Service duties to the parliamentary under-secretaries.

There are thus several politicians in the department, each of whom has important functions to perform. The remaining members fall into the administrative group, the military group or the scientific group. All have different professional backgrounds, experiences, and priorities, and therefore special effort is needed to achieve a working relationship. Conflicts of interest and outlook are bound to occur in such a large and diverse organization. The principal co-ordinating device is the Defence Council.

The Defence Council consists of the senior personnel of the department. The Secretary of State for Defence acts as chairman and the other senior politicians are members. Other members are the Chief of Defence Staff, the Chief Scientific Adviser, and the Permanent Under-Secretary of State. Ministers and representatives from other departments attend meetings as required.

The main function of the Defence Council is to consider major defence policy at departmental level. In addition certain regulations, orders and instructions, previously issued by Service Councils, are now issued by the Defence Council.

Immediately below the Defence Council, the Service Chiefs, Administrators, and Scientists are separately organized. The Chiefs of Staff Committee continues to meet under the chairmanship of the Chief of the Defence Staff. It is assisted by the joint efforts of the General Staff, Naval Staff, and Air Staff, which together make up the Defence Staff. The Chiefs of Staff are responsible for the conduct of actual operations.

Operational unity is supported by organization on a Defence rather than on a Service basis. Thus there is a Defence Operations Executive, a Defence Operational Requirements Staff, a Defence Signals Staff and a Defence Intelligence Staff. These are manned by personnel drawn from all three Services.

On a par with the Chiefs of Staff Committee is the Defence Secretariat, consisting of senior administrative class civil servants. The Permanent Secretary of the department, the right-hand man of the Secretary of State, is in command.

For some time, ministers with Service responsibilities were assisted by second permanent under-secretaries. Early in 1968 these were replaced by two functional second secretaries, one for Equipment and one for Administration, each assisting the corresponding Minister of Defence. Any inclination towards identification with a particular Service was thus formally eliminated at very senior official level. The Defence Secretariat, comprising these officials, is divided into sections which deal with such matters as programmes and budget, policy, and administration.

Although programmes are planned and costed on a functional basis, the defence budget was still being presented to Parliament in the form of separate Service Estimates in 1968. By 1970, however, it is intended that there shall be a unified defence vote. Parliament would then vote money for all three Services together.[46]

In a department as large and complex as the Ministry of Defence administrative skills are at a premium. Keeping the wheels turning is a considerable achievement in itself. And when the administrators also control the purse strings their influence is far from negligible.

The Chief Scientific Adviser of the Cabinet supervises the work of the Defence Scientific Staff. This includes a Deputy Chief Scientific Adviser, the chief scientists of the Navy, Army, and Air Force, a nuclear group, and others. The term "scientist" covers a range of backgrounds and interests, but broadly speaking the scientists constitute a group with sufficient homogeneity of outlook to distinguish them from the politicians, administrators and military men in the department. To weld these diverse types into a working whole is an organizational problem.

The Ministry of Defence is thus organized on a somewhat uneasy combination of functional and Service principles. The 1963 White Paper guaranteed the separate existences of the three Services, though it recognized their interdependence in modern warfare. The day-to-day management of the Services is the concern of an Admiralty Board, an Air Force Board, and an Army Board. The Secretary of State for Defence is officially chairman of all three, but normally the parliamentary under-secretaries deputize. The other members include the appropriate Service

[46] See *Statement on the Defence Estimates, 1968*, Cmd. 3540, HMSO, 22 Feb. 1968. The Statement announced two other changes. First, the appointment of a Deputy Chief of Defence Staff, responsible to the Chief of Defence Staff. His main duty is to produce proposals for weapons concepts which conform to defence policy and strategy. Secondly, the separation of responsibility for operations and policy, in that two Assistant Chiefs of Defence Staff have been appointed, one for Operations and one for Policy. The Defence Estimates for 1968–9 amounted to £2271 million, about 6 per cent of GNP, and 0·5 per cent less than the previous year.

Chief of Staff, Scientific Adviser, Second Permanent Under-Secretary, and their immediate aides.

In the terminology of formal organization theory, however, the basic principle embodied in the 1963 White Paper was unity of command. The Secretary of State for Defence, it lays down, "must have complete control both of defence policy and of the machinery for the administration of the three Services". His authority and responsibility is intended to "run unbroken through military, scientific, and administrative staffs throughout the Ministry".[47] Inevitably he must delegate much of his authority, but the basic aim is clear.

In practice complete unity of command is incapable of achievement. Unfortunately, however, dissatisfaction with the organization of the department is often based on the illusion that further administrative change will enable unity of command to be finally realized. There are a number of reasons why this cannot be so.

In the first place, the Secretary of State depends on the advice of numerous experts and specialists. Although he takes final responsibility for decisions, in many cases he can only accept what his "advisers" recommend. Those who are in the so-called line of command do not monopolize decision-taking to the exclusion of their staff or aides. Secondly, unity of command conflicts with division of labour, though both have been described as "principles" of organization. There must be a compromise of some sort, given that a compromise of principles is possible. But organizational theorists can offer little guidance as to the correct balance to be struck between the two. For this reason some writers prefer to describe such notions as unity of command as proverbs, or rules of thumb, rather than principles.[48]

Thirdly, in a department as large and geographically dispersed as the Ministry of Defence, the Secretary of State, and even the Defence Council, must delegate authority and confer discretion

[47] Cmd. 2097, p. 1, para. 9.

[48] On the conflict of "principles" of organization see H. A. Simon, *Administrative Behaviour*, Free Press, 2nd edn., 1965, ch. 2.

on subordinates. This at least modifies unity of command. In 1966 the headquarters staff of the Ministry numbered some 20,000 and there were over 100 officials with the rank of Assistant Secretary or above. Personnel were deployed not only in the Ministry of Defence itself, but in some thirty buildings spread over London and in research and other establishments outside the capital.[49] It is true, however, that modern techniques and methods permit more effective and unified control of large-scale organizations.

Even so, there is another administrative "rule of thumb", namely span of control, which lays down that there exists some limit, usually unspecified, to the number of people which any superior person or body can directly supervise or command. Because of the limit set by span of control, a large-scale organization has many levels of authority. The more numerous the levels, the greater the difficulties of communication, both up and down the hierarchy. This is additional to problems of communication between diverse groups occupying similar levels in the organization.

Communication may be excellent in the sense that each group fully understands the intentions and motives of other groups. But each tends to be unreceptive to policies and plans which they see as contrary to the interests or objectives with which they consciously or unconsciously identify. More often there are failures of communication because people in the same organizational whole have different backgrounds, experiences and values. All this may be concealed behind an atmosphere of formal politeness and co-operation in day-to-day administration.[50]

Unlike the Foreign Secretary, who is supported by a socially

[49] See article, Healey's monster, *The Sunday Times*, 25 Sept. 1966. By April 1968 the Ministry's headquarters staff was expected to total 16,730, nearly 7,500 fewer than four years earlier. See *Statement on Defence Estimates 1968*, Cmd. 3540.

[50] Difficulties of communication are increased in a new department because informal methods have not had time to develop. See Sir Geoffrey Vickers, Communication in economic systems, in Evan, Ayer, *et al.*, *Studies in Communication*, Secker & Warburg, 1955, pp. 77–80.

homogeneous administrative elite, in firm control of a relatively small department, the Secretary of State for Defence tries to control three elites, military, scientific and administrative. His task is complicated by differences *within* each elite, the most notable cause being inter-Service rivalry. In short, although reformers have striven to create a unitary structure, with a common purpose, the Ministry of Defence is best regarded as a coalition of interests. The structure of the department is important, but so too is the human variety and behaviour within it. The fact that some interests in the Ministry previously operated in separate Service departments is neither here nor there. Bringing them together in one department does not remove conflict, though it changes the terms and setting.[51]

The Chief Scientific Adviser to the Cabinet has suggested that the questioning, sceptical, authority-challenging attitude of the scientist is at odds with the demands of military organization. The latter requires acceptance of authority and habitual obedience. Moreover, the profession of arms in Britain, at least for the long-service officer, has traditionally been a gentleman's calling. An officer class exists with attitudes and values which are somewhat at odds with those of scientists, politicians and administrators, even though they may all support a certain political régime and economic system. The social status of the scientist is uncertain.[52] But the general Service officer has reason to believe that his own standing is subtly threatened by the role of science in modern warfare.[53]

In Britain, as elsewhere, the military are capable of suppressing their habitual obedience; on occasion they have shown some contempt for civilian authority. On the limited administrative front in Whitehall they have demonstrated considerable powers

[51] On unitary and pluralistic concepts of organization see A. Fox, *Industrial Sociology and Industrial Relations*, Research Paper No. 3 for Royal Commission on Trade Unions and Employers' Associations, HMSO, 1966.

[52] Sir Solly Zuckerman, *Scientists and War*, Hamish Hamilton, 1966, pp. 8–9.

[53] For example, see *Report of Committee on the Management and Control of Research and Development*, HMSO, 1961, paras. 192–4.

of stubbornness and resistance. It is easy to portray senior officers of the armed forces as military Luddites. But, like the Luddites, they are not stupid, but skilled persons facing an uncertain future because of technical developments. Tension between the military and various categories of scientists is therefore not unlikely.

There are also possibilities of conflict and misunderstanding between scientists and administrators. Many scientists have difficulty in communicating with persons who are not familiar with their disciplines. This is partly because each science has its particular jargon, known only to the initiated. The administrative class civil servant prizes lucidity of English expression, though in fact the class has its own jargon. Again, the scientist is apt to be a specialist, totally absorbed in a particular field or project, to which he attaches overriding significance. In contrast, the administrator is necessarily something of a generalist; and he is inclined to be cautious in order to keep his minister out of political trouble.[54] Of course, there are exceptions to these stereotypes, but some clashes of personality and temperament are probable.

There is no reason to suppose that relations between different groups in an organization are invariably marked by tension and conflict. The members usually have a common class background, though there may be subtle distinctions of social status. The structure of a department and standard procedures may help to minimize differences or to resolve them speedily. Organization along Service lines tends to give administrators, scientists and Service officers something in common. In the old Service departments the civil servants were the allies of a particular Service. At least one senior RAF officer has said some very kind things about the administrators in the former Air Ministry.[55] And in so far as the Ministry of Defence is still organized along Service lines, this sense of common interest, cutting across professional or functional differences, still exists.

[54] See Z. M. T. Tarkowski and A. V. Turnbull, Scientists versus administrators, *Public Administration*, Autumn 1959, pp. 213–56.

[55] Sir John Slessor, letter in *The Economist*, 11 June 1966.

Group and personal relationships in a department give rise to informal organization. The behaviour of members is conditioned by formal rules, procedures, and patterns of authority. But no formal plan is complete or exempt from evasion or modification in practice. The constituent groups of any department throw up their own leaders, who have considerable influence, even though they have no formal authority. They also develop their own practices, values, and expectations over time. These may or may not be compatible with the formal plan of organization. A great deal of training or learning occurs in an informal way. An informal system of communication will almost certainly exist. And most groups have informal contacts with outside bodies, which they exploit to achieve ends or to protect interests.[56]

This is of some significance for conflict within a department. Persons well down in the formal hierarchy may frustrate their nominal superiors in various ways, even in the most coercive organization. They may protest that innovations are unworkable, and subsequently do their best to see that they do not work. They may "drag their feet" or deny senior persons information, or feed them "censored" information. They may form unofficial cliques and factions. They may appeal over the heads of their superiors. They may inspire leaks and articles in the press. Interested MPs or pressure groups may be discreetly briefed and brought into the battle.[57]

In sociological jargon, however, such conflict may be functional. That is to say, it may contribute to the continuance of the department or its better performance. Decisions reached after struggles and manœuvres, in which no interest or point of view is neglected, may be superior to those which are imposed from above. Conflict is not incompatible with unity of command, providing it is accepted that "command" is not equivalent to the autocratic will

[56] See F. Morstein Marx (ed.), *Elements of Public Administration*, Prentice-Hall, 1959, ch. 13.

[57] See J. A. Van Doorn, Conflict in formal organizations, in *Conflict in Society*, Churchill, 1965, pp. 111–30.

of a single individual or group. In complex organizations commands, to be effective, must represent some sort of consensus. In a large department, such as the Ministry of Defence, an acceptable consensus is most likely to emerge when a miniature pluralistic system is operative.

When such a system is in being, authority tends to be willingly accepted. But attempts to impose decisions, by means of direct orders or coercion, are more likely to provoke resistance, evasion, and frustration. This is not to say that threats and coercion cannot produce desired results or should never be used. In the long run, however, frequent recourse to such methods arouses opposition, unless most members of the organization have been reduced to a state of abject servility, unworthy of free men.

Tension and rivalry are more probable in a department when economies are being sought. This is especially so in the case of the Ministry of Defence. When the Labour Party came to power in 1964 it imposed a ceiling on defence expenditure. The limit was to be £2000 million a year at 1964 prices. This meant a reduction of £400 million, or 16 per cent, on the expenditure contemplated by the previous Conservative Government.[58] Naturally there was apprehension in the Services as to where the axe was going to fall.

Even the most intensive lobbying by the aircraft industry failed to save the TSR 2. The RAF was promised the American F111K as a replacement, but this was also cancelled in a later economy drive. The Royal Navy had more cause for alarm. The Government resolved not to proceed with the building of aircraft carriers, but initially there was no reconsideration of commitments in the light of this decision, a fact which precipitated the resignations of the Minister for the Navy and the Chief of Naval Staff. Cynics argued that the Army, being already undermanned and inappropriately armed, faced fewer problems than the other two Services.

In July 1967, as a consequence of further economic difficulties, the Government announced a reduction in commitments outside Europe and fairly drastic cuts in Service manpower and supporting

[58] *The Defence Review*, Cmd. 2901, HMSO, 1966.

civilian employees.[59] But following the devaluation of sterling, in November, further cuts of £100 million were promised. According to the Secretary of State for Defence, this meant reaching the 1970–1 target of £1900 million, at 1964 prices, two years earlier than had been indicated only four months previously.[60]

The drive for economies reinforces demands for even tighter central control within the Ministry of Defence. The main target of attack is Service autonomy, because it is alleged to cause wasteful duplication and prevent standardization of weapons and equipment. Already schemes have been aired for more "functional" organization in the department. It is possible that the Chiefs of Staff will be replaced by officers with functional, rather than Service, responsibilities. The logical outcome of a strict application of the functional principle is the disappearance of separate Services, as in Canada. This would see the end of ministers with Service responsibilities, Service boards, and separate Service budgets. But so far no official pronouncement has indicated any government intention of taking this extreme course.

Within each Service, however, the functional principle is increasingly taken as the basis of organization, at least if changes in the titles of various Service commands are any guide. For example, Bomber Command and Fighter Command have been replaced by a new Strike and Reconnaissance and Defence Command. And the Army has abandoned the geographical principle, implied in the defunct Southern Command, in favour of new functional entities like Strategic Command. But all this is a long way from the integrated Service commands which have been proposed from time to time. For instance, a former Permanent Secretary of the Ministry of Defence has suggested the need for a Strike Command, responsible for all long-range nuclear and non-nuclear weapons, whether launched from aircraft, ships

[59] White Paper, *Supplementary Statement on Defence Policy*, Cmd. 3357, HMSO, 1967.

[60] Parliamentary Report, *The Times*, 28 Nov. 1967.

or land. There might also be a Training Command, and a Task Force Command for minor operations.[61]

Even if a single, integrated, British Armed Service does eventually evolve, there will still be a great deal of friction in a department like the Ministry of Defence, though it will take a different form. The department would still have its own internal political system, involving power, authority, leadership, conflict and consensus. A regular and persistent pattern of behaviour and procedure, designed to resolve conflict, would remain necessary. This internal political system could be classified as autocratic, oligarchic, despotic, democratic, pluralistic, and so on, according to its characteristics. And since it is possible to choose between alternative systems, the basis of departmental organization cannot be divorced from normative considerations.

[61] Sir Robert Scott, *The Fighting Man of the Future*, Alanbrooke Memorial Lecture, 1966, printed for the Honourable Artillery Company, p. 9. Also see Maj.-Gen. J. L. Moulton, *Defence in a Changing World*, Eyre & Spottiswoode, 1964, pp. 121–4 and 187–91.

CHAPTER 6

CENTRAL GOVERNMENT AND THE SOCIAL SERVICES

Functions and Economic Aspects

The major social service departments at the time of writing are the Ministry of Social Security and Ministry of Health, which are in the course of being merged, the Department of Education and Science, and the Ministry of Housing and Local Government. The Home Office also has important social service functions, especially with respect to children, some of which it may soon lose to the merged Ministries of Social Security and Health. Each department has its special functions and clientele, and each maintains links with different professional bodies and voluntary societies. They also have their own ways of doing things. Nevertheless, they have certain functions in common and these will first be discussed generally; they will then be examined with special reference to the present responsibilities of the Ministry of Social Security and Ministry of Health.

In this context, central government functions include policy formulation, the provision of resources in terms of finance, buildings, equipment, and manpower, the setting up of appropriate administrative structures, arrangements for appeals and complaints, publicity and education, supervision of local authorities and other bodies, planning and research, continuous reappraisal and modification in the light of experience and changing needs, and finally, what has been termed creative leadership.[1]

The determination of social policy is the most important of these functions. By social policy is meant those important decisions

[1] Sir George Schuster, *Creative Leadership in a State Service*, Hospitals and the State, Acton Society Trust, 1959. See Appendix (9).

of government, of general application, which are intended to lead to action designed to remove or ameliorate recognized social problems. But social problems may be deliberately ignored by governments. Even when they are not, they may not be regarded as urgent or requiring immediate action. In general, social problems are more obvious in times of unusually rapid economic and political change, for then, like troubles, "they come not single spies but in battalions". Transition from an agricultural economy to one which is predominantly industrial generates social problems, especially if the change takes place over a relatively short period. Subsequent development, from the initial to the more mature stages of industrialism, also creates problems, though probably not in such acute forms.

When and how a government will attempt to solve or deal with a social problem depends, amongst other things, on contemporary social philosophy, pressure group activity, the extent of the franchise, party political advantage, international comparisons, and the influence of mass media. The reports of royal commissions and academic and other investigations may also play a part. Often there will be several conflicting pressure groups at work. Some may demand vigorous government action, whilst others attempt to prevent or limit it, or guide it in a particular direction. At some point in time, however, recognition of social problems leads to the setting up of governmental agencies or departments, designed to provide services which will improve or make tolerable the present condition and future prospects of certain groups in society. In short, policy gives rise to administrative arrangements and decisions. These are connected with economic considerations in various ways.

It is clear, for example, that governments must decide the total amount of money they are prepared to spend on the social services over a given period.[2] They must also distribute this sum

[2] According to one estimate, the percentage of the gross national product allocated to the social services, including food subsidies, rose from 2·6 in 1900 to 11·3 in 1938 to 18·0 in 1950; it fell to 17·8 in 1961. Figures quoted in T. H. Marshall, *Social Policy*, Hutchinson, 2nd Paperback edn., 1967, p. 179.

amongst the various services, which are thus competing for scarce resources. But the social services are also affected by the general state of the economy and they, in turn, can affect the economic situation. Policy relating to the social services is thus bound up with economic policy.

It is unusual to regard money allocated to the social services as a form of investment, even though this affects the availability and quality of labour. The emphasis is more often on the allegedly unproductive character of social services.[3] As a result, they are vulnerable to cuts in government expenditure when there is a balance of payments crisis, because they are held to contribute to inflation. Even a service which can show an obvious economic return, or at least connection, such as technological or scientific education, is unlikely to be exempt from cuts since they are usually made across the whole range of services as part of a package deal. However, there are usually differences in the severity of cuts, depending on the influence and vociferousness of the professions affected and the support they receive from parties, clients and the electorate. But the extent to which social service expenditure is inflationary is a debatable point.

Social services are financed out of general taxation or by specific deductions from income. Money is either redistributed amongst consumers or spent on socially desirable ends rather than on consumer goods. It may be contended that raising national insurance contributions has a positively disinflationary effect. Certainly some economists see frequent variations in insurance contributions as a way of influencing total demand.[4]

In so far as they do affect total demand, social insurance schemes modify the severity of economic recessions by acting as a sort of economic regulator. When unemployment is relatively high, there is an increase in social security payments; the decline in total consumer demand is less than it would otherwise have been. But the potential or unmodified decline will not be exactly offset. This

[3] See J. K. Galbraith, *The Liberal Hour*, Pelican edn., 1963, ch. 2.

[4] For example, see *Report of Committee on the Working of the Monetary System*, Cmd. 827, HMSO, 1959, para. 517.

is because the principle of less eligibility is still accepted, in spite of exaggerated reports of its abandonment. Briefly, the principle is based on the assumption that work is inherently unsatisfying and that people will not work if they can enjoy the same real income via unemployment and other social security benefits. Hence total payments are normally designed to be less than what the recipient could earn, even though supplements related to previous earnings may be added to flat rate benefits.[5]

Because it can affect total demand, social policy is clearly connected with economic policy. And the adequacy of social security benefits, which are usually fixed for quite long periods, depends on the general economic situation, since their real value can be quickly eroded by rising prices. In a sense the economic departments are the most important social service departments. For whether prices are rising or not depends on the incomes and standards of living of people not in receipt of social security benefits, as well as on productive enterprise, whether public or private.

The quality of the social services is also affected by capital expenditure or investment and this too is clearly a matter of political economy. A great deal of capital expenditure is involved in the provision of houses, hospitals, schools, social security offices and other buildings.[6] The equipment required in, say, a modern hospital or school is also expensive. And both buildings and equipment are apt to become quickly obsolete in the face of changing policies, needs, and technological developments. It is clear, however, that if, for example, there are not enough schools, classes will be larger than is educationally desirable, and the ages of starting and leaving school will probably be adjusted to meet the resources available.

[5] Isolated exceptions to the principle are apt to receive excessive publicity. They often involve people whose earnings are very low relative to their needs and obligations.

[6] For example, it is expected that roughly £1000 million will be spent in England and Wales on hospital building during the ten-year period beginning 1966–7 and over £60 million in Scotland for the first five of these years. See *Britain: An Official Handbook*, HMSO, 1968, p. 143.

The manning of the social services depends very much on the payment of salaries sufficiently attractive to call forth a supply of labour of the right sort. If pay is low in comparison with what can be earned elsewhere, supply tends to fall short of requirements. And if conditions of work are relatively onerous, staff turnover is apt to be high. There may then be attempts to offset shortages by employing staff who are less well educated or trained. In some cases, as with the supply of civil servants or teachers, the central government is in a position to determine conditions and is therefore more or less directly responsible. In other cases, as, for example, with various branches of medicine, professional bodies can influence supply because they lay down qualifications and give recognition.

Enough has been said to indicate connections between economic policy and the functions of formulating social policy and supplying the social services with adequate resources. Most of the other functions previously specified need not be commented on at this stage, but one, that of setting up appropriate administrative structures, does call for separate discussion. Two questions arise in this respect. The first involves normative considerations. On what principle or principles *should* social services be organized and operated? The second question relates to actual practice. How do social services work in fact? This leads to a third question: How far is it possible to change or modify structures and procedures to make them approximate more closely to the ideal?

Administrative Principles and Problems

When considering how social services *ought* to be organized, it is tempting to state a strong preference for the clientele principle. Broadly, this means that the needs and convenience of persons who use, or who ought to use, the services should be paramount. This principle cannot be proved to be superior to all others, but in this instance it is often regarded as self-evident and in conformity with the assumption that nobody in need should be discouraged from making use of the services available.

Two things follow once the clientele principle is accepted. First, it is implied that administration should be predominantly local, in the sense of as near to the point of consumption as possible. For this reason local authorities are regarded as essential elements in the provision of most social services. Local administration lessens demands on clientele by reducing the distances they have to travel, with consequent saving in time and cost. And the more local the administration, the greater the prospects of face-to-face contact between officials and clients, with consequent humanization of the services. There is also less need for correspondence with geographically remote officials, who may use terms in written communications which many people find difficult to understand.

Secondly, a person or family in need usually requires help from several services, often provided by different departments or authorities. The convenience of clients demands that services should be integrated whenever possible. Just as in a health centre, where all, or at least many, forms of medical treatment are available, so there is a case for a single, locally situated, social services office or centre, dealing with most types of problem. Time is not lost travelling from one building to another and probably less waiting is involved. Furthermore, it should not prove necessary to repeat information for the benefit of different sets of officials and social workers. All this can be of considerable importance given that those who use the social services are often ill, old, under emotional or mental stress, and inarticulate.

Integration also has administrative advantages. One receptionist and one set of records may suffice, rather than two or more. Intensive use can be made of computers and other expensive items of capital equipment. Officials previously in separate buildings or departments may find it easier to co-ordinate their work. There are possibilities of making better use of training facilities. One social worker rather than several can visit clients in their homes and so on. But whether services are in fact clientele oriented, locally administered and integrated is another matter.

As with moral principles, administrative principles may be forgotten when they come into conflict with certain interests.

It is likely, for example, that the interests or convenience of administrators, social workers and other professional people will strongly influence both the structure and procedure of social service departments and organizations. It is not difficult for doctors or teachers to believe that what is good for them is good for patients or pupils. Officials and professional workers are apt to be better organized, more vocal and more influential than their clients. "Consumers" of all sorts are poorly organized. This is especially true of some consumers of social services, such as schoolchildren, the aged, widowed, destitute, mentally sick, and physically handicapped. They are not in a position to withdraw their custom if dissatisfied. Many of them are dependent on other people, who might be described as intermediaries, to express their needs and safeguard their interests.

Intermediaries include the members of voluntary societies, church organizations, and professional associations, as well as MPs, local councillors, and university academics. There is a great deal of diversity amongst them and it is difficult to generalize about their motives or how adequately they fulfil their role. They may have motives of which they themselves are not aware, or which they would be reluctant to admit publicly. For example, a local councillor may welcome the opportunity to serve on a welfare or children's committee, not because of what he can do for those in need, but because it will make him well known locally. An academic may be interested in carving out a niche as an authority on some social problem in the hope that it will lead to a university chair. A church worker presumably hopes that gratitude will incline people towards a particular religious persuasion. Intermediaries may be compensating for personal inadequacies or a disappointing career; perhaps they derive satisfaction from partially ordering the lives of other people in a way denied them in their ordinary work. In short, there are reasons for believing that the needs and interests of clients may get lost somewhere along the line.

Problems also arise when local authorities form the basis of local administration for social services. The structure of local government in Britain is unsatisfactory and has been so for many years.[7] County councils and county boroughs are the major local authorities in England and Wales outside London. But these and other categories mean very little in terms of population and financial resources. County councils, for example, range from Lancashire, with an estimated population of over 2 million and a 1*d.* rate which would produce more than £300,000, to Radnorshire, with a population of just over 18,000 and a 1*d.* rate yielding around £2000. Amongst county boroughs, that is towns and cities administratively independent of the counties, Birmingham has a population of over 1 million, whilst Canterbury has about 32,000.[8] Yet, in spite of these disparities, social service and other responsibilities are allocated to local authorities according to the category they happen to be in.

Clearly the social problems confronting a highly industrialized city like Birmingham, which dominates a large conurbation, are markedly different in scale, and even in kind, from those facing Canterbury. The position is further complicated by the fact that to make the best use of resources and to produce enough clients for some social services, such as mental health, very large areas and populations are necessary. But these same areas and populations may put too great a strain on other social services, such as secondary education, for which the same local authorities are also responsible. In addition, local authorities are supposed to exhibit a sense of community and to be rational political units. This is because people must be induced to serve as councillors.

Occupational and geographical mobility, however, which are generally held to have increased over the years, tend to undermine a sense of local community and the desire to participate in local affairs. This is especially so with respect to young adults, the better educated, and people in the professions. Areas vary in the calibre

[7] A Royal Commission is currently investigating local government structure and its report is expected soon.

[8] See *Municipal Yearbook*, Municipal Journal Ltd., 1967.

of their elected councillors since they are not equally subject to these and other influences.[9]

Both local councillors and officials are sometimes held to be more aware of the problems and needs of people living in their areas, and more responsive to their wishes, than are the personnel of central government. No doubt this is often true, but it is not universally so. There may be more petty-mindedness and narrowness of outlook in local than in central government. Local officials are at least as much inclined to adhere rigidly to precedent and the rule book as their central government counterparts. And few local politicians now campaign on the Joseph Chamberlain slogan of "high rates and a healthy city". Rather are local party politics fought in terms of keeping the rates down. In the past, local authority responsibility for poor relief was welcomed in some quarters precisely because parishes were inclined to be parsimonious.[10]

For these and other reasons, the central government in Britain plays a major role in the administration of all social services. But administration may still be local since departments can be decentralized, and regional and local offices set up which enjoy varying degrees of autonomy and discretion. Whether a service is formally administered by a local authority or by a local office of a Whitehall department, however, there are strong forces making for centralization.

First, there is the doctrine of individual ministerial responsibility and accountability to Parliament. Ultimately a Minister answers for the policy and quality of the service for which he is responsible. Secondly, the party in power at Westminster controls the legislature and hence the content of legislation relating to the social services. Thirdly, the scale and cost of these services, together with popular demands for universality and equality of standards, necessitate financing by the central government, with consequent

[9] See A. H. Birch, *Small Town Politics*, Oxford, 1959. On councillors generally see *Report of Committee on the Management of Local Government*, (Maud Committee), vol. 1, ch. 6; also vol. 2 of Evidence.

[10] For example, see D. Ricardo, *The Principles of Political Economy and Taxation*, Everyman edn., p. 62.

control. The only independent source of revenue for local authorities is the rates. Fourthly, centralization offers economies of scale in terms of bulk purchasing, standardization, and intensive use of equipment, common research and training facilities, and so on.

It might be supposed that central government control would encourage and facilitate the integration of social services. But successive governments, over the years, have responded in a piecemeal fashion to needs and demands. They have tended to set up a new department to deal with each problem as it arose. It has been necessary to co-ordinate their work via a non-departmental supervising minister at Cabinet level and through such devices as interdepartmental committees. Now, however, the tide is running strongly in favour of integration. The Ministry of Social Security is the result of one merger, not yet fully complete, and it is now to be integrated with the Ministry of Health. This seems an appropriate moment to consider the present functions and organization of these two departments. We may then conclude with some general observations on integrating social services.

Social Security[10a]

The Ministry of Social Security is occupied with the implementation of schemes relating to state pensions and social insurance. It has numerous clients and they constitute a unified clientele mainly in the sense that they all lodge claims or are recognized as entitled to benefits. To carry out its work the Ministry needs a network of conveniently situated local offices. But since much money paid out depends on evidence of contributions made over a long period, and because nearly everybody changes his job or place of residence at some time in his life, it is also necessary to have centralized systems of record keeping and to organize what is a national system from a headquarters office. Local offices are grouped under 12 regional offices which attempt to secure uniformity and co-ordination in their area.

At the end of 1966, in round figures, more than 44,000 out of a

[10a] See Appendix (10).

total staff of some 58,000 were employed in over 1000 local offices. Some 11,500 were working, chiefly on records, at central offices in Newcastle and Blackpool. Headquarters staff in London numbered just over 2000.[11]

The range of the Ministry's work is shown by the departments into which headquarters office is divided. These include one for war pensions, others concerned with industrial injuries, family allowances, national insurance benefits and contributions, and two dealing with supplementary benefits. There are also departments responsible for finance, establishments and organization, research and statistics, and legal and medical matters.

At headquarters, discussions take place about financial and other aspects of pensions and benefits, such as who shall come within the ambit of a scheme and on what terms. The principles underlying current policy are subject to review from time to time. Senior officials are in a position to influence policy and on occasion they may take the initiative.[12] The fact that most of the major decisions are made at the centre is evidenced by the absence of pressure group activity outside of Westminster and Whitehall.

Amongst the functions of headquarters staff, planning and research especially merit discussion. Planning social security, in the sense of controlling and influencing events with a view to attaining explicit objectives, is extremely difficult. This is because it can only be done satisfactorily as part of a larger plan which embraces all social services and economic policy. In some areas there is very little that the Ministry of Social Security can do. It is manifestly impossible to control the number of war pensioners, though this can be estimated with reasonable certainty, assuming that is that Britain is not involved in another major war.

With respect to such matters as retirement pensions and supplementary benefits, much depends on the age and sex structure

[11] *Annual Report Ministry of Social Security*, Cmd. 3338, HMSO, July 1967.

[12] See article, Twilight of Beveridge, *The Economist*, 18 May 1968. On what can be done by an astute official see references to Sir Robert Morant in B. Gilbert, *The Evolution of National Insurance in Great Britain*, Michael Joseph, 1966.

of the population. Here again there are limits to what the Ministry can do. Given existing moral codes, it is not possible to plan to reduce the number of people eligible for retirement pensions by opposing the trend towards the prolongation of life. Like Queen Anne, Malthus is dead. But, of course, the Government can try to foresee the social implications of the prolongation of life and this should affect the plans of the Ministry of Social Security.

Equally, the Ministry is not in a position to take unilateral action regarding living conditions and the concentration of population. Nor can it exert much influence on the level of rents in different parts of the country, though this has an important effect on supplementary benefits and on the adequacy of benefits generally. Its work is complementary to that of the Ministry of Health, Ministry of Housing and Local Government, and local authorities. But it is somewhat isolated from these other bodies, whereas sensible planning implies close collaboration.

Research, however, offers the Ministry greater scope to act on its own. In this context, research means not only the validation of theories, but also the discovery and presentation of facts which may prove useful in the formulation of policy and the evaluation of current operations. In 1966, for example, as a result of a special inquiry, a report was published which threw some light on the circumstances of retired persons.[13] The Ministry also compiles statistics showing retirement trends and the incidence of illness. These are of use to other government departments and outside organizations. Much of this information emanates from the records offices at Newcastle and Blackpool and from central offices in Wales and Scotland.

In spite of all this one may doubt whether the Ministry does enough research. It is apparently handicapped by lack of resources and suitable staff. According to one estimate, the Ministry has about 200 people working on research and statistics; the number varies according to the projects in hand. But only eighteen of these were found to be of senior executive grade or higher rank,

[13] See *Annual Report of Ministry, 1966*, Cmd. 3338, pp. 91–97.

and the figure included some people employed on information duties.[14]

The interests of clients are profoundly affected by decisions taken at headquarters. But most clients have direct contact only with local offices and their impression of the Ministry is derived from them. The organization of local offices is thus important from the public relations point of view. It must be remembered, however, that the Ministry of Social Security was only set up in August 1966 as a result of a merger of the former Ministry of Pensions and National Insurance and the now defunct National Assistance Board. Complete integration has not yet been attained.

The main purpose of the merger was to ensure that no one in need should be inhibited from applying for assistance. Invidious distinctions between pensions to which people were entitled and national assistance, for which one had to apply and show need, were to be abolished, in that both were to be collected from the same office. But accommodation and staff difficulties have slowed down integration and many local offices have not been integrated much further than the reception desk, clients then being directed to different officials or sections. There is some administrative justification for this since it takes longer to assess a new applicant for supplementary benefit than it does to answer an inquiry about a contributory matter. A certain amount of specialist knowledge is also involved.

In general, therefore, the work of local offices falls into two main categories, reflecting the origins of the department. One side of the office deals with contributions and payments connected with social insurance schemes. The other side is concerned with applications and payments relating to supplementary benefits, which are not dependent on contributions but on evidence of need or distress.

Contributory schemes allow local officials little discretion. The amount of benefit is laid down and what can be paid out, to

[14] A. Lapping, Social security: how new a ministry?, *New Society*, 8 June 1967.

individuals and in total, is really determined at the centre. In the main, local officials merely require a knowledge of the basic laws, rules, and precedents. Much of the work consists in the meticulous recording and checking of facts. Occasionally offices are working under pressure to get pensions to people entitled to them, especially when scales have been changed. In addition, local offices are subject to seasonal variations in the intensity of work because more people tend to be ill or unemployed during the winter months.

Although these functions are important and necessary, they are clearly associated with work of a somewhat tedious character. But local offices do offer alternative duties. For example, preliminary inquiries may have to be made about the circumstances surrounding a claim for an industrial injuries benefit. Occasionally deliberate fraud may be suspected. But this sort of investigatory work may not appeal to many officials. In any case, it is likely to be the prerogative of a few specialists.

Managers of local offices must attempt to overcome tedium because it can lead to a large turnover of staff. Furthermore, apathetic officials are apt to give clients the impression that they are there to be dealt with rather than served. This feeling is reinforced if procedure is too formal and offices are gloomy and uninviting. However, most clients concerned with contributory payments never see the inside of a local office of the Ministry of Social Security. At the most they may do so on one or two occasions only. Once entitlement to payment is confirmed, and this may be done by correspondence, benefits are likely to be collected from a post office or an office of the Department of Employment and Productivity.

On the supplementary side the position is somewhat different. Supplementary benefits come out of general taxation and scales are somewhat more elastic. They can therefore be related to individual circumstances. Officials thus enjoy some discretion. They must also exercise judgement in assessing needs. Even so, there are recommended and standardized scales and set ways of determining needs.

In this sort of work it is desirable that a sympathetic relationship should be established between officials and clients. Any suspicion of a grand inquisition, or humiliating form of means test, would be resented and deter people from seeking assistance to which they are entitled as members of the community. On the other hand, some probing into circumstances is necessary and this puts clients and officials on a different footing than in the case of contributory schemes.

Applicants may prove to be uncommunicative or inarticulate, through pride or ignorance or declining faculties. Sometimes people living in unpleasant conditions have to be visited at home. And it is a matter of some delicacy to inquire about their circumstances, such as the rents they pay, without arousing the curiosity of landlords, neighbours, and relatives. A great deal of help may be necessary with paperwork and documents, and rather complex matters have to be put in simple terms. Applicants may have to be put in touch with other social services, such as those provided by local authorities. Officials of the Ministry of Social Security should therefore have a broad knowledge of social services generally.

If it is to be well done this sort of work calls for special training. Some sort of formal qualification should probably be demanded. Little information is readily available about the education, training, age, and previous experience of people employed on various duties in the Ministry. One account of training in the now defunct National Assistance Board indicates that many officials are recruited fairly late in life, are therefore likely to be unestablished civil servants, and receive only the minimum amount of training.[15]

When the department is merged with the Ministry of Health it should be possible to offer better training and career prospects. But this depends on how far mobility between sections in the new department is encouraged. This may prove difficult since the tasks at present carried out by the Ministry of Health are of a

[15] K. R. Stowe, Staff training in the National Assistance Board: problems and policies, *Public Administration*, Winter 1961.

very different character from those of the Ministry of Social Security.[16]

Health

Both the Ministry of Health and the Ministry of Social Security look after the needs and welfare of certain groups of people in society. But unlike the Ministry of Social Security, which operates in a rather self-contained way, the Ministry of Health plays a supervisory role in a structure which is generally described as tripartite.

Within the health service in England and Wales there is first the hospital and specialist service.[17] This is administered through 15 regional hospital boards and some 333 hospital management committees. Teaching hospitals are run by 36 separate boards of governors. Secondly, there are the general practitioner services. These consist of the family doctor, ophthalmic and pharmaceutical services. They are administered by 134 local executive councils. Thirdly, there are local authority health and welfare services. These comprise a domiciliary maternity service, including antenatal care and the services of midwives and home helps; child welfare and preventive services, concerned with vaccination and immunization; the care of old people and the mentally ill; the provision of health centres; ambulance services; and the services of home nurses and health visitors. The authorities responsible are the councils of counties and county boroughs, the London boroughs, and the City of London. With the Minister's consent responsibility may be delegated to non-county borough and urban district councils with populations of over 60,000. In all, there are over 200 local health authorities.

Regional hospital boards usually have between twenty and

[16] On Administrative Tribunals connected with the Ministry of Social Security see its Annual Reports. For a study of activity in a central office concerned with records see N. Walker, *Morale in the Civil Service*, Edinburgh University Press, 1961, especially ch. 5.

[17] The Secretary of State for Scotland is responsible for the service in that country. The structure is basically similar.

thirty members who serve without pay. They are composed of people appointed by the Minister for a period of three years. He must consult universities, certain recognized medical organizations, local health authorities in each region, and other bodies when making appointments. Hospital management committees are appointed by regional boards in a similar fashion. Not surprisingly, boards and committees do not represent a true cross-section of the population. Hospital doctors and specialists, other professional people, retired persons, local councillors, and housewives predominate.[18]

The local executive councils consist of twenty-five members. Eight are appointed by the local health authority for the area, five by the Minister, seven by a local medical committee and five by local dental and pharmaceutical committees.

The health service is thus certainly not integrated. This is mainly because of historical factors and the resistance of various interests when the service was first set up. In particular, it is because of the opposition of the medical profession to local authority control.[19] Many problems result from the tripartite structure because the work of each part is related to that of the other parts.

Almost every health and welfare need falls partly on each of the three divisions though they are separately organized and financed.[20] General practitioners are contracted to executive councils but depend on local health authorities for auxiliary help, such as home nursing, and on the hospitals for specialist services. The quality of local health authorities is not uniform, with consequent variations in the burden on hospitals and general practitioners. Again, there is no precise definition of what is

[18] See H. Eckstein, *The English Health Service*, Oxford, 1959, pp. 187–8.

[19] See A. Lindsey, *Socialized Medicine in England and Wales*, University of North Carolina Press, 1962. Also H. Eckstein, *Pressure Group Politics: The Case of the British Medical Association*, Allen & Unwin, 1960.

[20] One estimate puts health service expenditure for 1966–7 at £1367 million. The approximate allocation is hospital service 55 per cent, executive councils 25 per cent, and local health authorities 20 per cent. See A. W. Miles, The health services, *Political Quarterly*, April–June 1968.

meant by "after care", and hence there is doubt about the point at which a patient should cease to be the concern of a hospital and become the responsibility of a local health authority. Both have a financial interest in putting off responsibility. Yet because of a shortage of hospital beds a mother may be discharged prematurely from hospital, which means that pressure is shifted onto her general practitioner and the home help and health visitor services of the local health authority. It is clearly undesirable that clients should be shuttled confusingly between the various parts of the service. And finally, the tripartite structure tends to make research more difficult and costly.[21]

Attempts are made to secure co-operation between the three parts of the service in various ways. It is apparent, for example, that there is a certain amount of interlocking membership. Local councillors who serve on the health and welfare committee of their authority are likely to be nominated to serve on hospital boards and executive councils. General practitioners may be co-opted to local authority health committees and so on. There are informal meetings and other contacts between officers of the various bodies. Ministerial circulars and memoranda urge collaboration. Standing joint committees may be set up for particular subjects and general purposes.

Such efforts are not always rewarded and they would not be necessary in a more integrated form of organization. In November 1967 the Minister of Health stated in the Commons that he was initiating an inquiry into the structure of the service. The results, which are expected to be published soon, will form the basis of further discussion.

The Ministry of Health itself reflects the tripartite structure, with separate divisions responsible for hospitals, executive councils and relations with local health authorities. Because it does not itself provide services it has only small regional or local units and in this respect too it differs from the Ministry of Social

[21] On these and other matters see D. Paige and K. Jones, *Health and Welfare Services in Britain in 1975*, Cambridge, 1966, ch. 2; and J. Parker, *Local Health and Welfare Services*, Allen & Unwin, 1965, pp. 77–85.

Security. In November 1967, out of a total of 4358 lay staff, 3219 were employed at headquarters. Its professional and technical staff of just over 1000 was about equally distributed between headquarters and the regions. There are many other differences between the two departments.

The Ministry of Social Security is not dependent on the co-operation and goodwill of long-established professional organizations such as those concerned with various branches of medicine. The success of the health service depends on people who in the main are not salaried officials in the civil service. Nevertheless, doctors must negotiate with the Minister over pay and conditions and this is the source of much tension.

Furthermore, the Ministry of Health must try to foresee the number of doctors, dentists, nurses, and so on which will be needed in, say, five to ten years' time. There is also the question of the type of doctor required. But the demand for the services of the various professions cannot be known too far ahead because this depends on things which often can only be guessed at, such as future standards of living, advances in medical science, and changing social habits, such as those relating to age of marriage and size of family. Similar difficulties arise in trying to decide how many hospitals to build and how to design and equip them. The Ministry of Social Security is not confronted with these sorts of planning problems.

Again, the Ministry of Social Security is not a major purchasing department but the Ministry of Health finances the purchase of expensive medical equipment and drugs. However, it is not easy to deny hospitals the latest equipment if boards, committees, and doctors are convinced it is necessary to save even a few lives. Moreover, it is the general practitioners who in the main prescribe drugs; and producers and dispensers are interested in maximizing profits and increasing turnover. The imposition of prescription charges on patients is unlikely to have much of a deterrent effect and any economies may be more than offset by increased administrative costs. When Mr. Enoch Powell was Minister of Health he encouraged the purchase of drugs for hospitals from Italy, which does not allow patents on drugs, and from communist countries which do not recognize Western patent rights.[22] In May 1968 the House of Lords threw out a clause of a Health Services and Public Health Bill which would have given governments the right to disregard patents in order to get cheap pharmaceuticals for general practitioner services.[23]

Moreover, because of the disintegrated character of the health service, the Ministry of Health has a leadership function which the Ministry of Social Security lacks. Opinions differ as to how far the Ministry of Health should attempt to impose its will on hospital boards, executive councils, and local health authorities. Too much interference might undermine local initiative or voluntary interest and effort; too little could be regarded as an evasion of ministerial responsibility, produce undesirable differences in standards, and make central planning virtually impossible.

Three basic attitudes have been suggested with respect to departmental leadership, namely, *laissez-faire*, regulatory, and promotional, indicating progressive degrees of central control. The Ministry of Health is placed in the *laissez-faire* category, meaning that it inclines to as little interference as possible, apart from the necessary fulfilment of its supervisory functions. The Home Office and Department of Education and Science are cited as respective examples of regulatory and promotional departments.[24] It would be difficult to place the Ministry of Social Security in any category because its power relationships with local authorities are minimal.

Finally, although there are administrative tribunals which deal with complaints and appeals against the decisions of both the

[22] See J. Enoch Powell, *A New Look at Medicine and Politics*, Pitman, 1966, ch. 6. Also see *Report of Committee of Enquiry into the Relationship of the Pharmaceutical Industry with the National Health Service, 1965-67*, Cmnd. 3410, HMSO, 1967.

[23] Parliamentary Report, *The Times*, 28 May 1968; also see *The Economist*, 8 June 1968, p. 79.

[24] J. A. Griffith, *Central Departments and Local Authorities*, Allen & Unwin, 1966, pp. 515–25.

Ministry of Social Security and Ministry of Health, they are differently composed and relate to different subjects.[25]

It is therefore apparent that the two departments have different functions or purposes and may be contrasted in many respects. What, then, is the case for integration?

Integration and Problems Involved

First, it is possible that the clients of the one department or service are also clients of the other department or service. For example, a person who is impecunious or unemployed may well be ill. Equally, a person about to be discharged from hospital may be in need of supplementary assistance. Even while he is in hospital his family may require financial help from the State. The reintroduction of prescription charges has pointed up the connection. People may be exempted if they possess a certificate from the Ministry of Social Security which shows they are in receipt of a supplementary pension or allowance, or if they are assessed as needing help to meet charges.

Secondly, both departments are interested in research and information relating to the incidence of disease, industrial injuries, problems of old age, standards of living and other matters. It may be possible to secure economies by such means as common research, standardization of statistics, and making more intensive or better use of computers and other equipment.

Thirdly, it may be argued that the Ministry of Health needs to strengthen its regional organization if it is to play a more positive role. The local offices of the Ministry of Social Security might provide the present Ministry of Health with more extensive contacts with local authorities and regional hospital boards; and the merger could bring the social security side more into contact with other bodies concerned with social problems.

Fourthly, an integrated department, offering a greater variety

[25] On tribunals connected with the health service see *Report of the Committee on Administrative Tribunals and Enquiries*, Cmnd. 218, HMSO, 1957, ch. 15. See Appendix (11).

of work and possibly better career prospects, might attract better staff and reduce staff turnover. Courses for general social workers, under the supervision of the Ministry of Health, could well be adapted to meet the needs of officials concerned with supplementary benefits work. And it would be possible to encourage the interchange of staff between local authorities and the new department, on either a temporary or a permanent basis.

Fifthly, it would no longer be necessary to have a non-departmental co-ordinating minister at Cabinet level blurring individual ministerial responsibility. Presumably the enlarged department would attract politicians of some standing in the parties and would command a seat in the Cabinet. Their appointment would signify the importance attached to the social services and social policy should be more coherent. There should be a reduction in the number of Cabinet and interdepartmental committees.

Finally, integration is related to what is happening at local government level. Local authorities have for some time been under pressure to co-ordinate and rationalize the work of their social service committees and departments. When legislation permits, a wholesale reorganization is anticipated. The reasons are plain enough. At present, families or individuals with problems are liable to be involved with a number of different local services, each trying to help with one aspect but often overlapping. The existence of separate services and agencies is confusing to the public. Often they do not know which department to approach first and they may be referred from one to another, asked to repeat information, and be visited by different social workers. Furthermore, the various services and departments compete for social workers and administrators using the same basic skills, even though some specialized knowledge is called for.[26] The inference is that there should be one main social service department at local government level.

At the moment, however, different local government departments have links with different central government departments.

[26] See White Paper on *Social Work and the Community*, Cmnd. 3065, HMSO, 1966. This relates to Scotland. A report is awaited from the Seebohm Committee with respect to England and Wales. See Appendix (12).

For example, child care departments come under the Home Office but health and welfare departments have their main contacts with the Ministry of Health. Supervision and directives emanating from different central government departments do not make liaison or integration easy within local authorities. Clearly the central government must put its own house in order. Nevertheless many problems are involved.

The Ministry of Social Security is still trying to secure the unification of work previously done by two separate organizations. Another merger at this time might not be appropriate.

It is possible that there will be a certain amount of competition and rivalry in the new department. For example, the health side might appear to be getting a disproportionate share of resources and senior posts. Particular spheres of authority and function may be jealously guarded. Many people prefer to be, or seem to be, bigger fish in somewhat smaller seas.

Status very often depends on the monopoly of functions closed to those without recognized qualifications. In a large and complex department there are bound to be professional demarcation disputes. Hence it may prove difficult to encourage contacts and mobility between different sections. And when professional status is uncertain, relations between different categories of social worker, and between administrators and social workers generally, can be very strained.[27] Attempts to develop common social work training courses, or to modify or tamper with existing courses, may only exacerbate ill-feeling.

Again, genuine integration depends to some extent on physical resources and the deployment of personnel. It remains to be seen whether more Ministry of Health officials will in future be posted to local offices at present run by the Ministry of Social Security. There is the further problem of deciding what to do with them if and when they arrive.

Finally, the new department will be large and diversified and there are managerial diseconomies of scale. The larger the

[27] See P. Leonard, Social workers and bureaucracy, *New Society*, 2 June 1966.

department the more complex, impersonal and bureaucratic it is apt to become. In the early stages communication is likely to be a problem because personnel will have had different experiences and training.

Probably many of these difficulties will be overcome or may never arise. Nevertheless, the history and operation of the US Department of Health, Education and Welfare might repay study. Although these areas of government are related, it has been observed that the constituent sections of the department largely go their own way.[28]

[28] J. D. Millett, *Organization for the Public Service*, Van Nostrand, 1966, pp. 47–48.

CHAPTER 7

THE STUDY OF GOVERNMENT AND PUBLIC ADMINISTRATION

Why Study Public Administration?

The word "public", in this context, denotes a type of administration distinct from more restricted or private forms. The first reason for studying public administration, therefore, is that it is, or should be, everybody's business. One might say that public administration was too important to be left to politicians and officials. The activities of governments affect whole communities in numerous ways, allegedly for the benefit of some common interest or purpose. In his role as a citizen or taxpayer, or as a member of a social class or occupational group, every individual has a legitimate interest in government.

Most modern governments claim to be representative in some sense. But experience shows that the claims of representatives to be serving the common interest are often false. Furthermore, they are inclined to deny the public information and to manipulate opinion. The best safeguards against deception and manipulation, apart from the maximization of self-government, are widespread interest and participation in public affairs.

John Stuart Mill justly observed that representative institutions may be instruments of intrigue and tyranny when public interest is lacking. And Rousseau thought that the more public affairs encroached on private in the minds of citizens, the better the constitution of the State.[1] A second reason for studying public

[1] J. S. Mill, *Representative Government*, Everyman edn., p. 179; J.-J. Rousseau, *Social Contract*, Everyman edn., pp. 77–78.

administration, therefore, is that it aids efforts to control representatives, knowledge, and understanding being necessary preconditions of effective public control.

The fact is that the common interest, or public interest, assuming such a thing to exist, is extremely difficult to define in any generally acceptable way. There are also differences of opinion as to how best to serve it. It is always probable that the "common interest" is no more than a political formula or façade, behind which governments rule, not in a neutral fashion, but on behalf of one of the contending classes or groups. If government has to do with the integration of society, there may nevertheless be such a thing as pseudo-integration.[2]

A third reason for studying public administration is that it is intimately related to the economic system. Thus it affects people in their capacities as employers, employees, and consumers. Modern economies are "managed" by governments, with varying degrees of success. The tide is running in favour of collectivization, even in capitalist systems. Technological projects are increasingly undertaken on an international scale, because individual states are too small to guarantee an adequate market, or lack the necessary resources. Such projects are initiated by governments and underwritten by them.

Governments no longer leave incomes to be decided by bargains struck between employers' associations and trade unions. Nor do they leave prices to be determined by market forces. Moreover, they run basic economic enterprises directly. And they have special responsibility for the national currency and trade relations with other countries.

Fourthly, it follows from all this that public administration affects the quality of life for the mass of the people; and this may be improved in various ways. The study of public administration here merges with ethics and metaphysics. These give rise to

[2] See M. Duverger, *The Idea of Politics*, Methuen, 1966, part 3, ch. 3, pp. 189–95, Paperback edn. Also see C. J. Friedrich (ed.), *The Public Interest*, Atherton, 1962; and B. Barry, The public interest, in *Political Philosophy*, A. Quinton (ed.), Oxford, 1967.

propositions which are not susceptible to scientific verification, but they provide a necessary starting point for social inquiry.[3] Many great administrators have been motivated by the vision of a "better" society—Sir Robert Morant, for example. There are countless ways in which governments can contribute to the maximization of physical and mental health and enjoyment. They include control over the use of land, the support of the arts, the encouragement of fine architecture and anything else which provides opportunities for widespread development of aesthetic appreciation.

Fifthly, study may contribute to improvement in a more limited sense. It may mean nothing more than discovering ways of securing greater economic efficiency in government, in the sense of lowering the costs of services, whilst maintaining or improving their quality. Or it may imply the introduction of more effective and satisfying methods in governmental organizations.

Sixthly, study is normally intended to clarify ideas and purposes, though there is usually an initial period of increased confusion. It enables things to be viewed in a new perspective. Frequently, the official, or practitioner of the art of public administration, is under constant pressure and finds it difficult enough merely to keep pace with the daily round of business and decision-taking. It is easy to lose sight of ends which are supposed to be served, or to be manœuvred into serving other ends. In sociological jargon, there may be a displacement of goals. In spite of the sceptics, formal study helps the public official to remain on course, or to reorientate his activity. Nevertheless there are certain difficulties involved in the study of public administration which need to be discussed.

Some General Problems of Study

A wit has remarked that, "the struggling for knowledge hath a pleasure in it like that of wrestling with a fine woman". But

[3] See J. Robinson, *Economic Philosophy*, Pelican edn., pp. 8–9.

such delights are rare in any study. And even a struggle with a fine woman is often the culmination of a prolonged and boring siege; study, too, has its *longueurs*. In public administration, as in other fields, a certain amount of uninteresting detail has to be mastered. It is true that the details of administration are often of limited importance, soon become outdated, and need to be comprehended in some broad framework of analysis. However, some details are significant and there is a definite problem of obtaining up-to-date detailed information about the working of government organizations in the face of official secrecy.

Another difficulty is that there is no agreement as to the precise boundaries of the subject. There is general recognition that it is a branch of political science, but political science itself overlaps with sociology, economics, and other disciplines. Furthermore, within political science, there is doubt about the area marked out for public administration. For example, do political parties fall outside its scope? At first sight it would appear so. But it would be impossible to explain the nature of the Cabinet, or the working of the Commons as an instrument of accountability, without referring to party organization. And parties cannot be realistically discussed without reference to class and other social divisions, which in turn relate to the structure of the economy and occupational differences.

Attempts are made to delimit the field of public administration by formulating definitions of the subject. It has been said, for instance, that it is the study of the executive branches of national, state, and local governments, and of boards and corporations set up by legislatures. Another definition suggests that public administration consists of all the operations designed to fulfil or enforce public policy. A third attempt contends that it is, primarily, the study of organizations which specialize in integrative and resource allocation functions for the whole of society; and also of organizations with productive or service functions which are sponsored by and integrated with governmental organizations. Yet another states that public administration is a study of what people want through government and how they set about getting it.[4]

There are many other definitions; some appear too narrow and others are very wide. On balance it is best to choose amongst the wider variety, since narrow definitions, strictly interpreted, exclude much that is relevant. Because it is a branch of political science public administration must be linked with a general study of politics, political theory and society. On this view it is something which involves much more than management, office organization, or computer appreciation, though these may form part of a course of vocational training for an administrative career.

To effectively analyse a system of public administration a knowledge of the basic structure and principles of political institutions is necessary. And it is important to understand that the formal division of functions and responsibilities is not necessarily that which actually prevails. What the student of public administration must strive to do is to continuously review whatever knowledge he possesses in terms of significant theories of politics, organization, and administrative behaviour. Above all, he should seek to relate systems of public administration to what he conceives to be the general working of democratic government.

It should now be clear that public administration is not what is called a "closed" system. If it were, it would scarcely merit the description of public. Because the system is open, it is subject not only to formal constitutional controls but also to social and political influences and pressures. A great many private associations are deeply involved in the process of public administration. Furthermore, economic, technological, and social developments continually interact with and modify the system of government, which is also subject to independent change.

[4] See Simon, Smithburg, and Thompson, *Public Administration*, Knopf, 1961; L. D. White, *Introduction to the Study of Public Administration*, Macmillan, 3rd ed., 1948; Parker and Subramaniam, Public and private administration, *International Review of Administrative Sciences*, vol. 30 (1964), no. 4; and M. E. Dimock, G. O. Dimock, and L. W. Koenig, *Public Administration*, Rinehart, revised edn., 1958.

The openness of public administration is one reason why it differs fundamentally from other types of administration. The objects, principles, relationships, and behaviour which prevail in a business organization, for example, are not necessarily to be found in government. In numerous ways a fully developed theory of public administration will differ from a theory of business administration or management.[5]

But just as there is no universally acceptable definition of the subject, so there is no orthodox general theory of public administration. The cynic may feel that teachers and students do not know what it is they are discussing or how to talk about it. It must be admitted that there is nothing equivalent to, say, the neo-Keynesian theories of economics, found in practically all standard economic textbooks in Britain and the USA. Thus students have to work out their own line of approach; but this has its compensations. They can certainly invoke the aid of well-tried methods and techniques. The main thing is to develop a sensible approach which can be applied logically and consistently to the analysis of particular problems or whole systems.

There are a number of methods which can be considered. For example, it is possible to see a problem or system mainly in terms of groups and group relationships. But it may be preferable, in a particular instance, to concentrate attention on some constitutional principle. Alternatively, it may be thought that the solution to a problem lies in the examination of some abstract concept, like "control", which is open to different interpretations and shades of meaning. It is possible that a comparison of systems or institutions will illuminate or uncover major influences at work. A deceptively simple approach is to analyse systems or institutions in terms of functions. Again, it is possible to borrow theories and ideas from classical writers, such as Bagehot, J. S. Mill, Marx, or Rousseau. And use can be made of modern theories of decision-taking, systems analysis, and so on. Some of these approaches merit further discussion.

[5] See J. D. Millett, *Organization for the Public Service*, Van Nostrand, 1966, ch. 1.

The Group Approach

Group or pluralistic theories of politics may be traced back as far as Aristotle, but they have been refined and elaborated over the years. It is only possible here to indicate, in a general way, some features common to all such theories.[6] All pluralists emphasize that what is called *the* public is really made up of numerous smaller publics. Under the microscope as it were, the public is seen to consist of groups or associations like churches, business organizations, trade unions, professional bodies, ethnic groupings and so on. An individual will have connections with more than one association or group, but in the main, whatever influence he has is derived from his membership and position in a group.

In varying ways all groups come into contact with or are affected by government. The State is but one association amongst many, though it has peculiar features which distinguish it from other associations. For example, membership is not normally voluntary and it has a legitimate monopoly of force over a defined territory.

The number of groups in existence in any nation-state and their aims and organization are closely related to economic development, social structure, and geographical and ethnic diversity. Thus an advanced capitalist system gives rise to classes and professions which are organized in a variety of ways. In modern group theories the tendency is to extend the idea of pluralism to the relations of groups *within* trade unions, firms, government departments, professional associations and other organizations.

One way of looking at public administration, therefore, is to see each situation in terms of the interplay of a series of informal

[6] For an elaborate modern group theory see D. B. Truman, *The Governmental Process*, Knopf, 1951. Also see E. Latham, The group basis of politics: notes for a theory, *American Political Science Review*, June 1952, reprinted in H. Eulau *et al.*, *Political Behaviour*, Free Press, 1956. The pioneer work is A. F. Bentley's *The Process of Government*, 1908, reissued by Principia Press, Bloomington, Indiana, 1949.

or organized groups. If this approach is adopted the first step in analysis is to identify significant groupings, each of which may be broken down into smaller groups or sub-groups. The next step is to consider their declared and undeclared objects, motives, attitudes, sources of power, influence, and tactics.

Any question of physical planning, for example, is likely to involve several organized interests. One study of a case of physical planning, for instance, is prefaced by a cast which includes seven central government departments, five local authority committees, several heads of local authority departments, a Wholesale Fruit and Potato Merchants' Association, the Fruit and Vegetables Organization, a firm of banana merchants, an engineering company, British Railways, and certain aggrieved citizens.[7]

Groups and interests are bound to develop and affect relationships within government departments, nationalized industries, and other official organizations. But such groupings are peculiar in certain respects. They operate in an environment which is subject to constitutional rules and the policies of the government. Thus departments are formally headed by responsible ministers. The institutional setting is an important conditioning factor on behaviour and procedure.

The authority of ministers and officials stems from the fact that they are supported by constitutional rules and laws. It follows that to see public administration merely as a process of interacting groups is somewhat misleading. The activity occurs within a framework of institutions and constitutional customs which condition behaviour. Public administration in Britain cannot be understood without an awareness of such constitutional principles as individual and collective ministerial responsibility. Even those rules which no longer seem to fit the facts may be important as myths which influence behaviour. For these reasons the group approach must take the constitutional framework into account.

Some writers who use the group approach lay themselves open

[7] F. G. M. Willson, *Administrators in Action*, Allen & Unwin, 1961, pp. 23–24. Also see list of interested parties in J. Long, *The Wythall Inquiry*, Estates Gazette, 1961, p. 139.

to criticism in this respect but this does not invalidate the method as such. However, group theorists have been criticized on other grounds. For example, they are said to neglect the concept of a public interest and the role of the state. It is further charged that they find little or no place for values, ideas and normative considerations in government, and that political society as a whole cannot be regarded as a cluster of face-to-face groups. And it may be remarked that the manner in which people are grouped is somethimes arbitrary and subjective, and that really significant associations, such as parties and class, are overlooked.[8]

In spite of these criticisms it would be a peculiar theory of government and organization which failed to take account of the structure and activity of groups. Furthermore, sophisticated group theories are exempt from many of the charges made. It can reasonably be argued that, in the absence of an acceptable general theory, certain group theories are the most satisfactory of all the unsatisfactory attempts which have been made to formulate one.

But in discussing groups, constitutions, systems, principles and myths one is inevitably using abstract concepts. And because concepts are often vague and ambiguous it is necessary to subject them to close examination. Moreover, the clarification of a particular problem of public administration may turn on what might be called the conceptual emphasis. Again, different systems of government are frequently compared in terms of concepts, rather than in terms of institutions, such as legislatures. It is therefore convenient to discuss concepts and comparative methods together.

Concepts and Comparative Methods

A concept may be defined as a general notion which is an aid to thought or study. Amongst the concepts which frequently

[8] For an extensive criticism of Bentley's Group Approach see L. Weinstein in *Essays on the Scientific Study of Politics*, H. J. Storing (ed.), New York, 1962. Also see R. S. Parker, "Group analysis" and scientism in political studies, *Political Studies*, Feb. 1961.

occur in discussions about public administration are: accountability, authority, bureaucracy, centralization, class, control, delegation, democracy, devolution, equality, group, interest, leadership, liberty, planning, power, public, regional, representative, responsibility, sovereignty, and state. The list is far from exhaustive, and all these words are open to different interpretations and shades of meaning. Whole books have been written about some of them. It is possible to arrive at different conclusions according to the sense in which words are used. Thus it may be decided that the British system of government is representative in one sense, but not in another.[9]

Again, a word like "control" may be given a "hard" or a "soft" interpretation. In the hard sense, one set of people may be said to control another when they effectively command or order them to do something, or when they severely limit their discretion. In the soft sense, control may amount to no more than guidance or influence. It is in the latter sense perhaps that the Cabinet is subject to the control of the Commons or the electorate. "Responsible" is another word which is open to emphases of this sort.

Distinctions are often made between "positive" and "negative" liberty. It is possible to play one meaning off against another in some fruitful dialectical exercise. But some concepts are so complex that continued brooding reduces the student to a state where he fears to put pen to paper, after the manner of the man who read a book on English grammar. On occasion it is wise to take refuge in an appeal to authority and to follow the usage of some writer of repute, with due acknowledgement.[10] To some extent, however, the student of public administration must dabble in linguistic analysis, but without becoming its slave.

Overconcentration on the analysis of words or concepts tends

[9] For various meanings of "representative" see A. H. Birch, *Representative and Responsible Government*, Allen & Unwin, 1964, pp. 13–17.

[10] Apart from standard classic texts see, for example, G. C. Field, *Political Theory*, Methuen, 1956; S. I. Benn and R. Peters, *Social Principles and the Democratic State*, Allen & Unwin, 1959; and H. R. G. Greaves, *The Foundations of Political Theory*, Bell, 2nd edn., 1966. Also see T. D. Weldon, *The Vocabulary of Politics*, Penguin, 1953.

to make discussion too abstract and remote from real life. At some point meat must be put on the conceptual bones. And the more examples which can be produced to illustrate or support an argument, the more convincing it becomes. Isolated cases may be untypical or misleading. In this respect comparative methods are necessary, because they widen the field from which evidence can be cited. But comparisons raise many problems.

It has been argued that meaningful comparisons between systems of public administration are not possible, because no aspect of government can usefully be considered in isolation from the total social system of which it is part. And each total system is a unique combination of factors. Thus it may be suggested that a comparison of executives in Britain and the USA is of little or no value, because the constitutions, history, geography, economy, social structure and cultures of the two countries are different. There are so many variations that it is not possible to establish major causal relationships, to which differences between the two executives can be attributed.[11]

Again, it is argued that there is no validity in comparing institutions which, though called by the same name, are differently composed and in fact serve different ends. Like must be compared with like. For this reason, it is said, it makes no sense to compare the Parliament of the United Kingdom with the Supreme Soviet of the USSR, though both are called legislatures. Some writers, therefore, prefer to compare systems wholly or mainly in terms of concepts like "power" or "leadership", rather than in terms of institutions. But there must come a point when institutions are brought into the picture, because institutional arrangements affect power, leadership, and so on.[12]

[11] For a general introduction to comparative methods see G. Heckscher, *The Study of Comparative Government and Politics*, Allen & Unwin, 1957. Also see R. Macridis, *The Study of Comparative Government*, Random House, 1955. For a critical look at methods and literature see L. Wolf-Phillips, Metapolitics: reflections on a "methodological revolution", *Political Studies*, Oct. 1964.

[12] For example, see Z. Brzezinski and S. P. Huntington, *Political Power: USA/USSR*, Chatto & Windus, 1964, pp. 3–6.

But comparisons need not necessarily be made between institutions or organizations in different countries. It is legitimate to compare, say, two government departments in Britain. And it is perhaps even more fruitful to compare the position and organization of one department at different periods of time—in effect, to use an historical approach. But even these types of comparison raise formidable problems when it comes to making generalizations or drawing conclusions, because numerous changes occur over time and it is difficult to identify cause and effect. Nevertheless, a case can be made out for the use of comparative methods.

Such methods enable us to see our own system of government in a wider perspective. They modify the insularity and partiality to which all peoples are prone, and therefore serve educational and liberalizing ends. Furthermore, one can better appreciate, say, the connection of physical environment and government when comparing the number and diversity of US agricultural pressure groups with the virtual monopoly of the National Farmers' Union in Britain.[13] Again, there is a strong trend towards the internationalization of certain aspects of public administration, assisted by improved communications. In considering an economic or defence problem, for example, it is usually necessary to understand both the similarities and the differences between government in various countries.

It may be that comparative methods will suggest solutions to particular problems or provide a basis for the reform of institutions. But, like the human body, the body politic is inclined to reject transplants and special treatment is necessary. Few ideas or practices can be exported or imported without undergoing considerable modification. They may not "take" at all in new conditions, or they may work in an entirely unexpected way. Thus the British Parliamentary Commissioner is not the exact counterpart of any Scandinavian model because there are numerous

[13] For Britain see P. Self and H. Storing, *The State and the Farmer*, Allen & Unwin, 1962. On the farm lobby in the USA see V. O. Key, *Politics, Parties and Pressure Groups*, Crowell, 5th edn., 1964, pp. 20–43.

differences between Scandinavian and British systems of government. Equally, it is possible to conceive the introduction of a British-type administrative class into the Federal Service of the USA. But, assuming it to be feasible, modifications would have to be anticipated and there would be implications for US public administration generally.

There are other, somewhat stronger, grounds for advocating comparative methods. They help us to gain a better insight into such tools of description or classification as federalism or democracy. Furthermore, if a science of public administration is to be developed, there must be attempts to formulate principles and generalizations which transcend national boundaries.[14] At the same time, comparative methods induce one to qualify generalizations. For example, if there is an "iron law of oligarchy", as Michels suggests, then it is less apparent at the national level in US than in British political parties. On the other hand, at state and local level, some US parties, in some states, are more oligarchical than British parties.[15]

Finally, it is reasonable to suppose that comparative methods which have served writers as diverse as Aristotle, Tocqueville, Bagehot, Bryce, and Duverger must have something to commend them. But there is no denying that such methods call for a great deal of sophistication, knowledge and exceptional ability. Tocquevilles and Bagehots are rare in any generation. And political developments have enormously increased the number of new nations, and hence the variety and complexity of systems to be compared.

The Functional Approach

Comparative methods really incorporate the other approaches outlined, or still others which have not been discussed. Compari-

[14] See R. A. Dahl, The science of public administration, *Public Administration Review*, vol. 7 (1947), no. 1, reprinted in *Administrative Questions and Political Answers*, Van Nostrand, 1966, C. E. Hawley and R. G. Weintraub (eds.).

[15] R. Michels, *Political Parties*, 1st edn., 1915. See Collier edn., 1962, with introduction by S. M. Lipset.

sons have to be made in terms of groups, institutions, constitutional principles, concepts and so on. One approach that requires mention, because it is widely used, especially by American political scientists and sociologists, is the functional method. In fact, it is more accurate to speak of methods, since there are different versions. They may be used in both comparative and non-comparative analyses.

The simplest versions would probably not be recognized as such by the more ambitious functionalists. It may be decided, for instance, that making governments behave is a function of legislatures in certain countries. The adequacy of their organization, composition and procedure may then be looked at from this point of view.[16] Again, one may consider what one believes to be the changing functions of the State, and then discuss the recruitment, training and general character of the civil service in terms of these functions.[17] This modest or simple version of functionalism has much to commend it.

But sophisticated writers distinguish between "manifest" and "latent" functions. Manifest functions are those ends and purposes which are supposedly served by some rule or procedure. Latent functions are other ends served by the same rules and procedures, but not generally intended or recognized by most people.[18] The manifest function of Question Time in the Commons is to secure the accountability of the executive. But departmentally inspired questions serve other ends. Again, the doctrine of individual ministerial responsibility serves the manifest function of accountability. But it also preserves the independence of ministers, because any interference with their policies by, say, a standing committee of the Commons may be said to infringe the doctrine.

The more elaborate versions of functionalism presuppose that structures perform functions in political and other systems. All parts of a system are interrelated, so that a change in any

[16] See K. C. Wheare, *Legislatures*, Oxford, 1963, ch. 5.

[17] For example, see W. A. Robson, Recent trends in public administration, in *The Civil Service in Great Britain and France*, Hogarth, 1956.

[18] See R. K. Merton, *Social Theory and Social Structure*, Free Press, 1957, pp. 19–84.

one part affects others to a greater or lesser degree. A system is essentially a series of "inputs", which flow into it, and a series of "outputs", which flow out of it. Inputs are converted into outputs by functions. Although systems are in a constant state of activity or flux, they are nonetheless enduring and relatively stable. Hence the concept of "equilibrium" is introduced. Basically this means that when something occurs to disturb the system, regulating mechanisms absorb the shock and maintain the system. Anything which tends to undermine the system is termed "dysfunctional".

All societies are conceived as having total social systems, which are broken down into less comprehensive systems or subsystems, of which the political is one. According to a leading functionalist, the thing which distinguishes the political system is its concern with legitimate force.[19] Thus political systems are occupied with decisions which are backed by the possible use of force or compulsion; and such force is considered "right" or "legitimate" by the majority of the people affected.

A political input is a demand that the government should make, or refrain from making, an authoritative decision about a particular matter. Such demands are said to be backed by "supports" of various kinds, e.g. pressure group activity, voting, payment of taxes, obedience to authority and attachment to the political régime.

The output or consequential side of the political system is made up of converted demands. It may include the regulation of activity and behaviour by means of legislation, a change of foreign policy, the provision or modification of a social service and so on. In the process of changing inputs into outputs the political system is said to articulate and aggregate demands, which are then converted into authoritative rules or decisions, subsequently made widely known, and enforced when necessary.

Clearly, in the process of converting inputs into outputs

[19] See G. Almond, A functional approach to comparative politics, in G. Almond and J. Coleman (eds.), *The Politics of the Developing Areas*, Princeton University Press, 1960, pp. 3–65.

public administration has an important role to play, since specialized governmental bureaucracies and agencies are necessary in any but the most simple of systems. However, it would take us too far afield to elaborate on the special place of public administration in functional schemes.[20]

Whilst functionalism has its adherents and uses, it has come in for severe criticism. In spite of its claim to be "scientific" and value-free, for example, concepts like "function", "equilibrium", and "legitimate" are both vague and value-loaded. It is not clear, for instance, how the majority which legitimizes a decision is calculated or how big it must be. And there are few clues as to what precisely leads people to accept something as "right", or whether mere passive acceptance is equivalent to legitimization.

Again, since all systems are depicted as incorporating regulatory mechanisms, working for equilibrium and maintenance, it is difficult to account for social and political change using a functional approach. Functionalism has a particular bias towards conservatism and the *status quo*. Furthermore, because it concentrates on a non-institutional approach, functionalism tends to ignore the fact that many political and governmental problems relate to organization. This considerably reduces its utility for the study of public administration.

It can also be said that functionalism tends to follow ancient classical theories in drawing false analogies between the state and machines and organisms. The governmental system, for example, is treated as a sort of neutral machine into which raw materials, or demands, are fed and which produces a flow of finished goods, or output. In fact, states are controlled by politicians and officials, who are far from neutral and who contribute their own special inputs.

No doubt functionalism can be defended against some of these criticisms. And as we have already seen, there is no approach

[20] For an introduction to functionalism see R. E. Jones, *The Functional Analysis of Politics*, Routledge, 1967. For illustrative material on terms used by functionalists, see H. V. Wiseman, *Politics in Everyday Life*, Blackwell, 1966, especially part 1, ch. 2. Also see O. R. Young, *Systems of Political Science*, Prentice-Hall, 1968, ch. 3.

which cannot be criticized on some ground or other. As things stand, it is simply a question of selecting what one considers to be the most satisfactory option.

It should be added that no system of public administration is unaffected by ideas and ideologies. Thus the ideas and theories of certain writers may be made the focal point of discussion. An acquaintance with Benthamism, and utilitarianism generally, illuminates British government. The ideas of the Federalists are an essential part of the study of US government. The influence of pragmatists, like Peirce, is also apparent in the US system. It is scarcely possible to overlook the significance of Marxism in the USSR and other communist countries. And of course Marxism, like other systems of ideas, tends to wear a local dress.

It would not be appropriate, in an introductory work, to attempt to summarize the work of modern theorists like Dahl, Easton and Simon. Those who have survived to this point must go to the original sources.[21] A Chinese proverb has it that a journey of 1000 miles begins with one step. But whoever sets out to study public administration embarks on a journey which has no end and he must follow a devious and complicated route.

[21] For example, see R. A. Dahl, *Modern Political Analysis*, Prentice-Hall, 1963; D. Easton, *A Framework for Political Analysis*, Prentice-Hall, 1965; and H. Simon, *Administrative Behaviour*, Free Press, 2nd edn., 1957. Also see H. Simon and J. G. March, *Organizations*, Wiley, 1958. For an overall picture of theoretical developments see W. J. M. Mackenzie, *Politics and Social Science*, Penguin, 1967. For an "unfashionable" but impressive normative essay see C. B. Macpherson, Post-Liberal democracy? in *The Canadian Journal of Economics and Political Science*, Nov. 1964.

CHAPTER 8

POSTSCRIPT: THE FULTON REPORT

THE Fulton Committee reported on the civil service after the main text was completed.[1] It found the main defects of the service to be:

(1) The prevailing philosophy of the amateur or generalist. Lord Simey entered a note of reservation and dissent on this point.
(2) The rigidity of the structure of classes.
(3) Insufficient opportunity for specialists to reach the top policy-making posts.
(4) Insufficient attention to managerial expertise.
(5) Lack of contact with the community.
(6) Inadequate personnel management and planning of careers.

To remedy these alleged defects and to improve the service the Committee recommended:

(1) The establishment of a new Civil Service Department.
(2) The abolition of classes and their replacement by a unified grading structure. It suggested that some twenty grades could contain all the jobs in the non-industrial part of the civil service.
(3) Recruitment of graduates with the best qualifications, aptitudes, qualities, and experience for jobs falling into one of the broad categories of administration.
(4) The setting up of a Civil Service College to provide training courses in administration and management and a wide range of short courses.

[1] Cmnd. 3638, HMSO, June 1968.

(5) The introduction of planning units, in departments which do not already have them, to be headed by a Senior Policy Adviser with direct access to the Minister.
(6) Less anonymity and more contact with the public.
(7) The transferability of civil service and private pensions, to encourage mobility and interchange between the private and public sectors.

Altogether the committee made 158 recommendations.

In a statement in the Commons on 26 June the Prime Minister said the Government accepted the committee's analysis, but not every criticism of the service. A Civil Service Department and a Civil Service College would be set up. Classes would be abolished after discussions with staff associations. Timing would depend on the availability of finance and the contents of reports awaited on the structure of local government and other matters. It was intended that new entrants should be given opportunities for working in regions outside London. It was accepted that the Prime Minister should be responsible for senior appointments in the civil service and that a minister of Cabinet rank should take on responsibility for the day-to-day running of the service and supervise its transformation. The Paymaster-General, Lord Shackleton, had been assigned the latter task.

Comment on the Report

1. The Civil Service Department

Broadly speaking, the Civil Service Department will take over the functions of the management side of the Treasury. Sir William Armstrong continues as Head of the Civil Service in the new department. Whether it is wise or practicable to have separate departments responsible for public expenditure and the running of the civil service remains to be seen. The staff costs of the service, excluding the Post Office, are some £850 million, and pay within the defence budget accounts for a similar sum. The Treasury is certain to retain an active interest in the running of the service, especially as its cost is directly related to management and the use and movement of personnel. Pay and conditions in the service are also connected with economic and incomes policy generally. The position of the Treasury may be strengthened in that it will suffer little loss of power whilst it retains control of the purse strings; but it is relieved of formal responsibility for running the service.

2. Structure and Career Patterns

It is possible that the abolition of classes will lessen the attraction of the service for holders of good degrees since they will no longer be more or less certain of clear and rapid progress to the summit. The chances of getting a good share of each generation of outstanding arts graduates are more doubtful. There is no reason to suppose that there will be a marked increase in applications from science graduates aspiring to embark on an administrative career. Graduates who have studied the social sciences would appear to be the main beneficiaries.

The committee suggests that new entrants should make their careers within certain divisions. Only two divisions are specifically mentioned, Financial and Economic, and Social Administration, though there could be others. The divisions cited are extremely broad. Some jobs would overlap them and others would not fall into either category. The committee is opposed to mobility between sections within departments but underrates their interconnection.

The committee states that the careers of all entrants should be determined by performance. But beyond recommending more and better personnel officers it is vague on the difficulties of selecting high fliers out of some 470,000 people hitherto categorized in 47 general and 1400 departmental classes. However unsatisfactory, these classifications do indicate particular experience and training. The heterogeneity of the service is rather played down by the committee. If new categories are not numerous enough to take into account the extremely wide variety of skills, aptitudes and qualifications required in different departments, individuals will have no clear idea of career prospects and may harbour vague expectations which are doomed to disappointment.

It is not the case that there will be equality of opportunity for advancement. A special training grade is recommended for graduates and the "best" non-graduates. But selecting the best non-graduates necessitates giving new entrants, early on, the right mixture of responsibilities and experience, whatever is meant by "right" in this context. One may doubt whether departmental duties can be allocated in this fashion. Moreover, opportunities for demonstrating talent vary considerably between and within departments. Again, they do not depend solely on the individuals concerned but on the calibre of leadership at various levels, on the facilities available, on work load, and on team work within a particular group or section.

The selection of non-graduate high fliers will initially rest with separate departments. Different standards and criteria may be applied. Initiative and enterprise are not invariably welcome in bureaucratic structures, especially at junior level. Those selected for advancement may be conformists, or deferentials who force themselves upon the attention of their seniors. As Sir Henry Taylor observed, "The arts of rising, properly so called, have commonly some mixture of baseness—more or less according as the aid from natural endowments is less or more."[2] One is tempted to posit an iron law of mediocrity whereby the rate of promotion is inverse to merit.

University graduates will still start with an enormous advantage. This is scarcely surprising since it is a function of the British educational system to make a preliminary categorization of people into those fitted for elite and non-elite positions in society.

3. Recruitment Favouring Certain Disciplines

A majority of the committee took the view that certain disciplines were especially relevant to public administration. They

[2] Sir Henry Taylor, *The Statesman*, Mentor edn., p. 73.

mention specifically social sciences, mathematics, physics, biology and engineering. This could be important if, as the majority recommend, Method 1 is retained but limited to papers in these or other "vocational" subjects. These preferred university studies would also carry additional increments in starting salary.

The majority appear to take a somewhat restricted view of public administration and what it entails at the highest levels. As one very experienced administrator commented, history is particularly relevant to government, concerned as it is with the growth and decay of civilizations and struggles to evolve forms of government.[3] Similar arguments can be advanced with respect to philosophy. It may be that philosophy and history will be squeezed in under the somewhat elastic heading of social science. It can certainly be reasonably argued that many social science courses are extremely narrow and abstract in content, and that a study of great literature, whether English or foreign, is at least as good a preparation for public service as mathematics or engineering. Furthermore, with the increase in the number of universities and other institutions of higher education there is considerable variety in the content, and possibly standards, of degree courses.

4. The Civil Service College

The setting up of a Civil Service College is clearly derived from the committee's preoccupation with expertise. To some extent it will be a more elaborate version of the Treasury Centre for Administrative Studies. If taken seriously it could be very expensive to run. Furthermore, one may doubt whether there are sufficient reserves of staff to permit large numbers of overworked officials to take time off on lengthy courses. Short intensive courses might well be the order of the day. It is not clear how much money will be available for research, mentioned as one of the functions of the college.

It is somewhat inconsistent to recommend that potential top

[3] Dame Evelyn Sharp, *The Sunday Times*, 30 June 1968.

civil servants should have more contact with the public and then advise the government to set up an institution which will prevent contact with people on suitable courses already available in universities. There seems to be no obvious reason why private enterprise should make use of a college specifically designed for public servants. Duplication of courses and research accords ill with the committee's point that more cost consciousness is needed in public affairs.

5. *Planning Units and Senior Policy Advisers*

There is little to object to in the idea of departmental planning units, staffed by youngish men, looking at long-term needs. It is questionable, however, whether practical ideas for the future can emanate from people not also involved to some extent in grappling with current administration and problems.

The suggestion that there should be a Senior Policy Adviser, with direct access to the Minister, is more debatable. Long-term research is apt to be connected with faults in current policy and administration. It will probably involve searching examination and criticism of the activities of several rather than of one department. In these circumstances relations between a Permanent Secretary and a Senior Policy Adviser could be one of continuous tension. Alternatively, the Senior Planning Adviser might feel obliged to hush up inadequacies, for political reasons or out of loyalty to the department and colleagues. Consultation and co-ordination with planning units in other departments could well prove difficult when they have different objectives in view.

It is far from certain that a Minister would benefit from having two top advisers, one for current activities and one for the long-term. Final responsibility for both aspects of policy is better unified in one man, the Permanent Secretary. The position is even more complicated if greater use is also made of outside advisers, as the committee suggests. A new Minister faced with a Permanent Secretary and a Senior Policy Adviser who do not agree might well be tempted to seek outside advice. If they do agree, he will find it difficult to resist their suggestions or to ignore them in favour of those of unofficial advisers.

Most permanent secretaries see themselves as Chief of Staff to a succession of ministers, rather than as managers of departments. In the transition period, an active but junior number two, in charge of personnel and reorganization, might well be more useful to departments than a Senior Policy Adviser.

Finally, long-term policy formulation has to be related to party politics. If departmental policies continue unchanged, irrespective of the party in power, as a consequence of the efforts of senior planning advisers, this will reinforce the view that the country is really run by civil servants and that the party system is a sham which offers electors no real choice of alternatives.

6. Less Anonymity

The recommendation that civil servants should be less anonymous and more communicative in public possibly connects with notions of an educated democracy and an accountable democracy. But many problems are involved. The relations between ministers and civil servants and between senior and junior civil servants could be adversely affected. It is not clear what demands would be made on the time of already overworked officials.

The committee suggests—that material collected and analysed in the course of policy formulation should be made public and that policy should be more openly discussed in the formative stages. This seems to overlook the fact that much advice is confidential. It would be extremely difficult to abandon confidentiality in many important areas of economic and foreign policy. And if policy were more openly discussed in the formative stages this could slow up the process of government since the Opposition, party factions, and vested interests could resort to delaying and obstructive tactics with greater hopes of success.

It is quite likely that some civil servants would welcome opportunities to defend themselves against the charge that they, rather than Ministers, are responsible for policy. Since they are highly intelligent, well informed, and very experienced in drafting answers to parliamentary questions which often conceal the real motives underlying policy, they have little to fear. The more so as it is far from clear what it is intended to do with them if their public statements are thought to be unsatisfactory. The doctrine of ministerial responsibility still has its uses.

7. *Mobility between Private Enterprise and Public Service*

The committee wishes to encourage movement and interchange of personnel between private concerns and the civil service. The different ends and character of private enterprise and public service tend to get overlooked. And, curiously enough, a report on the British economy published in the same week indicates that, if anything, industrial managers are even more amateurish than the administrative class is alleged to be.[4]

The dangers involved in too much of this type of mobility are ignored and no safeguards are proposed. The discretionary work of the civil service may affect the material prospects of particular firms and individuals and interchange clearly creates opportunities for favouritism and improper influence. Confidence in the impartiality of the civil service could be undermined.

Conclusion

Since the report itself naturally argues the case for the committee's proposals these comments have tended to concentrate on what can be said against them. It will be some five years before most of the recommendations are fully implemented and perhaps ten or more years before they show significant results. The long-term effect would appear to strengthen the influence of the bureaucracy at the expense of politicians. Somewhat harshly, but justifiably, *The Times* described the report as a thoroughly contemporary essay, heavy in technical appraisal of immediate

[4] R. E. Caves (ed.), *Britain's Economic Prospects*, Allen & Unwin, 1968.

problems and light on political reflection. In accordance with a long-standing British tradition it is quite likely to lead to the setting up of another committee, to inquire into the machinery of government.[5]

[5] See Appendix (13).

APPENDIX

1. p. 15, fn. 18. Mr. Crossman became Secretary of State for Social Services in autumn 1968 and headed the new Department of Health and Social Security. He retained responsibility for the co-ordination of all social services, including those outside his own department.

2. p. 38, fn. 4. The Commission is now part of the Civil Service Department. It retains its formal independence within the department.

3. p. 102, fn. 45a. The Select Committee on Agriculture ceases to exist at the end of February 1969, see H.C.Deb(775), 15 November 1968, cols. 827–38. The final report of the Committee should make interesting reading. Also see forthcoming article in *Parliamentary Affairs* by J. P. Mackintosh. Further committees have been set up on Race Relations and Scottish Affairs.

4. p. 119, fn. 70. Government proposals for the reform of the House of Lords are outlined in a White Paper, Cmnd. 3799, November 1968. This contains information on its present composition and party character. Partly to take the wind out of the sails of Welsh and Scottish nationalism the Government has also set up a Constitutional Commission to consider legislative and administrative devolution. For an introduction to regionalism and nationalism in Britain see J. P. Mackintosh, *The Devolution of Power*, Penguin, 1968.

5. p. 147, fn. 32 and p. 163, fn. 55. Sir Douglas Allen became sole Permanent Secretary in the Treasury after its management functions had been transferred to the Civil Service Department, headed by Sir William Armstrong.

6. p. 149, fn. 35. The past tense should now be mentally substituted in references to the Management Side of the Treasury.
7. p. 178, fn. 14a and p. 185, fn. 24. In autumn 1968 renamed the Foreign and Commonwealth Office.
8. p. 179, fn. 15 and p. 185, fn. 24. There was a considerable amount of reorganization and renaming of departments after the merger with the former Commonwealth Office, but still on the basis of geographical, political and functional principles.
9. p. 213, fn. 1. The leadership function has been complicated by consummation of the merger of Health and Social Security in October 1968. The new department is entitled the Department of Health and Social Security.
10. p. 222, fn. 10a. The past tense should be substituted in references to the Ministry of Social Security and Ministry of Health, p. 228. But the basic functions and problems remain unchanged.
11. p. 233, fn. 25. For a very useful brief work on administrative tribunals see H. Street, *Justice in the Welfare State*, Stevens, 1968.
12. p. 234, fn. 26. The Seebohm Report, Cmnd. 3703, was published in July 1968. For summary and comment see articles in *New Society*, 25 July and 1 August 1968, also available in pamphlet form.
13. p. 262, fn. 5. The Fulton Report has since been further discussed in both the Lords and Commons, see H.L.Deb(295), 26 July 1968, cols. 1049–74 and H.C.Deb(775), 21 November 1968, cols. 1542–1681. In the Commons the Prime Minister stated no outside committee on the machinery of government was planned. No decision had been taken to drop Method 1 but universities were being consulted. The Government rejected bias in favour of "relevant" studies in either Method, one reason being that it might close the door to suitable candidates. Other recommendations were still being studied.

INDEX